Place, Identity and Everyday Life in a Globalizing World

Place, Identity and Everyday Life in a Globalizing World

Harvey C. Perkins

David C. Thorns

palgrave
macmillan

First published 2012 by
PALGRAVE MACMILLAN

Palgrave Macmillan in the UK is an imprint of Macmillan Publishers Limited,
registered in England, company number 785998, of Houndmills, Basingstoke,
Hampshire RG21 6XS.

Palgrave Macmillan in the US is a division of St Martin's Press LLC,
175 Fifth Avenue, New York, NY 10010.

Palgrave Macmillan is the global academic imprint of the above companies
and has companies and representatives throughout the world.

Palgrave® and Macmillan® are registered trademarks in the United States,
the United Kingdom, Europe and other countries

ISBN-13: 978–0–230–57590–5 hardback
ISBN-13: 978–0–230–57591–2 paperback

This book is printed on paper suitable for recycling and made from fully
managed and sustained forest sources. Logging, pulping and manufacturing
processes are expected to conform to the environmental regulations of the
country of origin.

A catalogue record for this book is available from the British Library.

A catalog record for this book is available from the Library of Congress.

10 9 8 7 6 5 4 3 2 1
21 20 19 18 17 16 15 14 13 12

Printed and bound in Great Britain by
CPI Antony Rowe, Chippenham and Eastbourne

Contents

Preface

The book is the result of an extended period of collaborative work that we began in the early 1990s and which has explored the ways in which place, identity and every day are being changed in a globalizing world. Our work was helped considerably by the award of funding for a five-year research programme by the New Zealand Foundation for Research Science and Technology from 1997 to 2002. This programme first explored the meaning of home for New Zealanders, a central part of their sense of place and identity, and then moved to examine the growth and development of new residential areas, some in new suburban greenfield developments and others in intensifying inner-city areas and established suburbs. Exploring these themes in the context of global change, and reading the fascinating international literature produced by our colleagues in New Zealand and overseas, led us to examine debates about sustainable development, nature–society relationships, and refashioned notions of place and home that were emerging around these new ways of think about the management of human settlement. Given these efforts it seemed to us timely to try to bring this work together in a sustained treatment of the ways place, identity and everyday life could be understood within a world that was rapidly changing and which for some commentators was becoming 'placeless' as a result of more globalized understandings and connectivity and through the growth of 'virtual places'.

As we completed our book in the latter part of 2010 and the first three months of 2011 we experienced at first-hand the dislocation of our 'place' and 'home' in Christchurch, New Zealand, as a result of a series of damaging earthquakes, which for us dramatically reinforced the importance of place-based local experience in interpretations of the working out of everyday life. The first earthquake, on 4 September 2010, measured 7.2 in magnitude and since then the city has experienced many thousands of aftershocks. The initial earthquake did considerable damage to parts of Christchurch but a very shallow aftershock with an epicentre in the coastal part of the city measuring magnitude 6.3 on 22 February 2011 produced extremely intense vertical and horizontal ground shaking which led to the collapse of much of the central city and forced hundreds of thousands of tonnes of silt out of the ground through processes of liquefaction that spread across land and roads and brought vehicular movement to a halt. This aftershock also severely damaged the city's already fragile infrastructure, breaking underground cables and piping systems and cutting water and drainage and power to most of the city. Fortunately, some areas of the city suffered only minor disruption but for approximately 50 per cent of the residents in the central, east and south of the city there is, over five weeks after the aftershock, still no piped sewerage services, with many using portable toilets, facing power outages and living in houses that need extensive repair.

What we have experienced demonstrates the fragility of the urban environment when affected by extreme events and the challenges posed to our everyday lives when we can no longer rely on taken-for-granted supplies of water, power and the Internet! Of course without electricity, frustration levels rose as citizens were advised to go to websites for information they could not access and were then thrown back on more traditional media sources such as the daily press and the transistor battery-operated radio. Very quickly people in the city rallied; we saw an outpouring of local community sentiment and engagement as people got stuck in clearing streets and properties of silt, and making temporary fixes to houses. However the widespread destruction of houses, land, familiar building and popular recreational areas, together with the injuries and loss of life sustained in the city, also generated a deep sense of loss and grief and Christchurch has now been changed for ever.

Rebuilding will take years rather than months and as this reality sets in the communities within the city are struggling to deal with events which have undermined their sense of 'ontological security' as their relationships to people and places have been seriously disrupted. These events have given us a sharpened perspective on the contents of this book.

Many people have contributed to the development of the thinking that has shaped this book. We acknowledge the insights that we have gained from our students in our respective universities as we have engaged with them in our teaching. Particularly important have been those postgraduate students Natasha O'Dea, Natalie Nesbitt, Ben Peacey, Michelle Girvan, Elizabeth Wilson, Michael Nuth and Katherine Taylor with whom we have worked on summer studentships between 2000 to 2009 and also Mike Mackay for his Ph.D. research on DIY homebuilding and maintenance. We also have benefited from the interaction with colleagues in the International Sociological Association's Research Committee on Housing and the Built Environment, the European Housing Research Network, the Asia Pacific Housing Research Network, participants in the Australasian Housing Researchers' annual conferences and members of the Building Research Capability on the Social Sciences programme. Colleagues we have worked with on various aspects of the overall research programme deserve special recognition and these are Hazel Ashton, Ann Dupuis, Lorraine Leonard, Mike Nuth, Andrea Schöllmann, Suzanne Vallance and Ann Winstanley. We were also very appreciative of the comments from the reviewers who produced a very helpful and constructive critique of the first draft of the typescript, which enabled us to revise our work and extend it appreciably. Finally our thanks go to Anna Reeve for her support and encouragement through the publishing process.

Harvey C. Perkins
David C. Thorns
April 2011

Acknowledgements

The authors and publishers want to thank the following for their permission to use materials included in this book:

Statistics New Zealand for Figure 4.1, licensed by Statistics New Zealand for reuse under the Creative Commons Attribution 3.0 New Zealand licence.

Professor Eric Pawson for contributing his experience of the New York launch of the iPad in early 2010, in Chapter 6.

SASI Group (University of Sheffield) and Mark Newman (University of Michigan) for the use of Worldmapper material in Chapter 8.

Professor Karl. E. Case, Wellesley College, Massachusetts for the use of Figure 9.1.

Wheels24.co.za for the use of Table 8.1.

Figures and Tables

Figures

Tables

CHAPTER 1

Introduction

Introduction

This book examines a series of questions and debates about the inter-relationships between place, identity and everyday life and their connections to processes of globalization. While we discuss these ideas in greater depth in later sections of the book some brief definitions are in order. Our use of the term 'place' incorporates the many settings where people live out their lives as they engage in all of their many activities. Some places are used instrumentally, and while important in the course of events are not held in any particular regard by most people. Other places hold very great meaning for a variety of individuals and groups and are thus accorded high value. All aspects of people's lives are emplaced in one way or another. We use the term 'identity' to refer to the meanings attributed to individuals and groups by themselves and others. To an extent identity is created in self-conscious experience; but it is also influenced by forces not of our own choosing such as those associated with economy, culture and the social position and geographic setting into which we are born and then raised. People's conscious experience and the conditions in which they find their lives working themselves out combine to help constitute their sense of what and who they are. 'Everyday life' is the flow of social existence which is often routine and habitual, always embodied and temporal, often taken for granted and localized, and which for the most part changes incrementally but also sometimes dramatically. The meanings of place and identity are worked out together in everyday life such that sense of place and identity are often intertwined. Given the fluid and complex nature of everyday life it is common for the meanings of places to change, perhaps to take on several meanings and for people to have multiple and changing identities.

Why write about place, identity and everyday life in a globalizing world? Given the developments of the late twentieth and early twenty-first centuries, the scholarly emphasis on time–space compression, and the importance of 'virtual space and experience' in the daily lives of many people, it might seem odd to be spending time examining the social roles of traditional placed-based environments. Part of the answer to this question is that despite the increasing focus on the 'virtual' and 'mobilities', for most people, the experiences of everyday life are still firmly rooted in place and these are crucially important for informing us of who we are.

There are many ways to illustrate this. One of the authors of this book, for example, was travelling in 2006 by taxi to Dunedin City's Airport in the South Island of New Zealand after an information technology conference. In conversation with the taxi driver it emerged that he had lived his whole life in Dunedin, a city of approximately 120,000 residents, and had never travelled out of the country or to its northern regions. This is consistent with the experience of many people. It is easy to forget this and be distracted by the lives of the hyper-mobile, people who comprise only a small but influential minority of the global population. We note also that all of us, even the hyper-mobile, were raised in a place or places, and these settings imprint themselves on our identities, and allow us to answer the often asked question: 'where are you from?'. Our recollections of these places can often be nostalgically sentimental and filtered by time. It can thus be a disappointing experience to travel back to one's former home, finding that the places and people we once knew well have changed or gone, or that we have changed so much that connection with the place is no longer of value or interest.

Currently, scholars and policy makers who are interested in social, economic and environmental transformation are also investigating the connections between globalization and placed-based experience. Everywhere there is talk of change wrought by globalizing influences, but at the same time, many commentators recognize that most people live everyday in well-established and relatively stable local milieux. They are emplaced in significant ways and their lives are played out in interlinked spatial, social and bodily routines. Place and local context therefore continue to be very important for the crafting of everyday life within a changing, mobile and globalizing world. In this argument our senses of place and self are interlinked and created in an active process of day-to-day experience mediated by wider influences. As Marcuse notes 'every-day life is where the results of the social, economic and political systems in which we live are manifest and directly experienced – where they are shaped by the individual' (2010: 1).

This book therefore arises out of a desire to examine the tension between the social significance of place and the effects of globalization and to focus on the debates about place and identity and everyday life that have emerged over the latter part of the twentieth and early twenty-first centuries. These debates have been shaped by a recognition that there is a significant and growing awareness of our connection with each other across the planet. Developments in astronomy and in space exploration have revealed more of our planet and of the solar system, helping us to see that we are part of a greater whole. The images we now have of the globe from space and satellite imagery and the increasing accessibility of 'news' of events from multiple sources, which enhance and threaten our existence, have increased our global consciousness. But for all that, they have not necessarily diminished our sense of living in a 'local' place.

It should not be thought though that all aspects of the current conditions of life are new. Since the beginning of human migration and allied attempts to make maps and demarcate routes and areas of the earth's surface, people's lives have combined elements of the local and the global, the latter defined broadly as 'influences from afar'. What is new are the forms that the intermingling of local and global influences are taking, the speed at which they are being created and the compression that they bring to time–space. What previously took years to achieve now happens in minutes or even seconds with advanced high-speed digital transfers. Patterns of trade stretch across the globe bringing ideas, technologies and innovations in their wake, but today at a much faster rate than they did when the caravans made their annual journey on foot from Samarkand through present-day Afghanistan to the plains of India and along other parts of the Silk Road to China.

Within the social sciences, in such disciplines as sociology, human geography and anthropology, and their allied applied disciplines such as planning; housing, urban and rural studies; architecture and landscape architecture there have been debates about place, sense of place, identity, everyday life, globalization and their interconnections. These debates mark out contested intellectual territories and differences of opinion about the relative importance and contribution of local and global social, cultural and environmental influences in the creation of a sense of place and identity in people's everyday lives. They cover a wide theoretical spectrum from the humanistic with its focus on meaning and social constructionism, through to the structuralist with its emphasis on materialism and the power of the economy. Further, everyday life studies have been characterized by a variety of methodological approaches with each treating data differently. Some researchers take an ethnographic position and favour a deep exposure to places and people, while others prefer to work at a more distant macro and quantitative level of data collection and analysis (Mangin *et al.*, 2008; Perkins *et al.*, 2008a).

At the macro, and more structural level, systems analysis and the use of biological metaphors and analogies have been favoured. Thus, for example, the Chicago School in the 1930s used the idea of the ecological system and concepts from plant science to describe the incremental growth of Chicago, and by extension other industrial cities with high proportions of migrants in their populations. Other systems models drawing on mechanics and engineering, known generically as social physics, have featured the ideas of connectedness, flows and feedback loops to explain the structure of, and changes in, cities and wider rural regions. Structuralist perspectives with a Marxist influence have emphasized the economic determinants of city and regional life and argued that spatial structure reflects social class relations and the differential distribution of wealth and power (Castells, 1977, 1983; Harvey, 1973, 1989a). When advocates of such perspectives consider everyday life they see it as shaped and constrained by external forces, such as access to social, economic and political resources that often limit human agency. Further, they draw attention to the need for collective action by social movements to effect change to both individual and social conditions.

Attempts have also been made to overcome the tensions between those who would privilege structural conditions over human agency in social enquiry and vice versa. This has stimulated some researchers to attempt a reworking of this divide, the most notable of which has been Giddens' (1984, 1990) work on structuration (see also Thrift, 1983). As a result, over the last two decades, analysis has increasingly moved away from the somewhat dualistic approach created through the use of ideas about structure and agency, to one that is more flexible. This is highlighted in some of the commentary on globalization and the ways it affects people's everyday lives, and in turn how they help create the processes involved. Sociologists and geographers have attempted to elaborate the origins and mechanisms of globalization. These scholars see sense of place, identity and everyday life as being dynamic, shaped by a variety of fluid global economic, cultural and technological forces. Advocates of this approach also emphasize the possibility that people can assume multiple identities ranging from those created in association with traditional relationships such as those to do with kin, family and gender, through to senses of self and community emerging from the newer world of virtual relationships and social networking sites.

There are a number of perspectives on globalization, identity, sense of place and everyday life which have emerged as a result. Some scholars argue that while globalization is a very real and influential phenomenon, one of its counter-intuitive effects is to encourage local resistance to globalizing influences which in turn strengthens local expressions of identity and sense of place and therefore undermines completely any propensity for the development of cultural homogenization (Durrschmidt and Taylor, 2007). The same globalized influences that have been interpreted as creating cultural conformity have thus also aided the revival of threatened cultures and languages. In part this is a reflection of increasing mobility and the added ability, provided by new communication tools, to resist change and maintain cultural and linguistic connections. Others argue that globalization is a reified discourse which, while not representing anything particularly new in the working out of capitalism, definitely influences local activity as people act in accordance with the elements of the discourse. Still others argue for the relationship between globalization and everyday life to be conceptualized as lying at the intersection of the local and the global; that while identity and sense of place are created and maintained locally as people interact with each other and their immediate environments, these interactions occur within a decidedly globalized and dynamic set of circumstances. It has therefore become common to see scholars writing about identity and sense of place as being produced by local and the global forces in various combinations.

Other social scientists, working from a range of interpretative perspectives, and latterly, using poststructuralist analysis, have in contrast emphasized the role of human agency and cultural activity in discussions of change and stasis. This approach encourages an appreciation of the role of social actors, social movements, social groups, classes and individuals in the construction of everyday life. It also points to the risks of reductionism, partial explanation and flawed analysis inherent in explanations of change and stasis based on structural, technological or economic analyses. In their recent economic research, therefore, these interpretative and poststructuralist social scientists have focused on the role of individuals such as entrepreneurs and innovators as the early adopters and opinion leaders in new economic activities and also drawn on behavioural psychology to explain market failures (Elster, 2010).

Going further, these social scientists have argued that enhanced communication, tourism and mass migration have, on a grand scale, increased people's knowledge and appreciation of cultural diversity and highlighted, for a great many of them, the need to preserve rather than destroy differences. The greatest cultural diversity is to be found among the populations of global and other large cities because they are constituted through a mix of migration streams involving people from many ethnic backgrounds. Global cities thus face the challenges of social inclusion and exclusion, of maintaining social cohesion and building social capital within local and national communities. Notwithstanding the argument that urban population diversity can lead to an appreciation of difference, this process can also create anxiety and a fear of 'strangers in our midst', of people who speak different languages and have unfamiliar ways of living. This can also foster various forms of urban segregation and nationalist anti-immigration politics. Thus the consequences of global change are far from uniform with globalizing influences being mediated, blended and adapted as new technological, economic and cultural practices are incorporated by the residents of cities, towns and rural areas into their everyday lives.

Additionally, a number of these writers have begun to reject the usefulness of the local–global dualism, arguing instead for a network and node model of place relationships and identity formation. In this conceptualization we all exist at the intersection of constantly shifting networks of cultural and social influences, resources and ideas. There is no local or global, or grounded sense of place and social identity (at least in a sustained and stable form), just nodes of social, cultural, economic and environmental activity through which flow people, resources, ideas and power. This view has been influenced by writing about the rise of the information/networked society and new economies created around global spaces of flows.

It can thus be seen that the challenge for social scientists has been to find ways of characterizing the simultaneous experiences and expressions of change, stasis and resistance associated with globalization and everyday life. Many commentators working from a structuralist perspective have emphasized a top-down analysis which characterizes individual and collective agency as being constrained by economic forces and allied technological developments. In these terms it is new forms of technology and economic activity that have been responsible for changing people, places and cultural processes. The social, cultural and biophysical landscapes of urban and rural areas are shaped, for example, by technologies such as those associated with construction, transport, energy and telecommunications. They are also influenced by the position of products in national and global markets and the manifestation of technologies and economic outputs in the form of fixed and durable capital in the built environment such as houses, offices, factories, roads, farms, tourism facilities, etc. Such structures are said to change *and* constrain how everyday life can be expressed.

While we see the merit in some elements of the structuralist perspective, the way we view globalization is that it is a complex set of processes involving myriad interconnections and flows between the global and the local. This is illustrated, for example, in research into food and cultural practices. Falafel is a traditional Israeli staple food that was originally sold from small street-stands or storefronts as a 'fast food'. This relatively simple dish is made from chickpeas, oil, crushed red pepper and usually served in a pita pocket. It was considered a 'quick, messy, no frills street food, packing plenty of nutrition and value into a small portion' (Raviv National Identity, quoted in Lightman, 2010). Under the influence of globalization, McDonald's went to Israel with its food and new ways of selling and falafel migrated to the US. The result was a McDonaldization of the way falafel was prepared and sold in both countries. In the US falafel incorporated an expanded set of ingredients to meet local tastes and was sold through American-style fast-food restaurants. In Israel, what it means to eat falafel now covers a wider range of ingredients and some aspects of McDonald's practices were adopted to compete with the threat from the local fast-food market including expanding the scope of delivery by complementing the small street kiosks with seated dining areas. In both the US and Israel this had the effect of transforming local cultural practices. So what we see here is change in the mode of food production including differences in the ways it is prepared and consumed in the two countries reflecting the cultural contexts in which it is situated under conditions of 'globalization'.

Another example is sushi – a traditional Japanese food – now available in many countries. Some Japanese sushi chefs believe that globalization has devalued this form of cuisine because of poor practices adopted by inadequately trained chefs in countries other than Japan. It is the view of these Japanese chefs that their overseas counterparts have adopted this form of food without fully understanding its cultural context and methods of preparation. Staying with food momentarily, the growth of fusion food which combines elements and ingredients from a variety of 'places' is a another example of how globalizing processes are affecting our everyday activities and tastes and transporting elements of cultural practices from one context to another.

It is our position that globalization is in a new phase. We are living in an age of very rapid and fluid flows of information, ideas, goods and people which are having an effect at a variety of scales. If we are to understand this new phase, then emphasis has to be placed on the relationships between people's everyday lives and the variable manifestation of localities, cities, regions, national-level and global-level institutions and interventions, agreements and processes of government. We do not agree with much of the hype attached to popular interpretations of the 'current transformation' which privilege the effects of information and communication technologies (Carlaw et al., 2006). We therefore agree with Lipsey et al. (2005), who argue that set alongside such historically significant 'general purpose technologies' as writing, printing and electricity, the advent of micro-computer technology, while important, takes a secondary position. Electricity, for example, is of the most fundamental importance because without it many machines including computers and other new electronic media would not have been possible as we discovered after the earthquake that shook Christchurch, New Zealand, in February 2011. This disrupted power and Internet connections across the city, in some parts for two weeks, denying access to information, websites and links with family, friends and work colleagues locally and globally. What the new programmable computer technology enables is a more complex network of movement that has changed the way many people work, play, communicate and spend their leisure time. In these terms information and communication technologies are important because they have added to our repertoire of experiences but they have not replaced all our former practices and activities.

Structure of the Book

The book is organized into three parts. Part I, comprising Chapters 2 and 3, sets out the intellectual framework which underpins our analysis in the remainder of the chapters. Chapter 2 examines the ways that place, identity and everyday life have been interpreted and traces the theoretical developments and methodological approaches that have been adopted in the articulation of these ideas. This work draws on research mainly from human geography and sociology but also focuses on elements of history, planning, urban studies and landscape architecture. The chapter emphasizes the centrality of place-based experience in the construction of individual and collective identities and everyday life. Chapter 3 discusses how the idea of globalization and its relationship to everyday life have been conceptualized. The literature and debates are reviewed, and the chapter documents the shift from seeing globalization as primarily an economic and deterministic process to a broader set of interrelated processes encompassing economic, social, political, cultural and environmental changes played out in different ways and combinations in local, regional, national and international settings and places.

    Part II of the book, comprising four chapters, is entitled 'Organizing and Living in Our Everyday Worlds'. The first chapter in Part II, Chapter 4, examines the development, form and ways of life in cities and regions. The discussion centres on questions about the broad structural changes that have and are shaping people's capacities to create senses of place, and fashion their everyday lives in particular localities. It is argued that despite an increase in mobility, which is very much to the fore in global debates, the majority of urban and rural residents live out their lives in mainly local contexts. This is not to say that 'mobility' is an unimportant feature of many people's lives and we therefore discuss the various streams of current mobility and the people involved in them. These include hyper-mobile business and leisure travellers, internal and international migrants, and refugees.

Whether highly mobile or relatively sedentary, almost all people have some sort of sense of home, representing their connections to family, friends, social networks, landscapes and dwellings. Thus in Chapter 5 the scale at which the analysis is conducted is changed, and the chapter explores the meanings of houses and homes. The emphasis is on human agency and the ways people create a sense of home in their everyday lives. While the chapter primarily focuses on the connections between house and home, it acknowledges that the idea of 'home' is a much broader multifaceted and multilevel concept. The chapter reports research and analysis that has been carried out across a range of disciplines and draws predominantly from the results of qualitative social enquiry. In the final section of the chapter the global significance of second homes and amenity migration is discussed, which adds to the understanding of how places are linked and connected.

Chapter 6 discusses the intriguing role of virtual spaces and places in the lives of people who have access to computers, the Internet and cell-phones/mobiles. The chapter addresses such questions as: do these spaces and places constitute a new dimension in which everyday life is being played out? Are the Internet, World Wide Web and digital tech-nologies transforming how we work, live, build relationships and spend our leisure time? There are important connections between these ques-tions and debates about globalization and everyday life. The impact of these technologies is uneven and their spread greatest and most transfor-mative in the richer parts of the world but not exclusively so. A signifi-cant proportion of this chapter deals also with the important links between the development of these and related digital technologies and their use in various forms of personal and collective surveillance to enhance security and advance the interests of government and commer-cial organizations.

Chapter 7, entitled 'Places of Consumption', sees the focus shift to the ways everyday living and a wide range of places have been affected by the expansion of opportunities for consumption of an ever-increasing range of products and objects. The particular focus is on the relationship between leisure and consumption and how this relationship is profoundly important in the making of everyday life. The chapter discusses how a work-and-spend cycle has emerged in which leisure and day-to-day life has become increasingly linked to the consumption of an ever-widening range of commercial products, activities and services, often purchased on credit. This is illustrated by using examples from urban and rural areas in various countries.

The final section of the book, 'Part III: A Finite World', comprising Chapters 8 and 9, turns to the growing literature and debates surrounding the future shape of the city and countryside and whether these can be managed in a more sustainable way than has been the case in the past. As noted earlier in the book, there is a growing global consciousness of people's interrelationships with the natural world and the need to respect its fragility, infinite variety and delicate balance. A growing volume of research warns of the dangers to this balance and the sustainability of species as we recognize more clearly the impacts that humans are having on global environmental change. Sustaining places is thus central to the current urban and rural research agenda. However, as recent international conferences and the reports of International Panel on Climate Change (IPCC) have shown, finding solutions is a complex political process as it needs to address the economic, social, cultural and environmental dimensions of change. Chapter 8 draws on these wider, global debates, discussing attempts to sustain the city, the place where more than 50 per cent of the world's population now lives. Chapter 9 turns to the local manifestation of these attempts, focusing on sustaining housing, communities and neighbourhoods. This returns to the theme that runs through the book: that in order to understand and change how we view and use our world we need to explore how people live and experience the environment in their everyday encounters. We argue that this is where attitudes are changed and practices will be adopted that begin to make a difference. Chapter 10 examines two broad theoretical and methodological themes that have arisen from our discussion and that are relevant for the development of research agendas in urban and rural studies.

PART I

Establishing a Framework

This part of the book explores the framework that was introduced in Chapter 1 by focusing on how the analysis of everyday life and place has evolved. This is done through a review of the relevant literature and the exploration of the interconnection between place, space and dwelling and how within these spaces people shape their everyday living (Chapter 2). We see this as a dynamic emergent process which is increasingly influenced by a range of globalizing influences. This takes us to the second dimension of our book which is the processes of globalization. These are explored in Chapter 3 to complete the framing of our later chapters. Here again the emphasis is on process and element of change. Globalization is ongoing and evolving and is one of the most powerful transformative influences within our contemporary world.

CHAPTER 2

Place, Identity and Everyday Life

Introduction

The ways people live day to day in places and the influence that places have on how people identify themselves and interact with others is of considerable interest to social scientists and professional practitioners, including, to name a few: geographers, sociologists, planners, architects, engineers, landscape architects, property developers, housing managers, retailers, transport operators, recreation service providers, marketers and product designers. A way of thinking about this phenomenon is to say that the socio-spatial interactions of everyday life help people create a sense of place, themselves and others. This is a complex process and there is much debate about the relative importance and contribution of local and global social, cultural and environmental influences in the creation of a sense of place and identity in people's everyday lives.

Our purpose in this chapter is to discuss these debates, focusing on research into the connections between everyday life, place and identity. We want to examine in what ways, and the degree to which, emplaced local activity contributes to people's everyday lives. This is important in the context of scholarly and popular arguments which suggest that the influence of the 'local' is being eroded in the face of globalization. In doing so we will elaborate the work of social scientists interested in the connections between social events and settings which can be described as cultural contexts, created on the one hand by the variable capacity for action by individuals and groups and on the other by structural and cultural conventions and environmental limitations (Sztompka, 2008: 25). We will be discussing research that has been conducted using a variety of mainly qualitative methods such as participant observation, case studies, in-depth interviews and the interpretation of archival and printed material such as letters, life stories, family and community photographs and related film, video and digital imagery. These are methods used to examine the visible, observable and recorded aspects of everyday life in places.

Everyday Life, Place and Sense of Place

Sztompka (2008: 31–32) suggested that everyday life has several defining positive traits. The first is that everyday life 'is the observable manifestation of social existence' and always involves either distant or direct interaction with other people. Second, much of everyday life is routine and often cyclical or in other ways rhythmic over a variety of time periods. Good examples include such things as participation in work, employment, cultural events and recreation. Third, often everyday life is ritualized and habitual such as exercising at the same time daily, having a drink after work on Fridays, and attending weddings and funerals. Fourth, everyday life is embodied: it requires us to engage with others with all or some of our senses, and our capacity to participate in activities is enhanced or limited by our bodily characteristics. Fifth, everyday life has a temporal dimension where the actual or expected length of a social event affects its character. Sixth, many aspects of everyday life are taken for granted such that people are not often fully aware of their actions and motives. Finally, in Sztompka's terms, everyday life is localized, it occurs in particular spaces, many of which are integrally important to the activities involved. We would add that everyday life for the most part changes incrementally but also sometimes dramatically. It is therefore fluid.

It is Sztompka's latter point which links the social scientific understanding of everyday life to studies of place, sense of place and identity. These studies have been conducted over several decades and reflect changing academic fashions during that period. At the core of most place-related writing is the notion that places are more than just locations. Early approaches to this work were somewhat individualistic and emphasized mainly grounded local experience of landscapes and the people associated with them. In these terms, places are at the centre of everyday life. They are created by people, who in turn identify with them. As Relph (1976: 34) put it, 'people are their place and place is its people, and however readily these may be separated in conceptual terms, in experience they are not easily differentiated'. In its simplest form, sense of place therefore encompasses the idea that people, in the course of their everyday lives, form close relationships with the spaces in which they live. As they work, play, spend time with their families and friends, travel in their neighbourhoods and immediate environments individuals have positive and negative experiences in, and of, places and as a result ascribe meaning to them, themselves and other people with whom they interact (Buttimer, 1980; Lewis, 1979; Meinig, 1979; Relph, 1976).

Geographer Yi-Fu Tuan (1974) and landscape architect, J. B. Jackson (1994) saw this as an active process. Tuan used the term 'topophilia' to describe the relationships people establish with places, and wrote about 'place-making', the ways everyday involvement with particular settings forms close connections with landscape. He suggested that sense of place was the self-conscious evaluation of place by individuals, writing that 'sense of place … implies a certain distance between self and place that allows the self to appreciate a place' (1980: 4). A sense of place in these terms is sometimes only completely realized when a loss occurs, such as when a landscape has undergone change or a person is displaced.

A good example of such loss was documented during research into residents' reactions to rapid urban change in a small Southern US town, Chapel Hill, North Carolina (Perkins, 1988a, b, 1989). There, large forested urban lots with one or two houses on them were denuded of vegetation, the houses demolished or removed, and filled with medium-density multi-family housing, including apartments. Local residents who had habitually used these lots for casual neighbourhood recreation for many years, and appreciated their amenity value, felt their loss very greatly, and talked about their radically changed sense of place. This sense of place was associated with memories, meanings, moving events and the establishment of 'individual identity, security and concern' (Pred, 1983: 49). In Chapel Hill, residents were struggling with an emerging sense of place and new patterns of everyday life represented by the loss of both a biophysical landscape and opportunities for restful and intimate recreation with which they identified very closely.

So interpreted in this way, sense of place relates particularly to the routines of everyday life set in particular local biophysical landscapes. Relph (1976) wrote, for example, of sense of place as an evaluation of landscape. Jackson (1994) also exemplified this view arguing that a sense of place grows as people become accustomed to localities and learn to know their peculiarities. He believed that a sense of place is created in the course of time and is the result of habit or custom. In saying this he acknowledged that others with a landscape orientation believe that a sense of place is a response to features which are *already* there – either beautiful natural settings or well-designed architecture, a particular composition of spaces and forms – natural or manmade (151; see also Lewis, 1979). This latter point is reflected in Meinig's analysis of nostalgic American views of the New England, US, village. This landscape has a strong sense of place and symbolizes significant values: 'the best we have known of an intimate, family-centred, Godfearing, morally conscious, industrious, thrifty, democratic community' (1979: 165).

When incorporated into interpretations of regional identity, large geographic areas are drawn into debates about sense of place (Jansson, 2003). Choosing a controversial example to illustrate this point, Lewis described New Jersey in the US as: 'a state so conspicuously lacking a sense of place that most residents would think the phrase bizarre'. He wrote that Benjamin Franklin is supposed to have remarked that 'New Jersey served as part of a digestive tract that stretched between New York and Philadelphia, although he disclaimed knowledge about which end was which'. Lewis noted further 'that [others have alluded] to the Coastal Plain of southern New Jersey as an area where the sea withdrew in disgust' (1979: 29). Interpreted in this way, sense of place is the shared positive experience of the defining landscape characteristics of place. These characteristics can range from 'monumental totems ... to vernacular things, easily recognized as peculiar to a place and which are the object of general affection' (Lewis, 1979: 41–42; Wild, 1963, in Tuan, 1975). Landscape elements that may be of significance in one place or time may not make a contribution to sense of place in another.

Place, Everyday Life and Dwelling

Other writers have combined elements of these earlier interpretations of sense of place with alternative conceptualizations of place, landscape and everyday life (Feld and Basso, 1996: 9; Geertz, 1996: 262). One approach is associated with Heidegger's philosophical discussions of dwelling, as reworked by Casey (1993, 1998) and Ingold (2000). Dwelling in these terms can be defined as 'the rich and intimate ongoing togetherness of beings and things which makes up landscapes and places, and which bind together nature and culture over time' (Cloke and Jones, 2001: 651). This body of work has been used, for example, by a variety of researchers interested in the connections between nature, landscape and place. Cloke and Jones (2001), a case in point, studied how interaction between trees and people created place meaning. They used West Bradley Orchard, Somerset, England, to illustrate how orchards are places which are made by people *and* trees interacting together in a codependent relationship. Studies such as theirs show how places gain and reproduce their form and meaning in the working out of everyday life.

Bringing in the 'Social'

Other writers attempted to downplay the importance of individual encounters with landscape and highlighted social interaction in conceptualizations of place, sense of place and identity, while at the same time emphasizing the importance of local activity (Ley and Samuels, 1978; see also Duncan, 1978). These scholars relied on ideas about the ways meaning is created as people interact with each other in everyday settings around the use of objects (Blumer, 1969), and argued that place and individual and collective identity evolve in partnership. In this view, places and sense of place are produced by people interacting together, while at the same time their sense of who they are and how other people see them, their identity (or identities), is strongly influenced by the sites or localities in which they interact (Ley, 1981: 219).

Two quite different studies can be used to illustrate the significance and usefulness of this perspective. The first examined the relationship between rites of passage, physical spaces and objects. Silver (1996) used the phenomenon of students moving away from home to attend university to show how they took particular objects from their family home to their new university dormitory room as a way of bridging the social networks of those two places. They made choices about which objects to leave at home as anchors of prior identities, and the ones to take to university as markers of new identities. The latter, in time, were often reinterpreted in the light of new university experiences and either discarded or supplemented with newly acquired objects. Silver also made the point that the meanings of such objects differ by gender, suggesting that this transition to a new, albeit temporary home, illustrates how objects, physical settings, identity and gender are closely interlinked.

The second study, conducted in Glasgow, Scotland, bears the intriguing title 'Wine Alley: The Sociology of a Dreadful Enclosure' (Damer, 1974) and is a good example of how the ideas discussed above about everyday life, place and identity have been applied to interpretations of urban life. The term 'dreadful enclosure' refers to parts of cities or other areas that are synonymous with danger, pain and chaos and which gather reputations for moral inferiority. One such place was Wine Alley, a small, Corporation, slum-clearance housing estate in the Govan area of Glasgow, built in 1934. In its early 1970s redevelopment plan for Govan, the City Corporation proposed erecting three multi-storey blocks including two pubs, motor vehicle lock-ups and landscaping across the road from Wine Alley. Govan residents told planning staff that they couldn't see the point of such proposals because 'the "anymuls [animals]" from Wine Alley would sally forth from their ghetto, lay waste the landscaping, wreck the lock-ups, steal the cars, burn the multis to the ground, and mug, plunder and murder the inhabitants' (Damer, 1974: 223). The author set about trying to understand why such a pejorative label had been applied to the people of Wine Alley and concluded that it had its historical basis in competition for housing between Govanites and Wine Alleyites dating from the 1930s. Instead of housing the people of Govan at a time of very high unemployment and when very many of them were living in crumbling slums, the new housing estate was allocated to people from neighbouring Gorbals, an area with a reputation for being gritty and rough. Thus began a hostile place-labelling process by Govanites and the Corporation of Glasgow which characterized Wine Alley and its residents as *other*: lazy, thieving, dishonest good-for-nothings. Although this reputation had little basis in fact, and was actively resisted by Wine Alleyites, it influenced the ways they identified themselves and their urban neighbours, and affected their life chances.

These examples illustrate very clearly how place, sense of place and identity are created locally in everyday social interaction. Objects, physical spaces, built urban environments and the social groups associated with them are bound together in an iterative and intrinsically dynamic process which helps define the meanings of places and the people who live in them. These meanings have real effect in social, cultural and geographical terms.

Structure and Culture

Consistent with Sztompka's (2008: 25–26) conceptualization of everyday life and social existence it takes but a moment's thought to see that there are also bigger forces at work in the creation of the places and identities discussed above. As we have shown so far in this chapter, a focus on human action, known technically as agency, is important, for, as many authors have argued, people *do* make their own lives and create their own places and identities. But as Eyles also points out, they do so 'not necessarily or overwhelmingly in conditions of their own choosing' (1989: 109). Thus people's choices, and therefore agency, are constrained and enabled by their histories, cultures, subcultures, social class backgrounds, economic opportunities, positions of power and geographical locations (Giddens, 1984; Pred, 1983; Thrift, 1983; Eyles, 1985; Gregory, 1989). In the context of a discussion about everyday life and the ways sense of place and identity are created it can be said that they are influenced by the historical and current development of local and distant social interaction, deeply embedded cultural values and associated social relations and economic activity.

These are fundamentally dynamic arrangements. Shields' (1991) work on social spatialization amply demonstrated this where he infused discussions of place-making and identity with a strong sense of fluidity, emphasizing the need to examine place relationships at a variety of scales, and incorporating influences from multiple parts of distant or local social and economic networks. In these terms, places, like identities, are multifaceted, emergent and contingent. Ideas such as this opened the way for significant changes in empirical studies of people's place relations. A good example was Eyles' (1985) examination of the sense of place of residents in a small English town. While the study was undeniably local in orientation, there are clear hints in it of people's senses of place and identity being created locally but also being channelled by the influences of wider capitalist market-oriented processes and cultural developments. They also involve a combination of social and landscape elements. Eyles' study participants indicated in their interviews that they lived where they could find employment or otherwise make a living and created a sense of place that is as permanent or temporary, strong or weak as conditions permitted. Some people stayed in the locality for a long time and put down roots and made strong social, familial and environmental connections. Others, often out of necessity, had a much more instrumental connection with place and people, seeing their investment in the locality as fleeting and necessarily shallow. For still others, place and social relationships were limited by a sense that they had no control over their lives. Whatever their situation the relationships these people had with the locality in which they lived could best be described in terms of senses rather than sense of place because of the multifaceted and changing nature of their lives. Eyles (1985: 122–126) listed ten dominant senses of place articulated by his research participants. They included:

1. **Social sense of place** – place was socially significant and social relationships had place significance
2. **Apathetic–acquiescent sense of place** – no strong sense of place at all. Underlying this sense of place was the notion that some people felt that life, including place, is largely meaningless; or that the possibilities of controlling one's life and one's place were very limited.
3. **Instrumental sense of place** – place was a means to an end and its significance depended on whether or not goods, services and opportunities were available.
4. **Nostalgic sense of place** – dominated by feelings towards place at some time other than the present.
5. **Commodity sense of place** – place was seen as an ideal place which is quiet, safe and had certain valued facilities and types of residents.

This sense of place was held by residents who were employed in professional/managerial/technical occupations. Place was a commodity which was purchasable, useable and exchangeable, and saleable, and after a time able to be discarded for another.

6. **Platform/stage sense of place** – place was like a stage on which life is lived out. Similar to commodity sense of place, but distinguished from it by the establishment of stronger, longer-lasting, social attachments to place.

7. **Family sense of place** – place was family interactions and attachments.

8. **Way-of-life sense of place** – the research participants' whole way of life was bound up with a specific place.

9. **Roots sense of place** – unselfconscious attachment to place.

10. **Environmental sense of place** – place is not important for its social, familial or transitional meanings but is an aesthetic experience. Place is something to be lived in.

These dominant senses of place illustrate the point that groups and individuals may have differing and multiple senses of place in a particular setting. These shift as the local and wider contexts of residents also change. Family or friends may move away, which for those remaining may erode long-held social attachments; threats or enhancements to the local landscape my change environmental senses of place, employment opportunities may become more stable and thus allow previously temporary residents to strengthen their relationships to local people, activity and sites; or alternatively, economic conditions might deteriorate at a national or global level undermining the performance of local businesses and changing people's working lives, incomes and social and place relationships.

History and Conflicting Senses of Place and Identity

Massey (1994a, b, 1995) added a further element to these analyses. She argued that senses of place should also include interpretations of people's histories and their self-interested attempts to create places, such as those associated with boundary marking; place-naming; offensive and defensive tactics; claims about the appropriateness of, and priorities for, land use; memorializing; building; promoting; and the development of formal policies favouring particular groups, cultural practices and land uses (Berg and Kearns, 1996; Massey, 1994b, 1995; Norton, 2003; Williams, 2002). This approach to place-meaning works against the belief that places have only one past, and therefore one meaning, created by residents of long-standing.

Egoz *et al.*'s (2001, 2006) New Zealand study of the ways conventional and organic farmers interpret and react towards each other's farming and landscape management practices is a very good example of the relevance of Massey's contribution to the sense of place debate (see also Egoz 2000, 2002). Farming in New Zealand and its rural landscapes have their origins in nineteenth-century British colonial settlement and contribute significantly to the nation's income *and* collective senses of place and identity, despite the fact that 85 per cent of the country's population is urban (Statistics New Zealand, 2001). The country's well-established conventional farmed landscape looks controlled and tidy. Organic farming, on the other hand, is based on more recent and different values and organic farmers share a world-view based on working in harmony with nature. They oppose the application of chemical fertilizers and herbicides, and organic farms typically have 'weedy' landscapes containing long grass and untrimmed hedgerows.

These differences in landscape aesthetics often cause conflict when conventional and organic farmers become neighbours. Their farms illustrate the ways landscapes symbolize beliefs and everyday practices, and how new landscape introductions challenge established senses of place. In the conventional farming community, a neat, tidy and closely grazed landscape tells neighbours that a farmer is managing her or his land well and is capable of hard work. Proponents of organic farming interpret this conventional landscape as representing irresponsible land management. Conventional farmers view organic landscapes as an example of inefficient land use and laziness. Thus the co-location of organic and conventional farms shows how places may be managed in a number of ways by different groups and therefore have multiple and shifting identities as time passes.

Going Global and Mobile

Massey (1994a, b, 1995) also focused critically on the effects of globalization on everyday life, place meanings and sense of place. Some writers have suggested, for example, that globalization may homogenize experiences in and of places across the globe or even deny the possibilities for close place attachments. The widespread use of television and the development of shopping malls are suggested as mechanisms through which people have the same experiences of places whether they are in Europe, North America or Oceania. But this is too simplistic, and Massey takes a different view, acknowledging the fluidity and diversity of place meanings and the ways that, in the past and present, the 'global' and 'local' have always been implicated in the construction of each other; that they intersect in the construction of place. The experience of everyday life and the meanings of places are influenced by the ways power is distributed (see also Berg and Kearns, 1996). But the power of people and organizations to affect place-meaning should not be thought of as dominant and unchangeable. Rather, as its basis has 'continually to be renewed, recreated, defended, and modified' so too will it be 'continually resisted, limited, altered and challenged' (Williams, 1977: 110–113). Thus, as Massey (1995: 188–190) put it 'the identity of places, indeed the very identification of places as particular places, is always in that sense temporary, uncertain, and in process'.

Consistent with this perspective, Sheller and Urry (2006) in their review of 'mobilities' research have argued for 'going beyond the imagery of "terrains" as spatially fixed geographical containers for social processes, and calling into question scalar logics such as local/global as descriptors of regional extent' (209). Unlike writing which emphasizes strong attachments to place and locality and the creation of consequent identities, Sheller and Urry emphasized the need to reject what they call *sedentarist* theories in social science and suggested that we should inject a sense of mobility into the study of everyday life and therefore accept the theoretical importance of distance, change and placelessness.

Massey (2004), Amin (2004) and Thrift (1999, 2004) have contributed to this line of thinking in their discussions of relational space and the politics of place. From this perspective, a place is a centre, node or location through which flows diverse networks of people, ideas, resources, practices, etc. which have long histories. Places are therefore 'spatial formations of continuously changing composition, character and reach' (Amin and Thrift, 2002, quoted in Amin, 2004: 34). Massey elaborated this argument, noting that 'If space is a product of practices, trajectories, interrelations, if we make space through interactions at all levels, from the (so-called) local to the (so-called) global, then those spatial identities such as places, regions, nations, and the local and the global, must be forged in this relational way too, as internally complex, essentially unboundable in any absolute sense, and inevitably historically changing' (2004: 5). Amin took this conceptualization of place to discuss what he calls a 'relational politics of propinquity' (2004: 39). This politics arises when groups sharing the same spaces have to negotiate cultural change and diversity, including claims about the appropriate use of resources, such as land, all of which are constituted increasingly through distant attachments and influences (see also Macnaghten and Urry, 1998).

The way in which in relational terms, everyday life, sense of place and identity are constantly changing can be illustrated by returning to the example of conflict between conventional and organic farmers in New Zealand outlined above (Egoz *et al.* 2001, 2006). There, historically well-developed ways of farming, senses of place and local landscapes are changing as a result of market opportunities in, and ideas from, distant settings. Organic agriculture is growing in New Zealand. Its landscapes are based on new meanings and beliefs and a sense of place shared by a growing group of farmers and their urban sympathizers. Conventional farmers have to date resisted it, but the mainstreaming and global corporatization of organic agriculture may limit this resistance because it presents alternative agriculture in a new light. Mainstreamed organic production is a large-scale activity and more mechanized than subsistence forms. In New Zealand, this is likely to create farming landscapes of the 'middle way', somewhere between the neat and tidy landscape of conventional agriculture and the messy landscape of the smallholding organic farmer. It is not possible to predict the detailed features of the new rural landscape mosaic but it seems likely that more diverse production landscapes will be associated with political contests between existing and new rural interest groups, the members of which have varying and conflicting senses of place and identity.

Conclusion

In this chapter we have discussed arguments about place, identity and everyday life. Our reason for doing so has been to show that for several decades scholars have conducted research which shows that place-based experience is a defining characteristic of everyday life for most people, notwithstanding the fact that they are influenced by, and contribute to, wider social, economic and cultural currents. Recent writing on sense of place and identity has taken account of debates about 'globalization' and its variants in discussions of 'mobilities' and 'relational space' and to varying degrees has suggested an erosion of local influences in everyday life. For us these developments underscore the need for a more detailed and critical examination of such debates and we begin to do this in the next chapter.

Further reading

Cloke, P. and O. Jones. 2001. 'Dwelling, Place and Landscape: An Orchard in Somerset'. *Environment and Planning A* 33, 649–666.

Eyles, J. 1985. *Senses of Place.* Warrington: Silverbrook Press.

Ley, D. 1981. 'Behavioural Geography and the Philosophies of Meaning', in *Behavioural Problems in Geography Revisited* (eds.), K. R. Cox and R. G. Golledge. London: Methuen.

Massey, D. 1995. 'Places and Their Pasts'. *History Workshop Journal* 39, 182–192. 2004. Geographies of Responsibility, *Geografiska Annaler* 86, 5–18.

Relph, E. 1976. *Place and Placelessness.* London: Pion.

Sheller, M. and J. Urry. 2006. 'The New Mobilities Paradigm'. *Environment and Planning A* 38, 207–226.

Sztompka. P. 2008. 'The Focus on Everyday Life: A New Turn in Sociology'. *European Review* 1, 21–37.

CHAPTER 3

Everyday Life in a Globalizing World

Introduction

The world is globalizing. People are connecting in an increasing number of ways. The working out of these developments over the past 50 years or so has raised questions about whether we are now living in a new epoch. But despite globalization there are still deep and enduring differences among the earth's people, and considerable, and in many cases, growing, inequalities in access to resources and services across the globe. The impact of change is thus uneven. It is clear also that in the face of globalization the ways everyday life is constituted are still shaped by local experience of place, and by where people live locally, regionally and nationally and by the access they have to resources and opportunities in those settings. It is important therefore not to fall into the trap of seeing global change as creating a sense of universal cultural and economic homogeneity. Our task in this chapter is thus to set our examination of place, identity and everyday life within a broader, global, context but still recognize their intrinsically unique, variable and fluid dimensions.

Writing about Globalization

The time at which globalization began has been a source of considerable controversy. For example one view is that:

> Two dates 1494 and 1969 stand out as important moments in the history of the world as a global place ... Since the fifteenth century, people have slowly come to think of the world as a global place. This process was aided by the

25

widespread use of maps and globes in schoolrooms ... and in 1969 the astro-nauts' photographs of earth gave currency to the idea of the world as a global place. (Shaffer, quoted in Khondecker, 2000: 17)

The reason for the choice of the first date, 1494, was that in this year Columbus 'found' the new world of the Americas and helped to initiate a period of colonial expansion and increased trade bringing new commodities and social practices into European countries and creating new forms of wealth and the rise of the mercantile class to challenge the power of the established landed classes. It also heralded dramatic changes for the people and environment of the new-found lands. The second date, 1969, was the year 'man' landed on the moon and created a set of new images of planet earth and gave us a greater sense of being globally connected, changing our images and understandings of how our earth fits within the solar system (Robertson, 1992). Globalization can be thought of as an increased level of economic, political, social, cultural and environmental connectedness. This means that globalization is a multidimensional and multi-causal process that is still unfolding rather than something that is completed. To an extent the determination of phases and causes relates to whether primacy is given to economic processes or social and cultural ones. For some writers, for example, Wallerstein (2000) and Friedmann (1995) explanations are shaped by the development of capitalism and a world system that has created a system of dependency and exploitation with core nations dominating maritime and then later industrial production as the industrial capitalist system become dominant in the eighteenth and nineteenth centuries. These arguments then shift to the development of Fordism – mass-production-commodity-based economies in the twentieth century that internationalize production through the rise of a new international division of labour (Froebel et al. 1980). Then in the late twentieth and early twenty-first centuries this system has been transformed into the latest phase of globalization through the formation of more flexible arrangements reflecting a shift to greater linkages of products and markets and the integration of financial management facilitated by new forms of communication technologies (Jessop, 2002). The alternative explanation, developed by Robertson (1992) is focused on the globe and its culture rather than the nation state and its economy. He thus explores ideas around global consciousness which he sees as a relatively new phenomenon:

Globalization as a concept refers to both the compression of the world and the intensification of consciousness of the world as a whole ... both concrete global interdependence and consciousness of the global whole. (8)

The compression of the world as an outcome of globalization is agreed upon by most writers but what Robertson (1992) shows is that this is not just about economic processes but about social and cultural ones as well. As the writings on globalization have expanded, the range of topics covered has broadened so that in thinking about it in the early part of the twenty-first century it is necessary to see this as a set of processes that encompass economic, political, social, cultural and environmental change. These will be elaborated after we look at the growth in writing about globalization from the 1980s.

The literature on globalization shows that it was in the 1980s that sociologists and geographers began writing actively about globalization. Its increased currency reflected changes in the economic, political, social, cultural and environmental relations between and across countries. Over the following years the underlying theme of all the writing on globalization has been about the ways formative influences have shifted to the global level, leading to the remaking of national, regional and local boundaries and everyday relationships. The precise connections between these levels have been debated. Researchers have focused on the causative influence of global processes as opposed to national and local ones. They have examined the extent of, and possibilities for, resistance or reworking of these changes at a local level, and the desirability of doing so. The globalization agenda has spawned many new terms such as 'glocalization' to refer to the interconnection between the global and the local. For some writers, not to say readers, this proliferation of terms has confused rather than improved the clarity of debate.

It is important to be critical when approaching the notion of globalization. In their examination of the development and use of the term, and the ideas it represents, Robertson and Khondecker (1998) observed that:

> In spite of a number of attempts on the part of social scientists to conceptualize globalization in a careful analytical fashion, there is now so much loose and negative talk of 'globalization' that serious scholars of the compression of the world as a whole, in long historical perspective, face the increasingly difficult task of maintaining their intellectual seriousness in the face of slipshod and often heavily ideological employment of the word. (26)

While it is true that popular and academic writers have used the term in many different ways this does not mean that it is of little analytical value. Our view is that just because globalization has been widely discussed does not mean that there is no place for more discussion.

Furthermore, Robertson and Khondecker (1998) point out that a key component of globalization is the 'compression of the world': that the world has been 'shrunk' and more attention is now given at the economic and political level to relationships between transnational organizations and institutions. These relationships have been facilitated by new information-transfer technologies such as telephone/faxes, cellphones/mobiles, computers, scanners, digital cameras, etc. which have become integral parts of the everyday working and recreational lives of a growing number of people.

Other writers have drawn attention to the political nature of the term. Held, for example, suggested that globalization is:

> Primarily an ideological construction: a convenient myth which in part helps justify and legitimate the neo-liberal global project, that is, the creation of a global free market. (2000: 5)

This interpretation illustrates the point that writers can take positions within any debate, especially one that is widely discussed, and appropriate terms to suit particular interests. This, again, does not mean that we should abandon the use of ideas such as globalization but that we should be careful how we enter the debate and use the term.

One outcome of globalization that seems clearest is the interconnected nature of the global economy and the ways that an event in one part of the world can significantly and rapidly influence other parts. A good example is the global credit crunch that shook the world in late 2007 and precipitated a global economic crisis. It began with financial instability in the United States where loans were made to people who had little hope of repaying them but in the expectation that property prices would keep booming; when the bubble of economic optimism burst, falling property values caused finance and allied institutions and companies to collapse. This sent the world markets into a tailspin which by 2008 had led to a global recession. The impact has been widespread with people's livelihoods being affected, their savings eroded, wages cut and houses lost. This has affected consumer demand and led to governments around the world intervening to try and shore up financial institutions. Material conditions, the availability of jobs, income, housing and food are key resources for the constitution of our everyday lives. So alongside the financial and material crisis caused by the credit crunch we have also had a global crisis of identity, safety and security. These combined crises have been interpreted by some writers as a failure of modernity and rationalization. Others have placed them in a broader category of global risks such as those associated with terrorism, climate change, genetic modification and pandemics (such as SARS and bird flu).

Is Globalization Anything New?

One of the key areas of debate among theorists is the extent to which globalization is a new phenomenon or a stage in an evolving process. Debate as we have noted continues about when it began and the path that it has followed and thus how new it is. Some see it as being continuous with the past rather than as a radical departure. Others interpret it differently and place greater emphasis on what is changing rather than staying the same. Some, such as Robertson and Khondeker (1998), take the position that the emergence of a more 'global' world is not new and that we have been increasing both our knowledge of, and engagement with, the world over many centuries. They see the present phase of global change as part of an unfolding pattern of expansion initiated by the movement of people outwards from the European states to find new worlds to explore, exploit and settle in the fifteenth and sixteenth centuries. Throughout this period the increased speed of travel and communication alongside improved navigation were crucial to the patterns of this expansion.

This approach to globalization was adopted by Winchester (2003) in his history of the 1883 volcanic eruption of Krakatoa entitled *Krakatoa: The Day the World Exploded*. He told the story of how, by that time, much of the world, and certainly those parts that had been colonized by the European powers, were linked together in webs of commercial interest helped in significant part by the existence of underwater and terrestrial telegraph cables. So when Krakatoa in the Sunda Strait between Java and Sumatra, in what today is Indonesia, erupted so catastrophically, it took very little time for the news of the event and its aftermath to be reported in the newspapers of Europe and its settler colonies across the globe.

Another analyst who encourages us to take the long view is Wallerstein, who commented that:

> Globalization is a misleading concept since what is described as globalization has been happening for 500 years. Rather what is new is that we are entering an 'age of transition'. (2000: 249)

He also indicated, however, that simply to see the present as a linear extension of the past 500 years is not sufficient and that we need to appreciate that we are now in an age of rapid and significant 'transitional' change. The existence of a 'transition' or 'transformation' is a position held by a number of analysts with respect to globalization. They, like Wallerstein, identify rapid changes but are not yet certain of the outcomes (Giddens, 1990); so one significant aspect of these analyses relates to the speed of change rather than change itself. The last 20 or so years of the previous century up to the present do stand out as a period where change has seemingly speeded up. Faster and larger aeroplanes have enabled more people to travel and at lower cost. Electronic communications systems have enabled people to interact across borders without moving. New forms of wealth generation have not been as limited by geographical constraints and have operated globally.

Emerging from these debates are three broad positions. These represent the *optimists, transformationalists* and *pessimists* (Held, 2000). The optimists see globalization as a positive and inevitable trend; it is not possible to withdraw from the system because the economic, political, social and cultural networks are so intertwined and complex. They argue further that the global system is being remade around new transnational institutional forms. Thus nation states are declining in their significance and need to form alliances and networks to retain their capacity to influence the system. In this view the global system is dominated by economic forces and interactions and the need to generate wealth. Additionally, with the demise of the socialist alternative, the dominant mode of production is liberal capitalism built around expanding markets and consumer choice (Ohmae, 1996).

The transformationalists believe the changes that are occurring will rework many key relationships at both global and local levels (Giddens, 1990). They are less certain, however, that the outcome is known or inevitable, and emphasize the important agency of the key actors in the new global system. They thus turn their attention to the activities of transnational corporations, the ways that forms of governance are emerging via treaties and international organizations (e.g., the Group of Eight major economies (G8), European Union (EU), Organization for Economic Cooperation and Development (OECD), etc.) and to the role of social movements. Just as transnational corporations have emerged as key players, so too have transnational non-governmental organizations (NGOs). Good examples include environmental and peace movements such as Greenpeace, various women's movements, and first nation and indigenous rights groups which are actively engaging around the use of information and communication technologies to link themselves and develop their global campaigns. The recent success of the anti free-trade movements at getting their message onto the international agenda indicates how social movements are still significant players, effectively challenging the economic and political interests of the transnational corporations.

The final position on globalization is that of the pessimists who argue that nothing much is changing and there is very little that is new. Many pessimists share the economic determinism of the optimists but draw different conclusions. For the pessimists, capitalist economic relations continue to dominate as in the past but increasingly at an international level. They argue that this is to be expected given the accumulative nature of capitalism so nothing much about the 'global hype' is in fact new or novel. One group of pessimists, the regulation theorists (Jessop, 2002; Aglietta, 2000) interpret recent changes as a shift in the basis of economic and social regulation. This shift has been from welfare-based systems regulated by political compromise between employers and workers to moderate wage increases for state provision of welfare benefits and full employment to a more flexible system based around increased levels of individual responsibility and contracting. Integral to this are new global flows of information and products which change the balance of power between capital and labour allowing the restructuring of production, labour markets and welfare provision to increase international competitiveness (Yeats, 2001). In order to understand these differing interpretations we need to explore the interrelated processes that are thought to shape globalization and the context for our everyday lives in the twenty-first century.

The Processes of Globalization

Globalization is best seen as a set of interrelated processes rather than as something that has happened and has been finished. It is ongoing and in that sense not complete. There are five key processes: the economic, often seen as the central process; the political; social; cultural; and the environmental (Figure 3.1).

Economic Globalization and the Rise of Neo-liberalism

Identifying globalization with changed economic relations is one of the major strands in the academic literature and the one that dominates popular discussion. This work originated with the 1970s downturn in the world economy which signalled the end of the post-Second World War period of economic growth which had seen steady expansion within the OECD member countries. The political response to this economic crisis was to restructure national economies along neo-liberal lines by adopting policies strongly influenced by monetarist economics. These policies contrasted dramatically with the neo-Keynsian economic approach that had underpinned development in the period 1945 to the late 1960s in which state policies were designed to intervene in national economies to maintain the rate of growth, employment, welfare provision and wage levels – the latter often via accords with organized labour. The alternative neo-liberal economic approach was adopted because in the Western economies neo-Keynsian policies had failed to provide sufficient return to capital to ensure investment in new forms of economic activity (Lash and Urry, 1987; Thorns, 1992; Kelsey, 1997). The new policies marked a shift away from state-organized demand management towards the control of inflation and the creation of more competitive and less-regulated environments. Crucial to this was the dismantling of subsidies and border protections to allow the freer flow of goods and services. This was seen as a way of reducing costs and creating a restructured set of economic activities and labour capacities and wages. Critics argued that neo-liberalism thus facilitates a 'race to the bottom'; for as one country adopted this approach and succeeded in cutting its costs of production and labour so others were forced to undercut to maintain a competitive advantage.

The shift of productive activity, particularly manufacturing, from nation states in the developed to the developing world created further pressures for the adoption of a globalized neo-liberal policy: the free-trade agenda. Global bodies such as the World Trade Organization (WTO), World Bank (WB) and International Monetary Fund (IMF) were all key players who used loans and trade liberalization rounds tactically to increase accessibility to markets through reducing restrictions on trade between countries. The key elements of this policy focused on increasing free trade; deregulating financial markets and freeing currency exchanges; encouraging greater internal and international competitiveness by removing tariffs and

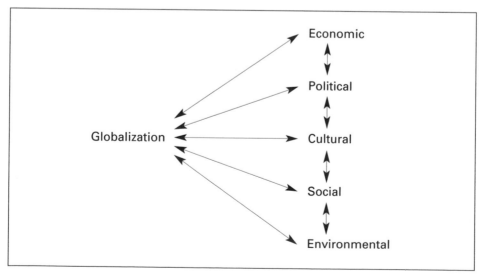

Figure 3.1   Globalization Processes

subsidies and enhancing consumer choices. This programme reflected the increasing centrality of finance capital within the new system of economic relations.

Friedmann reflected on these neo-liberal changes, defining economic globalization as:

> a loose combination of free trade agreements, the internet and the integration of finance markets that is erasing borders and uniting the world into a single lucrative but brutally competitive market. (1995: 18)

The importance of information and communication technologies is clear here. Trading within the world's stock exchanges is now focused on the computer screen. This has transformed the trading of shares and management of investment portfolios. Information from around the world is brought before the brokers and they make their decisions on the basis of what they see on their computer screens. Time and space are collapsed in this trading world because its activities take place from many sites and at all times of the day and night at different places around the globe.

Friedmann (1995) also drew attention to the erasure of borders. This is taken up by a number of economic globalization writers who argue that the nation state is losing its significance in a world of global financial and information flows. Investment is now therefore no longer geographically constrained and industries operate globally so national borders matter very little. Some commentators argue that when states do intervene they often get it wrong and prevent the system working efficiently, and so they advocate for the minimization of state activity, a greater reliance on the market and the free flow of money, goods and labour (Ohmae, 1996).

The final element of Friedmann's (1995) assessment of globalization is the rise of a brutally competitive marketplace. As capital in the new globalized economy has a limited attachment to place, production centres, such as offices, factories or farms, locate only where it is competitively advantageous to do so, and economic activity moves to where labour is cheapest or raw materials least expensive. This may depend in turn on the incentives being provided by particular governments in the form of infrastructure provision and tax concessions. Consequently the bargaining power of capital relative to states and labour has been considerably increased. Ireland, for example, was often cited in the 1990s as a great success story of smart economic policy helped by its geographic location on the edge of the EU representing a market of over 300 million people. Its favourable tax policies for overseas companies meant it was very attractive to US capital and considerable investment came from that source. Also in the 1990s other small nations studied the Irish experience to see what might be learned. In New Zealand, for example, some commentators suggested that with the right kind of positioning similar advantages might be created. It was soon realized, however, that the distance from substantial markets with a wealthy population made replication of the Irish experience unlikely. Of course in light of the experience of the 2007 global credit crunch and Ireland's dramatic economic collapse, commentators who once praised the Irish approach have become very quiet and others note that in the global competition small countries with floating currencies can find it difficult competing for capital and controlling their own fate.

A key driving force in the current global system is the transnational corporation. Many of the major global companies have total revenues far greater than many nation states. The computer giant IBM, for example, at $US78.5 billion has about the same revenue as Egypt ($US75.5bn.) and greater than the Czech Republic ($US54.9bn.) and New Zealand ($US67bn.) (Held, 2000). Transnational corporations are dominant in the financial, banking, media, entertainment, information and communication technology sectors. Global companies such as Disney, Time Warner and News Corporation are now powerful players, shaping ideas and everyday social and cultural practices around the world. Disney, for example, owns theme parks in Asia (Japan and Hong Kong) and Europe (France), in addition to the parks in the United States at Anaheim in California and in Florida (Hirst and Thompson, 1999).

One of the key aspects of the rise of the transnational corporation is that these organizations are considered to be relatively indifferent to territory and have little attachment to the long-term requirements or interests of the nation states within which they operate. The workers employed in such companies do not, however, have the same mobility and thus are vulnerable to the global shifts that occur when managers decide to abandon a production site for others that are more profitable. Local labour forces are also in a weaker position with respect to their employers because if wage levels are not competitive then the global corporation can threaten and then decide to move its operations elsewhere.

The intensified nature of this international competition has meant that some governments have cut their welfare provision, wage and tax rates to make themselves a more attractive prospect for international capital (Yeats, 2001). New Zealand is a good example, where in the 1990s, pursuing a neo-liberal political agenda, the government cut social security benefits and passed the Employment Contracts Act 1991 to discipline unions and restrict wage increases as a significant step towards making the local economy more attractive to transnational investors (Kelsey, 1997).

The growth of the global economic system over the past 20 years has by no means benefited all people. The gap between the rich and poor has continued to grow, with the distance between the richest 20 per cent of the world and the poorest 20 per cent doubling in the past ten years. Further, 358 billionaires control assets equivalent to the assets of 45 per cent of the world's population. The world's largest item of expenditure continues to be weapons of warfare, about $US750 billion per year. The amount of money associated with illicit drugs follows a similar trend (Castells, 1998). Such global inequalities bring us to the questions of equity, social exclusion and social integration. Excluding people from the mainstream of society creates urban ghettoes and a rural and urban underclass of marginalized and deprived people. It wastes human potential and can become a destabilizing societal factor. Data from the United Nations (UN) show that rural workers and member of the urban working class, especially those who had worked in the industries that have been restructured in response to changes in technology and international labour markets, are the people most adversely affected (UNCHS, 1996, 2001a, b).

Political Globalization

In geopolitical terms, the era from the end of the Second World War to 1989 was shaped by the 'cold war' which divided the West from the East. The cold war centred on the establishment of the North Atlantic Treaty Organization (NATO) and the Warsaw Pact in the 1940s and a system of political relations around containment and counter-threat. This was associated with the nuclear arms race and the belief that security, peace and stability in Europe could be maintained by having a capacity for overwhelming armed response. Beginning in the 1950s, the continued growth of the EU, formerly the European Economic Community (EEC), and its huge market potential also contributed as a major political, economic and social force in the differences between West and East.

Political globalization took a dramatic step forward at the end of the 1980s when the Berlin Wall, which had symbolically divided the world between forms of socialism and liberal capitalism, came down and the cold war ended. Germany was reunited and Berlin again became the capital. The rapid disintegration of the former USSR led to the creation of new European states, reflecting the rise of 'nationalisms' which had been suppressed. The changes in the southern part of the former USSR around the Black Sea have been extensive as has the crumbling of the former Yugoslavian Republic and the creation of Croatia, Bosnia, Montenegro, Slovenia, Serbia and Kosovo, and the generation of ethnic conflict leading to substantial numbers of refugees moving from the region. The collapse of socialism in Europe has also had its corollaries in other regions, including Asia and Central America.

These processes have reinforced the notion of the 'borderless world' discussed above in the context of the transnational corporation and the flow of globalized finance, credit transfers, floating exchange rates and convertible currencies, low- or no-tariff regimes and freer trade. This situation has meant that many political and economic analysts now suggest that there is 'no other way' than to follow a globalizing agenda. Ohmae is one such analyst who has raised the question of the lessening importance of the nation state, noting that:

> nation states no longer posses the seemingly bottomless well of resources from which they used to draw with impunity to fund their ambitions ... they have to look for assistance to the global economy ... and invite it in. (2000: 239)

The new globalizing political agenda has privileged international organizations and institutions. These include, first, organizations which represent governments. The UN, for example, is taking a leading role in resolving international disputes, delivering humanitarian aid and improving development options and health practices. But the power of these international organizations and institutions is not absolute. The wars in Iraq, Afghanistan and Libya have raised significant questions about the ability of the UN to take effective action against the world's strongest powers. The outcome of wars such as these and the subsequent 'peace' is likely to show whether or not the world has only one truly global power with the military and economic strength to impose its will on the wider international community. The second kind of international institutions are NGOs that have formed strong global networks and had some success in shaping policies and decision-making.

Cultural/Social Globalization

Globalization also has a significant social and cultural dimension associated with the flow of knowledge and our understandings of the world. One powerful imaginary is of the world as a single global community based on universal principles associated with utopian movements and visions of a new world. An alternative image is that of Huntington (1993, 1996) who sees the world polarized between the West and an emergent Islamic–Confucian axis. Here the axis is not economic but about values and religious philosophies sharpened by the rise in religious fundamentalism in both Christianity and Islam. There is though a link with

economic and political globalization as these movements intersect with
the rise of new global powers such as China and the growth of militant
Islam in many parts of the developing world and in the 'construction' of
the war against terror by the Bush administration after the events of 9/11.

One of the key contributors to the shaping of the changing social and
cultural understandings and images of the world is the rise of a global
media which has created a trend towards a more homogenized popular
cultural experience. Increasingly all nations and peoples are being
exposed to a common diet of television, films and news media transfer-
ring the same information and values across national boundaries. The
question then becomes if we are all increasingly embracing a common
'US–Western' culture and its attendant consumerist and individualistic
lifestyles, does this also mean that our social and cultural differences are
shrinking? The answer is yes and no. While there is undoubtedly an
increase in the similarity of experience, cultural and social globalization
does not necessarily mean total homogenization and in some cases can
represent increasing diversity (Thorns *et al.* 2010).

To the extent that our differences are shrinking this represents what
some analysts interpret as being the ultimate triumph of modernity,
reflecting the success of attempts to enhance processes of capitalistic
rationality, efficiency and standardization, which Ritzer has termed
McDonaldization (Ritzer, 1998; Bauman, 1992). The global expansion of
McDonald's and other fast-food chains (Schlosser, 2001) is a particularly
good example. But, paradoxically, the extent to which our differences are
diverging is also a key cultural and social affect of globalization and less
pessimistic writers see the increase in knowledge about the world as
aiding in the celebration of cultural differences rather than homogeneity.
Staying with the example of nourishment, a good illustration of such
diversity is local resistance to fast foods and the production of regionally
different 'fusion cuisine' and 'slow foods'. Even in the case of some well-
established brand products these principles apply. It has been reported,
for example, that Nigerians drink more Guinness beer that do the people
of Ireland, where it is traditionally brewed. But this is 'Nigerian Guinness'
not the drink that is served in Europe. It is a 'thick, treacly tipple, a bit
like cold Horlicks, with a shot of Bovril in the bottom'. It more closely
resembles the once 'Dublin-brewed Foreign Extra Stout made extra alco-
holic and extra thick to keep during long sea voyages'. This Guinness is
made using hops, barley but also from African-grown sorghum and it is
served chilled, not at room temperature (Owen, 2007: 40). So, here then
is evidence of both the dominance of standardized mass culture and
regional cultural differentiation sitting alongside each. Interestingly, the
latter often sees local food producers using the marketing techniques

developed by the global companies to enable them to sell their products to wider markets and thus stay financially viable.

Elements of cultural and social globalization are directly connected to advertising and marketing. The power of advertisers and the way that they can influence global events such as major sporting competitions, for example, World and European Cup Soccer and the Olympic Games, to suit television and sponsors has become more pronounced. Increasingly such events are now shaped by global and pay television channels. On a smaller scale, but still showing the power of the media and sponsorship to shape the event, is the shifting of sporting events to the night-time to suit sponsors and television audiences rather than players or the fans who actually turn up to watch the game in the stands. This happened to New Zealand's All Black Rugby Football test matches which have all been played under lights in the winter season when the temperature in the South Island can fall close to zero degrees centigrade.

Print and electronic media also have the power to represent and create images of places and cultures in the minds of people located throughout the world. Feature films are good examples and again we can turn to New Zealand experience to illustrate this. There has been a recent rise in interest in making films in New Zealand; partly because it is a convenient location but also to show something of its cultures and landscapes. This was demonstrated in the use of New Zealand as a location for the *Lord of the Rings* trilogy and the *Last Samurai* both of which depended on the country's dramatic scenery. *Whale Rider*, on the other hand, a film that draws upon Māori culture was shot in New Zealand because its people are a significant component of the story. What these cases show is how the film and media industry is differentially using the 'local' to produce films for the 'global' market.

A further dimension of the global media relates to the ways we know about events around the world. Information about, and images of, the dramatic and riveting unfolding of the September 11, 2001 attacks on the US, and subsequent 'terror events' since, were, for example, instantly sent around the world by global satellite television. Similarly, the 'war on terror' launched in the wake of 9/11 has also been waged on the screen and people around the world are shown versions of the war in Afghanistan – mostly dominated by Western-controlled media, such as CNN, Sky News and BBC World, but an alternative voice has been provided by Arab media station Al Jazeera. Consequently, knowledge of these events has become available to considerable parts of the world's population as they have happened. For many, the 9/11 events took over their day as they watched the live telecast and saw over and over again the planes striking, exploding and creating a fireball that led to the burning and collapse of the twin towers of the World Trade Center in New York City. Less spectacular and thus less often shown was the subsequent crashing of a plane on the Pentagon – the centre of US military administration. These events underscored some of the key changes that have created a more 'global world', but which have also influenced the everyday lives of many people in particular localities.

Events such as these, and particularly the ways information about them has been transmitted to such large numbers of people in such a short period of time, and in turn affected their ideas and practices, have led to a vigorous debate about whether the world has now changed so extensively that we need to revise our former ways of thinking and analysis. Taking the 9/11 events again as an exemplar, let us think first about how we found out about them and grasped their enormity. We were able to see these things because of the all-pervasive presence of the camera and the power of the media. The events were captured in real time – so it was easy to assume that what we saw must have been accurate and truthful. But as the events and debate about their significance unfolded the issue of the 'truth' of the interpretation became contentious. Newspapers ran articles a few days after 9/11 indicating that people had turned to the Internet as an alternative source of information because they distrusted television. One source that became popular was the Pentagon website.

This highlights how the World Wide Web has become one of the new ways of knowing the world in the 'global age'. For some people it appears to be more accurate because it is an open rather than controlled space where all views can be presented. The growth of social networking sites such as Facebook and Twitter have been very influential in this regard raising questions about how these different forms of 'information' are to be assessed and evaluated. It also points to the collapse of previous notions of space and time. Distance no longer serves as a barrier to communication. Knowledge is no longer confined to specialist repositories such as those of the 'expert' or the academy. Seemingly, all are free to engage and understand.

At one time most of the news we received from afar was distilled through various interpretative lenses: newspapers and other media, books, articles and educational institutions. The advent of the Internet has opened up a new means to 'discover' the truth and this has challenged the authority of traditional forms of text. Now people with digital access can 'surf' the net and 'discover' for themselves. This appears to provide accessible 'information' unconstrained by national borders and state agencies who wish to shape what their citizens see and do. The liberating impact of the World Wide Web could of course be an illusion. Others, in fact, process the 'information' that computer users search and interpret as reliable and true. The search engines commonly used are not neutral and can be influenced to privilege particular sites and sources. Material that is placed on the Web is a collection of often unverified and unverifiable information and may distort and obscure just as much as data from more conventional sources. Nevertheless, the digital information and communication technology revolution has created new opportunities to stay in touch across national and international borders and has had a significant impact upon our ideas about place, identity and nationality.

Cultural and social globalization is also influenced by permanent and temporary migration and transborder movement of people. This has increased since the last decades of the twentieth century. In the early part of that period, in 1990, 80 million people were living outside of their country of birth, 1.7 per cent of the world's population at that time. These migrants are moving both voluntarily and against their will, with refugees being driven from their homelands because of wars and ethnic conflicts of various kinds. These migration streams blur cultural lines and make national cultures more complex. In Britain, for example, the multi-ethnic and multicultural nature of immigrants often poses challenges to dominant national cultures and creates tensions around the nature of identity. One consequence is that people feel alienated by these changes to their surrounding streets and neighbourhoods. They are confused by change and blame migrants which can lead to a rise in nationalist sentiment in defence of established local culture. Migrants are sometimes blamed, for example, for the lack of safety on the streets, a decline in the quality of public transport, shabby urban landscapes and a breakdown in public civility, but in reality these are much more likely to be related to the restructuring of welfare provision, inadequate pensions and housing allowances, and the absence of public and private investment in infrastructure.

Migrants are an easy target and have been used as part of political campaigns in, for example, European elections. Similarly, in the 2001 Australian Federal election the case of the Tampa boat people was used to justify a strong campaign against illegal immigrants. The 2002 New Zealand elections saw the New Zealand First Party campaign for greater screening and limitation of immigration. The presence of culturally distinct ethnic groups can also generate hostility and fear and lead to outbreaks of violence and racism. Illustrations of this include the 2005 urban riots in the *banlieues* of France, areas with high rates of unemployment, crime and significant numbers of foreign-born residents. In this case the riots involved the burning of cars and public buildings at night starting on 27 October 2005 in Clichy-sous-Bois. Similarly, and also in 2005, there were a series of racially motivated riots and mob violence in

Cronulla, New South Wales, Australia originating from attacks fuelled by alcohol, which turned to violence when a young man of 'Middle Eastern' appearance was seen on the beach. This attack led to further violent incidents over subsequent days.

Other forms of migration are also noteworthy. Tourism is an example of temporary cyclic migration which has significant connections to processes of cultural and social globalization. This is because tourism is now one of the world's largest industries and brings people of many cultures together in often fleeting but still consequential ways. In this sense globalization manifests as a set of day-to-day 'lived experiences' at home and abroad. Travel brings people into touch with different cultures and experiences of history, food, lifestyles, activities and landscapes which leads to a growth in awareness of others and the integration of such experiences into everyday lives. A huge electronic and print-based industry exists to support tourism as exemplified by two recent BBC publications: *Unforgettable Things to Do Before You Die* and *Unforgettable Places to See Before You Die* (Davey, 2004; Watkins and Jones, 2005). Both these books are designed to inspire, offering ideas about where to go and what to do for those with sufficient funds to engage with 'the other'. In the process of all this seeing and doing (Urry, 1990, 1992, 2002; Perkins and Thorns, 2001) the destinations to which people travel are changed and in some respects develop a sameness which stimulates still further rounds of tourism seeking new and exotic sites and experiences (Cloke and Perkins, 1998, 2002).

In some Western cultures, tourism has become a rite of passage for members of particular social classes. A good historical example is the grand tour in continental Europe of wealthy British and Northern European men from the mid-seventeenth to nineteenth centuries and of Americans in the late nineteenth and early twentieth centuries. In the twentieth and twenty-first centuries many young middle-class New Zealanders have sought exotic stimulation by having what they call their overseas experience, known colloquially as 'OE' (Wilson, 2006). In the past this invariably meant going to work in Britain with often multiple side tours to continental Europe and for a small group a major overland trip through Asia or North America before their arrival or after their stay in the UK. Today, greater diversity is now apparent in these global journeys with an increased interest in South America, South-East Asia and Australia. Further, having an overseas experience has become more global, sought by young people from many countries taking a 'gap year', or longer, to travel and explore the world after high school and before going on to tertiary education or employment.

The experiences of these young people, and the other migrants discussed above, are, among others, captured in Sheller and Urry's

(2006) review of the new mobilities paradigm mentioned briefly in Chapter 2. They began their review with the statement 'All the world seems to be on the move' (207) and then reinforced this point by referring to 'asylum seekers, international students, terrorists, members of diasporas, holidaymakers, business people, sports stars, backpackers, commuters, the early retired, young mobile professionals, prostitutes, armed forces' (207), all using the world's aeroplanes, buses, ships, trains and private motor vehicles. Thus, 'internationally there are over 700 million legal passenger arrivals each year (compared with 25 million in 1950) with a predicted one billion by 2010; there are four million air passengers each day; 31 million refugees are displaced from their homes; and there is one car for every 8.6 people'. With respect to tourism, and in the context of a discussion of the Internet, they noted that there will soon be one billion users worldwide and that this has led to the emergence 'new forms of "virtual" and "imaginative" travel' which are being combined in unexpected ways with physical travel (207). German Moltz (2006) reported that the everyday life of travel is often mediated by the Internet. As people travel they often post itineraries and journal entries on 'round-the-world' websites which allow their friends and family to follow their progress and respond to it. So, simultaneously they are writing stories about their travel and are the subject of surveillance and interaction from a distance. The people who are watching are at the same time travelling vicariously and imaginatively.

The final element of cultural and social globalization we will discuss relates to religion. In one of President Bush's speeches immediately after September 11, he invoked the image of the 'crusade' against the evil empires. This was interpreted by many as the constitution of a new global antagonism, between 'Christian liberal capitalism' and 'Muslim fundamentalism'. Whether or not this was precisely what was intended, the appeal to religion as part of the response to 9/11 and its intertwining with nationalism has been a notable characteristic of responses to the terror attacks. Subsequently, the people who took responsibility for them described the conflict as part of a 'jihad' or holy war, positioning themselves against President Bush's 'crusade'. Since that time the US and its allies have attempted to break the link between 'religion' and 'terrorism' in order to build a broader international coalition of support for the 'war on terror'.

Staying briefly with religion, it seems clear that as a result of a global diversification of knowledge, a decline in certainty and the breakdown in trust relationships identified by social capital theorists among others (Putnam, 2000) new forms of fundamentalist and individualistic religious and spiritual expression have strengthened. They have become important for the exploration of identity and meaning in everyday life for their adherents.

Environmental Globalization

Many analyses of globalization have failed to consider the environment. This is limiting because seeing ourselves and our futures as closely aligned with the integrity of 'planet earth' is a significant aspect of a new global consciousness. This awareness manifests itself in many ways including a new view of the natural and the social worlds. It is also represented in the growth of myriad local, regional, national and global political movements (Macnaghten, 2003). In the context of a discussion of place, identity and everyday life this is very important because today many people are significantly influenced by concerns about the environment and engage in practices about which they are passionate. These include activities such as recycling, composting, vegetable gardening and various community-based environmental restoration projects. These local expressions of 'environmentalism' are an outgrowth of an appreciation since the 1960s of the world as a single global ecosystem. This change came with the growth of the environmental movement and space travel. In the late 1960s the landing of people on the moon significantly changed our images of the globe. We saw pictures taken from space of planet earth, we saw detail of the earth through satellite and other images which had not been possible before. Added to this has been the advent of Google Earth. It is hard after such events not to see the world as a single place.

The growth of environmental consciousness and the identification of a wide variety of environmental 'problems' has led to the proliferation of global institutions, fora and agreements to address the risks to the health and well-being of the planet's environment as well as the growth in new awareness of the limitation to growth and the need for a reassessment of our relationship to nature. The development of modern society through the nineteenth and twentieth centuries was shaped by attitudes that saw nature as something that had been understood by science and brought under control by technologies that allowed its abundance to be used to enable the standard of living to rise. Growing concerns with respect to the limits of growth and the planet's capacity to sustain the form of development being pursued led to a range of new agendas at the global political level from the mid-1960s. These are being worked out in varying ways in all countries, not just those which are wealthy or endowed with large science and environmental management budgets. Research currently being conducted in the mountainous Mustang region of Nepal indicates that in that country an environmental transformation is under way which reflects global influences and local action around questions of environment and development (Thakali, 2011, pers. comm.).

The first global environmental conference was held in Stockholm in 1972 to consider the need 'for a common outlook and for common principles to inspire and guide the peoples of the world in the preservation and enhancement of the human environment' (UN, 1972). Over the next decades there was growth in environmental science and research arguing for new ways of thinking about the relationship between science and nature (Michelson, 1976; Catton and Dunlap, 1978). A significant global forum in the 1980s was The World Commission on Environment and Development (WCED, 1987), which introduced the concept of sustainable development. This requires the countries of the world to consider the impacts of development for both present and future generations. The global debate around this prescription has led to two major summits, Rio de Janeiro in 1992 and Johannesburg in 2002. In 1997 another important landmark was the signing of the Kyoto protocol as part of the UN framework on climate change. Initially this was signed by 37 countries and came into force in 2005. Under its jurisdiction the signatory counties agreed to reduce their greenhouse gas emissions by 5.2 per cent of their 1990 levels by 2012. By 2005 191 countries had signed. Two developed countries which did not sign up were the United States and Australia. International debates and conventions brought the questions of, and interconnections between, climate change, pollution, availability of clean water, poverty and social justice much more prominently onto the world stage and sharpened the debate between developed and developing countries with the latter arguing that limitation of their development through new climate change-based restrictions should not inhibit their ability to develop and modernize their economies and improve their standard of living. Further debate took place in Copenhagen towards the end of 2009 on what should replace the Kyoto protocol indicating that the debate around the impacts of global environmental change are now deeply political and a globally agreed plan of action at the institutional and political level has yet to be achieved.

While geographers have for over half a century attempted to integrate local and global natural and social environmental concerns into their work (see e.g., Kates and Burton, 1986a, b) this has not been the case for most sociologists. But as they have grappled with the debates around the form and nature of globalization and late modernity sociologists too have increasingly rethought the conceptual separation between the 'natural' and the 'social' worlds and called for their reintegration (Giddens, 1990; Macnaghten and Urry, 1998). One of the most recent significant sociological contributions has been around the concept of risk and how both individuals and social groups develop their responses to living within the contemporary global world (Beck, 1992). Beck and others have drawn attention to the need to locate the debates about global consciousness and changes in understandings of the relation between the social and the natural within the context of changing modernities (Durrschmidt and Taylor, 2007). The new uncertainties about the future of planet earth that have heightened our concerns about our safety and security such as 'food scares' with respect to such things as salmonella in poultry and antibiotics use in food animals as a result of industrial production methods, the bovine spongiform encephalopathy (BSE) outbreak in the UK in meat, the problems with contaminated milk in China and the 2011 earthquake, Tsunami and radiation leaks from nuclear power plants in Japan bring an awareness of increasing threats to our everyday lives. One consequence is the growth in both our concerns about what we eat, and how we maintain our bodies, and this has led in turn to a growing interests in natural therapies and organic foods. The renewed interest in 'natural' products and healthy lifestyles reflects what Macnaghten (2003) sees as a move from seeing 'nature as out there' to seeing nature as 'in here'. The renewed focus on our bodies is about the examining of our personal and moral concerns and reshaping our daily living practices to reflect changing values and understandings arising from shifts in our global consciousness (Blowers, 1997).

Conclusion

In this chapter we have further developed our position that globalization is multidimensional, multi-causal and constituted around a number of interconnecting processes rather than having one single form. The globalization of the world has been occurring over a long time period. As both social and geographical mobility and movement (physical and now virtual) of goods, people, information, financial transactions have increased we have extended our knowledge of the globe. This has been facilitated and expanded by opportunities for land-based travel and broadened horizons through air and space travel and the arrival of the Internet. These shifts in knowledge moved us from seeing the world as flat to understanding that it was round – and that it was part of a solar system and universe the extent of which is still unknown. Movement and mobility have been seen by some as the defining characteristics of the most recent phase of globalization as these have speeded up and space and time have become more compressed. However we can also observe that mobility and movement is caused by a range of factors some voluntary as when people choose to move for education and work to enhance their quality of life and some forced when migrants are refugees from famine, war, and political and religious persecution. The processes which have helped create and operate within globalization include a range of interacting economic, political, socio-cultural and environmental factors that operate at various levels from the global to the regional to the national and the local. It is our view that the ways these processes shape and reshape our everyday living is not a simple top-down determination. Rather they provide opportunities for ongoing engagement which provides the context for understanding the complex outcomes that we see and that show us that there is not only one way that the world is being changed and one outcome of globalization. Globalization is an ongoing process that is a work in progress not a finished state and thus our understanding and theories need to centre on the dynamics of change and appreciate both the structural changes that are occurring and the capacity of people and communities to reshape their futures through their engagement with each other and through forms of social action. Thus as we explore place, identity and everyday life further in the Part II we will work through an analysis of the intersection of structural shifts and everyday engagements and how we craft our sense of who we are and respond to change.

Further reading

Overviews

Durrschmidt, J. and G. Taylor. 2007. *Globalization, Modernity and Social Change*. Houndsmill: Palgrave Macmillan.
Held. D. (ed.). 2000. *A Globalizing World? Culture Economics, Politics*. London: Routledge.
Sassen, S. 2007. *A Sociology of Globalization*. New York: W.W. Norton.
Waters, M. 2001. *Globalization* (2nd edn). London: Routledge.

Economic

Friedmann, J. 1995. 'Where Do We Stand: A Decade of World City Research', in *World Cities in a World System* (eds.), P. Knox and P. Taylor. Cambridge University Press.
Hirst, P. and G. Thompson. 1999. *Globalization in Question* (2nd edn). Cambridge: Polity.
Wallerstein, I. 1980. *The Modern World System II*. New York: Academic Press.

Political

Held, D., A. McGrew, D. Goldblatt and J. Perraton. 1999. *Global Transformations: Politics, Economics and Culture*. Cambridge: Polity Press.

Holton, R. J. 1998. *Globalization and the Nation-State*. Houndsmills: Macmillan.
Larner, W. and W. Walters. 2004. *Global Governmentality: Governing International Spaces*. New York: Routledge.
Ohmae, K. 1996. *The End of the Nation State*. London: HarperCollins.

Social/Cultural

Appadurai, A. 1996. *Modernity at Large: Cultural Dimensions of Globalization*. University of Minnesota Press.
Bryman, A. 2004. *The Disneyization of Society*. London: Sage.
Marcuse, P. and R. van Kempen. 2000. *Globalizing Cities: A New Spatial Order?* Malden, MA: Blackwell.
Ritzer, G. 1998. *The McDonaldization Thesis: Explorations and Extensions*. London: Sage.
Robertson, R. 1992. *Globalization: Social Theory and Global Culture*. London: Sage.
Robertson, R. and W. Garret (eds.). 1991. *Religion and Global Order*. New York: Paragon.

Environmental

Beck, U. 1996. 'World Risk Society as a Cosmopolitan Society? Ecological Questions in a Framework of Manufactured Uncertainties'. *Theory, Culture and Society* 14(4), 1–32.
Macnaghten, P. 2003. 'Embodying the Environment in Everyday Life Practices'. *Sociological Review* 51, 63–84.
Macnaghten, P. and J. Urry. 1998. *Contested Natures*. London: Sage.
Satterthwaite, D. 1999. *The Earthscan Reader in Sustainable Cities*. London: Earthscan.

PART II

Organizing and Living in Our Everyday Worlds

Part II addresses a series of key aspects of the transformation of place, identity and everyday life. We begin in Chapter 4 with the focus on some of the major structural changes that have taken place over the last 200 or so years and created the settings where the population of the world now live. This provides the context for Chapter 5 with its emphasis on one of the most intimate and central aspects of everyday living – the experience of home and house. This is where important parts of our identity are formed and from where we launch ourselves into the wider world. We examine how the idea of home is multifaceted and multidimensional and has stimulated a range of debates and analysis. These are presented in this chapter and then returned to in Chapters 8 and 9 when we explore the connections between housing and the creation of sustainable human settlements. Chapter 6 takes up the issues surrounding the relationship between real physically bounded spaces and the new spaces of virtual worlds that have become a more significant part of our daily experience. The expansion of these virtual worlds has created new tools for both communication and surveillance which highlight the tensions between our quest for greater security and the risks this poses to individual freedom, protection of identity and personal information. There are strong links between virtual technologies, consumption and leisure and in Chapter 7 we show how the expansion of consumption in a wide variety of settings has become one of the driving forces of contemporary life. We explore the extension of commodification and the creation of new products, services and settings through the use of traditional print-media, radio, television and web-based lifestyle advertising and taste and place-making. At the end of Chapter 7 we turn to the development of concerns about the expansion of consumer culture and the questions this raises about its impact on resource availability and the environment and thus whether it can be sustained into the future.

Organizing and Living in the
Everyday World

Chapter 4

Cities and Regions

Introduction

For the first time in human history the majority of the world's people live in cities and towns. As we discuss in later chapters, rural areas are still very important social, economic and environmental settings, but our focus here will be on the ways urban environments are constructed in the interaction of structure, individual agency and immediate social relationships. We will examine the processes contributing to urban form and how they are affected by individual and collective action. While drawing on information about the experiences of urbanization in a number of countries, we will mainly emphasize data from urban studies in the US, Europe and Australasia because of their early experience of the combined processes of industrialization and urbanization. It is important to note at the outset that the processes we discuss in this chapter have not worked themselves out uniformly in all countries and regions. There has been very great variability in national and regional experiences.

Analysis of Urban Growth

More structurally inclined analysts have dominated much urban analysis. They have interpreted the structural elements of society as the key determining feature of city form and activities. Cities in these terms are 'growth machines' (Logan and Molotch, 1987) and are the engines of economic and population change. An increasing proportion of the world's population lives in mega or world cities which are home to millions of residents. Many of the world's largest cities have populations of between 15 and 30 million and are still growing. The scale of what constitutes 'the urban' has thus changed dramatically. Cities are the places to which migrants are drawn in their search for jobs, housing and more vibrant life experiences. They are the places where material and non-material values, and normative expectations, are formed and reinforced, often challenging past practices and ideas. Cities are therefore sites of innovation and heterogeneity where like-minded people can relate and find support and encouragement. The anonymity cities offer means that people are able to experiment and change their everyday living arrangements and practices more easily.

Much of our thinking about cities is shaped by the experience of the last 300 years when new technology and economic systems combined to create rapid industrialization and urbanization. In Western Europe this began in the eighteenth century and spread to the New World in the twentieth century. The distribution of population changed from being predominantly rural to urban with the main forms of employment changing from agrarian to industrial activities thus dramatically changing the way people lived and worked. A consequence for many people caught up in this change was unemployment and poverty rather than an increase in their quality of life. The experience of this world was vividly portrayed by social commentators and reformers, and in Dickens' novels, Hogarth's cartoons and in magazines such as *Punch*. One such writer in 1773 wrote of 'thousands of people starving, perishing for want in every part of the nation ... I have known one woman in London picking up from a dunghill of stinking sprats, and carrying them home for herself and her children' (quoted in Stuart, 2008: 100)

Social scientists who were interested in these changes focused on the transition from rural to urban ways of life, placing emphasis on the effects this had on everyday living. The rural was classically characterized in terms of 'community': the close-knit network of family and locally determined relationships. In the rural, the rhythm of life and work was shaped by the seasons and home and work were not seen as separate (Tönnies, 1956). Industrialization and urbanization brought factories and shift work, regulation by the clock rather than the seasons, and a more sophisticated and differentiated division of labour required to carry out necessary tasks. In the growing industrial cities, functional interdependence provided the glue that held the social world together as people were increasingly dependent on each other to make the new society work (Durkheim, 1960).

Industrial Cities

The first industrial cities grew from the mid-eighteenth century in Britain in a way that created social and spatial segregation by class and activity.

Attempts to model these cities showed that they comprised 'zones', characterized by particular combinations of people and activities (Burgess and Bogue, 1964). Engels' (1971) analysis of Manchester at the time of the industrial revolution, for example, found that as cities grew around industrial activity, the demand for labour also increased and tenements were built in close proximity to factories to house the new workers. Engels, a friend of Karl Marx, and deeply influenced by his writings, interpreted the emergent patterns of urban living as a product of industrial capitalism. In the Marxist view industrial capitalism was an essentially exploitative system, generating profit out of the labour power of industrial workers; in cities, this system ensured that 'workers' and 'owners' were both spatially and socially separated, thus creating distinctive urban districts and cultures.

Other writers in the late eighteenth and nineteenth centuries drew attention to these divisions pointing in particular to the segregation of poor new industrial workers in rapidly growing cities. Many of these writers were social reformers who both analysed the city and advocated for change to living conditions. Charles Booth was a good example. He studied the connections in London between low income, poverty and other forms of social disadvantage including morbidity and mortality rates. Booth (1903) mapped these and found strong correlations between urban social and spatial segregation.

Some of the nineteenth-century urban health problems identified by these researchers stemmed directly from unplanned growth. This led to overcrowding, poorly built housing and inadequate sewage and drainage infrastructure. Drinking water supplies were often polluted and contained water-borne diseases. The connection between contaminated water and disease was not revealed until early epidemiologists demonstrated that water in London from different pumps created variable local health outcomes. As a remedy to the problems of unregulated growth, planning regimes, large-scale public works, civic improvements and regulation of construction were initiated at the beginning of the twentieth century. This began to improve public health and those aspects of well-being amenable to change by manipulating the biophysical environment of the city.

Ways of Life in the Industrial City

Early twentieth-century analysis of city life was influenced by the work of sociologists at the University of Chicago, known as the Chicago School. Burgess, one of the key figures in this school developed a model of the city based on a series of concentric circles that made up distinctive 'zones' moving out from the central business district to the outer suburbs. The dynamism of the model was derived from the science of plant ecology to describe what he termed 'urban metabolism and mobility'. This led Burgess to suggest that cities expand outwards as each outer zone is invaded by new residents whose former zone is filled by people migrating from nearer the city centre. In addition to this outward expansion and succession there were also antagonistic and complementary processes of concentration and decentralization in the inner city (Burgess, 1967). Robert Park, another of the founders of the Chicago School, and origi- nally trained as a journalist, was more interested in the ways areas of the city grew and became home to particular subcultural populations. He also encouraged his students to spend time in the 'field' observing and experiencing life in the city to deepen their understanding and analysis. This led him to the conclusion that the city combined a physical struc- ture with particular patterns of social organization. For Park the city was:

> A state of mind, a body of customs and traditions, and of the organized atti- tudes and sentiments that inhere in these customs, and are transmitted with this tradition. The city is not, in other words, merely a physical mechanism and an artificial construction. It is involved in the vital processes of the people who compose it, it is a product of nature, and particularly human nature. (Park et al., 1967: 1)

Park thus recognized the agency of city residents and their ability to create their own ways of life.

Wirth (1938), a later Chicago School writer, also drew attention to the heterogeneous forms of urban social life. Like Park, he was interested in the spatial distribution of subcultures and the ways they were expressed in different modes of everyday living. His particular interest was in the ways that ethnicity and international migration to the US lay at the centre of this urban differentiation. Millions of migrants went to the US during the early part of the twentieth century from Europe seeking a new life in a new country which they saw as a land of opportunity. Their arrival in the US is today celebrated at the former immigration station on Ellis Island in New York Harbor which has been renovated and turned into an immigration museum dedicated to educating visitors about the immi- grant experience. Between 1892 and 1954 approximately 12 million steerage and third-class steamship passengers from mainly Europe were legally and medically inspected before being allowed to enter the US. One of the fascinating stories told at the museum is that many migrants returned home disappointed, but the majority stayed. They swelled the populations of cities such as New York and Chicago, brought their languages, traditions and religious practices and created the various 'zones' into which the cities were separated. Different cities reflected the way these 'social factors' interacted, thus creating so many ways of living. These were explored in ethnographies of the city that highlighted rich social and cultural diversity and the formation of 'urban villages'. Gans (1962), for example, studied the Italian Americans living in the West End of Boston and showed how they formed a socially cohesive society in which peer groups, kinship structures and language were crucial to the integration of this local community and its everyday social practices.

The pattern of internal urban differentiation in the United Kingdom was different from that of the US. While there was also international migration from Europe to cities such as London, Birmingham, Liverpool and Manchester it was not on the scale of that experienced in the US. The industrial revolution stimulated significant rural–urban migration in the UK; as the industrial cities grew, urban working-class 'communities' developed socially and spatially around employment in traditional industries such as dock work, ship building, textile milling, mining and steel making. These communities existed intergenerationally in particular places and were reinforced through the interaction of extended kinship ties. British research showed how class, space and kinship were interwoven and helped fashion a particular set of everyday practices. Young and Willmott's (1958) *Family and Kinship in East London*, for example, illustrated how life in London's East End centred on the street and the 'local' pub; with there being one pub for every 500 households.

Simmel was another writer who analysed the rise of the cities in the early part of the twentieth century. He focused his attention on the psychosocial impact of urban life arguing that:

> The psychological basis of the metropolitan type of individual consists in the intensification of nervous stimulation which results from the swift uninterrupted change in inner stimulus. (1969: 410).

The new metropolis was filled with strangers, fleeting encounters and many relationships rather than the smaller number of deep connections that characterized life in the countryside and small town. In Simmel's analysis the new urban social relations were based on a set of exchanges regulated and valued in monetary terms. Money, how much people had, and how they displayed and used it, formed the basis of the ways people and relationships were valued in the city. This idea was taken up by Veblen (1970) in his theory of the leisure class. He noted the importance of possessions among the American upper classes and the ways they were displayed as markers of social status and achievement. Ideas such as these were taken up by subsequent writers in their analyses of the suburban expansion of cities. Their particular focus was on how wealth was displayed in the consumption of particular goods and services (Gans, 1967; Berger, 1960; Bryman, 2004)

Twentieth and Twenty-first-Century Urbanization

The Automobile and Suburbia

Twentieth-century urbanization was driven by economic imperatives associated with industrial expansion based around the assembly line and the marketing of a growing array of goods and services. This helped increase the focus in everyday life on income and choice as the essential ingredients in shaping the life course and lifestyles. Allied to this form of modernity was a set of political and administrative arrangements which ensured that the great majority of citizens were able to earn wages sufficient to allow them to consume mass-produced goods and services. Linked particularly to the experience of North Americans, this system became known technically as 'Fordism', named after Henry Ford, who appreciated that to sell his assembly-line-built cars it was necessary to pay workers a high enough wage to make buying one affordable. Ford thus produced the Model T at a price that would make it accessible to the working population. His pioneering efforts led in time to the growth of mass markets for a wide range of standardized commodities. The growth of this commodity range was directly stimulated by the expansion of owner-occupied suburban housing on large gardened lots. To develop and maintain their new houses and gardens households purchased and created further demand for such 'consumer commodities' as washing machines, refrigerators, televisions, lawn mowers and power tools (Castells, 1998).

One estimate is that in the twentieth century more goods and services were created for sale than in the previous centuries combined (Lipsey *et al.*, 2004). This level of production and consumption fundamentally changed the form and nature of urban life and made the home a central site for a range of activities including work and leisure; and in the developed countries the amount of domestic space consumed per person gradually increased. The digital revolution towards the end of the century increased the technological complexity of the home environment and new forms of everyday living and working significantly.

Widespread motor car ownership had a profound effect upon the shape of cities and their ways of life during the twentieth century. Whereas in earlier times people had walked or used horses, industrialization introduced the possibility of building cities based on mass transit as transport modes moved from horse-drawn to electric trams, cable cars, railways, underground systems and buses to private transport, so creating the car-dependent cities of the mid-twentieth century up to and including the first decades of the twenty-first century. Suburbia mushroomed in the post-1950s decades and the use of public transport fell away (Gans, 1967). Private motor car ownership allowed the growth of suburban areas comprising largely detached single-family housing. The suburban expansion of cities in the west of the United States, Australia, New Zealand and Canada were very much shaped by the automobile and these are among the cities in the world which have the highest ratio of cars to their population and the least well-developed and used public transport and cycle-way systems. This makes these cities particularly vulnerable to fluctuations in the availability and price of oil.

The easy availability of the car also produced a particular kind of suburban family life based around automobility (Sheller and Urry, 2006). Cars have been an obvious element of popular culture, celebrated in pictures and song. *American Graffiti*, a 1973 film, is a pertinent example, with its portrayal of youth culture and the car as a cult acquisition. Road movies have also been an important genre. The love affair with the car continues unabated today. It is a vital part of the identity of many people in developed countries who see cars as an integral part of their lives. For a very significant minority, all things to do with cars as both machine and as a cultural symbol are well illustrated by the widespread popularity of motor racing and such television programmes as *Top Gear*.

As suburbanization flourished, city centres and their local governments fought for survival as residents left for the urban periphery where everyday life and leisure was based around individualized modes of recreation and travel. At the same time, downtown areas became congested with traffic, particularly during business hours. Parking became difficult. Road widening to accommodate increasing car usage disrupted local communities and retailers, and was expensive and often contested. Progressively, in some cities, retailing, commercial and other economic activity and most of the remaining wealthy citizens left for the suburbs, leading to dramatic inner-city collapse. In other cities this flight to suburbs was only partial. This process caused fiscal problems for local governments because it weakened the tax base of inner-city jurisdictions where middle and high earners had been replaced by lower-income occupants and those with multiple needs and high dependency (O'Connor, 1973). The physical fabric of the city also decayed, with whole city blocks sometimes comprising abandoned buildings. This eroded living conditions still further and fuelled continued out-migration.

Local politicians and their allies in business and national governments responded with a raft of inner-city redevelopment and revitalization initiatives which by the 1970s resulted in a reverse migration in many cities and Yuppies, young upwardly mobile households, and Dinkies, dual-income, no-kids households, started to move back into areas that were being renewed or 'gentrified'. Further interventions to control traffic flow including road narrowing and street calming through to congestion charging and pricing schemes for people who wanted to drive downtown and park their cars assisted in furthering this trend. This process was supported by government housing redevelopment subsidies in many cities as well as being actively pursued by property developers and allied financiers wishing to profit from this back-to-the-city movement. It resulted in significantly renewed or rebuilt downtown residential areas and increased land and property values. The other side of the picture was that the former often low income residents of these inner-city localities, many of whom rented their properties, were forced to move to find cheaper accommodation which often was located on the suburban periphery. Such relocation affected their choice of work and increased their time and travel costs and so restricted employment options (Smith and Williams, 1986).

Restructuring, Rust-belt and Sunrise Cities

This intra-city change was accompanied by new forms of global restructuring beginning in the mid-1960s. A new form of global competition emerged from South-East Asia, Central and South America where labour costs were lower and technology and production plants were newer. Manufacturing enterprises moved to these lower-cost zones creating a new international division of labour, a more globally structured system of production and distribution, and competition between cities and regions with some winning and others losing (Froebel *et al.*, 1980). In the areas of decline, industrial restructuring affected urban populations through redundancies and unemployment. Closures of mines, shipyards, steel mills and railways particularly affected male manual skilled and semi-skilled jobs and the communities in which they worked and lived. Some of these workers were able to make the transition to new jobs through retraining, but by no means all. The cities involved often experienced a steady decline and out-migration leading to regional shifts in employment opportunities. Between 1955 and 1985 the United Kingdom had a 10 per cent reduction in its industrial workforce from 47 per cent to 37 per cent (Massey, 1984; Lash and Urry, 1987, 1994).

One industry that took a 'king hit' in the restructuring of the 1970s was the automobile industry with significant shifting of production from the US and UK to Japan and Southern Europe, and South America, leaving US cities such as Detroit, in Michigan, severely affected (Bluestone and Harrison, 1986; Zukin, 1995). Car making was a major employer in the United States but since the mid-1980s this industry has been restructured a number of times and reduced in size. 'In effect, Detroit's three major car makers General Motors, Ford and Chrysler were making vehicles that Americans no longer wanted to buy and as a result with the current recession the city now has … an unemployment rate of 28 per cent … higher than during the Great Depression' (*The Press*, November 2009: B4). The latest round of closures and layoffs occurred as a result of the post-2007 global financial crisis and recession and has led to further significant reductions in production and rising unemployment. A recent US government bailout and restructuring was organized to enable the car industry to survive the current global recession.

The declining urban areas of the formerly dominant industrial countries became known as 'rust belt' cities. These cities were notably among those discussed above that experienced fiscal crises and difficult adjustments, in turn stimulating a search for new forms of wealth generation and renewal in the areas of services and knowledge-based activity such as information and communication technologies (Lipsey *et al.*, 2005). This was often aided by government intervention polices to stimulate redevelopment of land and economic activity. In this process, former industrial land has been used for residential, recreational, commercial and retailing activities. The London Docklands development is one such renewal programme that has affected the former working-class community in London's East End. The Docklands development was a mix of residential and commercial office development which required the dismantling of docks made redundant by the shift to containerization and the demolition of older-style terraced housing. These changes remade the local 'community' that had centred on older forms of association based around shared work and living conditions within the docklands.

In Australia, Sydney's Homebush Bay, the site developed initially for the 2000 Olympic Games, is another example of the remaking of a former indusial landscape. This site was a polluted area that had previously been a mixed-use industrial site with a slaughterhouse, brickworks and electrical battery production plant. As part of winning the bid to host the Olympic Games, managers of the site were required to redevelop it to high environmental standards. The site now contains a number of major sporting facilities including a swimming-pool complex and Australia Stadium used for cultural and sporting events such as important games of Australian rules football, rugby league and rugby union. The site also contains an important conservation area for the rare green and golden bell frog (*Litoria aurea*) and supports innovative approaches to sustainable use of urban water. Hotels and office blocks are appearing and residential accommodation is planned. The planners believe that this area will develop into a new 'community' where people will live and work connected to the wider Sydney region by an integrated public transport system comprising a bus exchange linked to the metropolitan rail system.

Neo-liberal national and city politics, as outlined in the section on economic globalization in Chapter 3, influenced these urban-restructuring processes and affected the provision of, and access to, social services and other resources. At its heart neo-liberalism is an attempt to shift the balance between determination and freedom of choice lying at the centre of many of the contemporary arguments about the role of the state and levels of personal responsibility. The neo-liberal agenda has encouraged a greater degree of personal and family responsibility for health and well-being, managing risks and creating security in old age (Larner and Walters, 2004). In the area of government-funded welfare, universal payments were abandoned and replaced with benefits targeted towards those defined as having the greatest 'need'. With respect to urban development these changes have favoured private market-based solutions. People on lower incomes have been given monetary support to make rents and house purchase more affordable rather than the state providing houses directly (Kemp, 2007; Thorns, 2009). The ethos underlying this approach is that by using income supplements, tax credits or vouchers, known technically as demand-side interventions, those receiving government assistance have increased choice and reduced stigma. It also limits people's dependency on the state and therefore taxes. The expectation is that the 'market' will respond by providing an affordable flow of housing for rent and/or purchase. This has encouraged the selling of public housing and the encouragement of owner occupation in many cities (Duncan and Constantino 2011).

In contrast to the rust-belt cities discussed above, those that benefited from the growth in services are known as 'sunrise' cities. They emerged, for example, in locations favoured by elderly people for retirement, such as Florida and Arizona in the US and the Gold and Sunshine Coasts in Queensland, Australia. Tourism centres also count among the sunrise cities. Good examples are the coastal resort towns of North America, South-East Asia and Australia and mountain resorts such as Queenstown in the South Island of New Zealand. Other cities have grown around specific types of leisure-based consumption, for example Las Vegas and Atlantic city around gambling and Orlando in Florida and Anaheim in California as the sites of theme parks. The development of these latter urban areas demonstrates the power of 'media and entertainment capital' which lies behind the development of these parks. When the Disney Corporation was looking for a site for its new Disney World and EPCOT Centre it was able to extract planning and other concessions from the State of Florida by using the threat of locating elsewhere. Consequently, the Corporation achieved virtual autonomy over the site's development. The trade-off for the State was the economic activity stimulated by park visitors and expenditure within the State (Bryman, 2004; Fogelsong, 1999).

Sunrise cities, and other cities that have continued to grow strongly, have recently incorporated an interesting variant of suburban development. This is the themed suburb or master-plan community which is also sometimes gated to protect property values and assets and the safety of residents (Dupuis and Thorns, 2008). These developments have proliferated in various countries because of demand from members of the ageing but longer-living baby-boom generation (the post-1946 birth cohort) and provide high-quality retirement and recreational facilities and opportunities for residents. These forms of urban development offer a range of accommodation, purchase or lease arrangements and facilities and services. In part their growth is motivated by feelings of insecurity arising from increased social and cultural diversity leading people to wish to live with others like themselves and who share the same values and attitudes towards social relations and activities. In such 'communities' norms can be enforced by local management and by protocols and covenants which were agreed to as part of buying into the 'community'. Such rules often specify conditions with respect to the keeping of pets, where washing can be hung out to dry and the maintenance of gardens and lots.

One very significant form of sunrise city grew in regions which specialized in research and the development of innovative high-technology and production systems (Piore and Sabel, 1984). An early example was Boston with its Route 129 high-technology corridor close to Harvard University and MIT; but the US cities of California's Silicon Valley stand out as being the best-known examples. They have been used as models for the creation of science parks as a part of regional development initiatives in Europe, South-East Asia including Singapore, the Middle East, Australia and New Zealand. Creating clusters of like employment strengthen the possibilities for both formal and informal social engagement where the new generation of hi-tech workers of the dot.com generation can meet and develop their ideas and socialize. Such communities, for example, those in California, generally have a high level of recreational and entertainment facilities which reflect the demands of this new emerging class of high-spending often dual-income households.

At the centre of the existence of these technology-oriented sunrise cities is the idea that information and knowledge, their creation, management and dissemination, is the key to profitable production. Early writers on these developments such as Drucker (1969) and Bell (1973) saw this as part of a move towards a 'post-industrial' economy and society. The initial focus on 'information' shifted in the 1970s to a greater emphasis on 'knowledge'. As Stehr (1994: 122) put it: 'the origin, social structure and development of the knowledge society is linked first and foremost to a radical transformation of the structure of the economy'. The information economy requires new forms of flexible organization based on networks (Castells 2001, 2007; Urry, 2000). This development has been accompanied by a re-emphasis on 'human capital' as an individual good, which is said to enhance the earning capacity of the individual and recognize more strongly their contribution to overall wealth generation. Consequently, entrepreneurial innovators and knowledge managers have become the key to economic growth and change.

This process has profound spatial implications which are still working themselves out. Theoretically, at least, the networked knowledge society allows people to live and work in global villages and cities. People can now carry out their work from home, a 'hot' desk, their car, while travelling around the world, connecting through the Internet using their laptop computer, Blackberry or iPhone. They have less need for travel, and places of work don't need to be fixed in one place. A radical view of this would have people interacting in virtual spaces, and with towns and cities becoming unnecessary. This is a utopian vision of unpolluted and mobile cyberspaces. In many respects it is also an example of exaggerated hype. The reality is somewhat different, as we live increasingly in two worlds at once. The first comprises congested cities; the rigid physical world of clogged roads, which is inefficient and moves slowly, and the second, the immaterial world of computers and communications which is much more fluid and rapid. The expanding use of computers and allied electronic gear is also not without its physical problems. It creates its own forms of pollution in the form of computer waste as these greedy technologies become rapidly obsolescent (Carlaw et al., 2006). Socially, and culturally, these futuristic visions appear to suggest that people can live without having a sense of place and that the presence of other humans could ultimately be done away with for much of life's activity. But this idea of living without tangible social and place relationships contradicts what we know and have discussed in Chapter 2 about the fundamental importance of face-to-face contact with family, friends, workmates, those with whom we do business and recreate, and connections to the wide range of environmental settings in which these contacts occur. The existence of trusting relationships is very important in many areas of human endeavour and it is by no means clear that these are easily made and sustained using electronic communication.

Flexibility and Consumption

Nevertheless, the advent of electronic information and communication technologies has introduced a desire for more flexibility in aspects of urban life. As a result of the post-1970s restructuring and the growth of service industries, employers strove to create a more flexible workforce. Thus women and part-time and temporary workers increased their level of workforce participation. Additionally, it became commonplace for commodities to be manufactured globally rather than in one location (Jessop and Ngai-Ling Sum, 2006). This has created much greater local instability in employment and in the revenue base for cities. Cars and aeroplanes can be designed in one country, using computer technology, and the details of components sent around the world to manufacturers or suppliers, and the car or aeroplane can the assembled at yet another location. Parts for the European Airbus, for example, are sourced from many countries. The advantage of this system to producers is that labour costs can be managed globally giving greater flexibility. Suppliers and employees are not as well-off in this arrangement.

Computerization has also aided the creation of more flexible and consumer-driven variation in commodity production as flows can be varied more easily 'on demand'. The spatial interconnectivity and fluidity that is inherent in these new manufacturing processes means that cities are now linked to a global economy characterized by great mobility of capital and where the control of finance is the key to wealth creation. The dominant cities are those that have become the financial command-and-control centres of the new urban networks (Friedmann, 1995; Sassen, 1991, 1996, 2007; Graham, 1999). These cities are at the nodes of the new cyber networks that are a crucial part of the information highway that links the globe and provides the technology for globalized accounting and financial markets.

Urban retailing, too, has globalized with dramatic effects. Shopping areas are dominated by super malls containing a standardized set of 'outlets' whether these are in Hong Kong, Bangkok, Sydney, New York, Los Angeles or Edmonton or in the Gulf States, or in the retail complexes of the major international airports. There is also evidence, however, of a counter-trend against the growth in retailing homogeneity; indicating a revival and recognition of the value and celebration of 'local' shopping cultures and places. Travellers are attracted to these localities as well as to the high-fashion, air-conditioned and highly internationalized shopping malls. In places such as the central streets of Bangkok, Thailand, the pavements and open spaces between the modern high-rise malls are taken up by street traders and sellers displaying their goods. These are informal, temporary and shifting retailing spaces and activities, present through the day and much of the night servicing locals and visitors. In other cities, Singapore, for example, the authorities have reversed a former policy of clearing the older areas of shops and houses. These are now interpreted as an asset, redeveloped to encourage a more diverse urban fabric.

Urban analysts have debated whether these changes represent a transition in which cities are being increasingly influenced by consumption rather than production. In some respects this question is based on a false dichotomy, because clearly, the two activities are connected; but the debate really centres on the relative strength and importance of forms of activity that generate wealth. Much of this links to the idea of moving to a symbolic economy of signs in which cultural consumption has an impact on the refashioning of the landscape (Lash and Urry, 1994). The creation of European cities of culture through competition across Europe has led, for example, to the reimaging of a number of cities as has the designation of historical areas of cities as UNESCO world heritage sites. Many cities now invest in a 'brand image' to promote themselves, often drawing on 'league tables' that are produced around the liveability of cities, or their 'health and air quality', the festivals or events that they support (Kearns and Philo, 1993).

Labour Demand, Migration and Urban Cultural Diversity

It is impossible to fully comprehend twentieth and twenty-first-century cities without understanding labour demand, migration and their effects on urban cultural diversity. The decades of the 1950s and 1960s were generally expansive times as the world economy recovered from the Second World War and growth returned. Production shifted from war manufacturing to commodity production to satisfy a growing and more affluent population. This was a time of strong employment growth. Initial industrial development was led by the traditional manufacturing industries based around coal, steel, shipbuilding, railways and consumer commodities such as cars and household appliances (Massey, 1984). In Europe where many houses had been destroyed during the war there was huge demand for house construction and this, along with the post-war baby boom, stimulated a housing expansion which led to a wave of suburban growth.

The UK economy in particular expanded strongly and continued to have a dominant place in global industrial production. The demand for labour outstripped supply which both encouraged women into the workforce and migration from the 'Empire and colonies'. In the 1950s and 1960s, therefore, West Indians, Indians and Pakistanis migrated in high numbers and changed the face of British cities. This brought new forms of urban segregation and tensions as these migrants concentrated in inner-city housing (Rex and Moore, 1967). They brought their religions, festivals, foods and entrepreneurial activities with them, many entering the market by buying small businesses such as corner shops, dairies, food outlets and taxis. These new streams of migrants therefore increased cultural diversity and brought alternative ways of life into the places they settled in including new religious practices that challenged some of the taken-for-granted norms of social behaviour.

In the UK these patterns were cross-cut with a concerted effort to replace decaying inner-city industrial housing with high-rise housing estates in the 1960s in the hope of improving social well-being; but what the planners failed to understand was that while the old housing was decrepit, and residents were not financially well-off, the working-class communities in which they lived were very robust. The destruction of the housing and the relocation of residents to new modern housing had the effect of breaking established ways of life and creating a good deal of stress and social dislocation. Life in the new estates was influenced by distant and spatially dispersed social relations, and leisure that was either supported by commercially provided public activity or was home centred. Television was particular important. The leisure opportunities that were available away from home continued to diversify as a range of commercially provided experiences became available such as the cinema, bowling alleys and bingo grew.

While permanent migration from other countries changed the physical layout and cultural life of cities, alternative, temporary migration, created other issues. Some European countries drew upon their former colonies to recruit the labour they required (Potts, 1990; Held *et al.*, 1999). In many countries, such as Sweden and Germany, labour market needs have been managed by using 'guest workers', temporary migrants on limited-stay visas. The presence of these migrants has led to issues around citizenship rights in these European countries. Inevitably, some of these temporary migrants overstay their allotted residency period illegally and while they are often left alone during good economic times, in periods of economic recession and high unemployment calls are made increasingly to repatriate them to their native countries. This occurred outside Europe as well, and for example in New Zealand in the late 1970s, leading to controversial 'dawn raids' by police and immigration officials to locate and remove those migrants thought to be in the country without the appropriate documentation (Loomis, 1990; Spoonley, 1988). In other countries many 'foreign' workers have entered either illegally or without permission to live and work for significant periods of time. Because they are undocumented they are very vulnerable to exploitation as a source of cheap labour. Just because they are illegal doesn't mean they are unneeded or unwanted by the host economy. In US debates about illegal migrants it has been shown that returning the 'illegals' would seriously deplete the numbers of people available to work in many of the less-attractive low-paid service occupations.

A further factor stimulating global migration, and therefore the composition and situation of urban populations, is changing national population numbers and distribution. In 1999 the population of the world reached six billion having doubled in just 39 years from three billion in 1960. Since 1999 a further one billion has been added and expectations are that this will continue to increase, peaking at around nine billion in 2045/2050 (Chamie, 2010). That means a further two billion people to house and the likelihood is that the majority of these will be urban dwellers. The total population is shaped by fertility and mortality rates. The distribution of population across the world is determined by rates of growth and decline in different regions and localities and by migration of the population both internally and internationally. The patterns of fertility or birth rates show that the greatest growth will occur in less-developed countries of the world with the African population set to double from one billion to two by 2050. The Asian population with the exception of Japan and the Republic of Korea will grow from 4.2 to 5.2 billion. In many European countries and in the Republic of Korea and Japan, however, the birth rate is now well below the replacement level of the total fertility rate of 2.1 births. In Italy and Spain, for example, it is around 1.3 children, so these populations have relatively few children but rising numbers of elderly people due to the large-birth cohorts in the two decades after 1945.

These issues are not just relevant for the people of European countries but have also been a feature of those parts of the US, Canadian, Australian and New Zealand populations that are of European descent. With this comes a concern for the future balance within national populations and whether there is sufficient future capacity to maintain services and economic productivity. Pressure is growing in Japan, for example, for a change in migration policy to ensure that there will be sufficient labour to help pull the economy out of recession. Japan's chronic financial difficulties, and the high housing costs to which they have given rise, has created a 'lost generation' unable to afford, housing, marriage and family life (Hirayama and Ronald, 2008; Hirayama, 2011) which in turn has made it difficult to increase birth rates.

The imbalances of population noted above have created an unfavourable dependency ratio, that is, the number of people not in the workforce under 16 and over 65 relative to those in the workforce, which has consequences for pension support and care for older age groups whether they are still in their own homes, retirement villages or in rest homes and has raised both fiscal and social concerns. Many European countries rely on migrants to maintain their declining working-age population and to provide care for their older citizens. Further, globally, these demographic changes have begun to alter the balance of power and economic strength across the regions of the world. China and India, now two of the most populous and economically dynamic nations with high economic growth rates, are likely to increase their relative global position. Both these countries have a significant global 'diaspora' which contributes to their global power and position. The Chinese diaspora, for example, has been calculated as the third largest global economy.

In Australia, New Zealand, US and Canada labour market needs in the 1950s and 1960s stimulated migration. These streams of migrants were initially from Europe where people affected by depression and wartime looked to a 'better life' in the newer societies and expanding post-war economies of these countries. This stream of migrants began to further diversify the population through both adding to and extending the range of ethnic communities in many cities. As for the UK, discussed earlier, the migrants added new dimensions to urban life: new cuisine, different festivals, languages, dress and leisure pursuits and new sporting codes.

The Australian case is instructive. Since 1945 seven million people have chosen to migrate to the country, and a further 700,000 have arrived through humanitarian and refugee programmes contributing to a total population in 2010 of 21.5 million (ABS, 2010). The majority of the migrants have settled in urban areas creating a series of distinctive sub-communities. In the 2006 census 24.6 per cent of the total population was overseas born with 29.7 per cent from North-Western Europe, 16.7 per cent from Southern and Eastern Europe and 12.6 per cent from South-East Asia. Overall, the population consists of over 200 ethnic and language groups. In the 1950s and 1960s, for example, Italians and Greeks supplemented the traditional UK migrants and these were then further complemented by Turkish and Middle Eastern migrants, and refugees and migrants from Asia (such as those from China, Cambodia, Laos and Vietnam) (Collins, 1988). Population growth in Australia, the US, Canada and New Zealand is likely to continue because they are still attracting a net inflow of new international migrants. In the last 30 years the streams of such migrants have become increasingly diverse in both language and culture as entry on the basis of skills has become the key criterion in assessing eligibility for permanent migration.

Multi-ethnicity is therefore a significant aspect of twenty-first-century urbanization. In many large cities residents recognize themselves as possessing many ethnic identities forming what have been called ethnoscapes which now enrich and enliven urban life (Appadurai, 1996). People with multiple ethnicities are now more likely than in the past to describe themselves positively, as for example Greek Australian, Turkish Australian or in Canada Caribbean Canadians.

Auckland, in New Zealand, is an interesting example of one of the globe's most ethnically diverse cities (Thorns *et al.*, 2010). The data in Figure 4.1 show the expected rates of increase of the main ethnic groups that make up the city's population. The European group is the largest component but it is the one with the lowest fertility rate so will decline as a proportion of the total population and may even decline in absolute numbers (at the lowest projection). In contrast Māori, Pacific and Asian populations are all set to grow in absolute numbers and as a proportion of the overall population. For the Māori population the increase is predicted to be 1.4 per cent a year to reach a total of 820,000 by 2026. The Pacific population will increase, but at a faster rate, 2.4 per cent, due

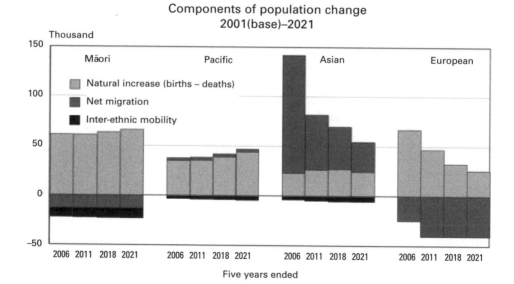

Source: Statistics New Zealand

(1) Ethnic population projections from series 6. New Zealand population projections from series 4.
(2) People who identify with more than one ethnicity are included in each ethnic population.

Figure 4.1   Population Change by Ethnic Group

to its age profile and fertility rate, and is predicted to move from 300,000 to 480,000. The Asian population, drawn from a range of countries with significant differences in language, ethnicity and religious affiliation, has the fastest expected growth rate of 3.4 per cent. An increase of 380,000 is projected by 2026, bringing the total to 790,000. The Asian increase is largely driven by their net migration rate of five times the natural increase so the actual increase may well be influenced by immigration policy and economic changes in New Zealand over the projected period. Māori and Pacific population growth, in contrast to Asian increases, is mainly influenced by births reflecting fertility rates averaging 2.6 whereas for European and Asian women these are between 1.7 and 1.8. The age distribution is also an issue with a higher proportion of older Europeans contributing to the differential fertility rates and growth potential across different ethnic groups.

One of the consequences of these population changes and streams of in-migration is that Auckland is now home to over 200 ethnic groups. This greatly increased diversity is reflected in the fact that 17.5 per cent of people in New Zealand speak two or more languages. Current data indicate that a growing proportion of the population are multi-ethnic, sometimes identifying with three to four ethnicities. Multiple responses were permitted to the ethnicity question in the 2006 census and a considerable number of people chose to record their multiple ethnicities. This makes comparison with other years difficult, but highlights the complexity of cultural diversity in contemporary New Zealand.

The increasing cultural diversity of countries was also well illustrated in the 2010 football World Cup competition where the national sides demonstrated the varied ethnic make-up of their populations. Discussion, for example, of the German national side drew attention to the number of players in the side who were descendants of recent migrant families including one of its young and rising stars. This team's diversity was also encouraged by the rise of a global market for sports stars who move from one country to another to advance their careers and may well enjoy multiple citizenships.

One form of migration that attracted attention in the 1960s and continues to be an issue is the 'brain drain or gain'. The concern in the developing countries is that their brightest and best trained are being educated and drawn away to fill skilled positions within the developed economies removing potential leaders and expertise to enable local development. From the 1960s to the 1990s about one million scholars and students moved from developing countries to Western ones (Jeanpierre, 2010). The country that has gained the most from this migration is the US which has established itself as the dominant player in this global market for 'knowledge workers' with science and engineering graduates being preferred. In the US there are approximately 595,900 overseas students with a quarter of these coming from China and India, with the Republic of Korea also being well represented. After the US, Western Europe (UK, France, Germany) and then Australia are the next most popular destinations for students. Overseas tertiary and secondary students since the 1980s have been seen as sources of talent and revenue, given that they pay fees and live in the country where they study and spend money in the local economy. The scale of the loss of students to their home countries can be seen in figures for the numbers who remain after their study is completed and seek and find employment. Fifty per cent of those who entered the US on temporary study visas in 1998 were still there in 2010 (Jeanpierre, 2010). It is Indian and Chinese postgraduates who were the most likely to remain in the US.

Conclusion

People's everyday lives are being reworked through global urban change. The size, density and population mix of cities is becoming more heterogeneous as a result of migration and the resulting increased ethnic and cultural diversity. Urban spaces are also being reformed. The world is getting smaller in the sense that it is now more known and visible. This allows us to see both what is similar and what is different. We can share in events as they happen and feel part of both a global and local community. The new technologies of communication, including the 'mass media' and the Internet and a range of individualized media, allow an increased differentiation of taste; but we are being influenced in our habits and practices by subtle advertising and the pervasiveness of some standardizing cultural tropes. At the same time, access to the wider global media enables more control over at least some parts of our lives.

This chapter has explored the tensions between structural constraints and human freedom and choices. When we think about the political economy of the city we are viewing this question from the perspective of the system as a whole rather than that of the individual actor. We have therefore addressed the questions of how the city gets organized, the shape of its economic underpinning, how wealth is distributed and who gains and who misses out, and how structural changes play out in everyday life. In writing about this latter question Chaney (2002: 37) drew our attention to the underlying contradiction that prevails in our everyday living. There is an 'incompatibility between the messy particularity of everyday life and the drive to order, control, and the rationalization of the dominant discourse'. Chapter 5 returns again to focus on the particularity of every-day life by examining the roles of our houses and homes in our lives.

Further reading

Harvey, D. 1989. *The Condition of Post Modernity*. Oxford: Basil Blackwell.
Jessop, R. and Ngai-Ling Sum. 2006. *Beyond the Regulation Approach: Putting Capitalist Economies in their Place*. Cheltenham: Edward Elgar.
Massey, D. 1994. *Space, Place and Gender*. Cambridge: Polity.
Smith, M. P. and J. R. Feagin. 1987. *The Capitalist City: Global Restructuring and Community Politics*. Oxford: Basil Blackwell.
Sassen, S. 1991. *The Global City: New York, London, Tokyo*. Princeton, NJ: Princeton University Press.
Thorns, D. C. 2002. *The Transformation of Cities*. London: Palgrave Macmillan.
Zukin, S. 1991. *Landscapes of Power: From Detroit to Disneyland*. Berkeley, CA: University of California Press.

CHAPTER 5

Houses and Homes

Introduction

The ways that houses and homes have been conceptualized depends very much on whether houses are seen as commodities to be traded, or as secure places for living. From a structuralist perspective, housing 'is fixed in geographical space, it changes hands infrequently, it is a commodity which we cannot do without, and it is a form of stored wealth which is subject to speculative activities in the market' (Harvey, 1972: 16). The owner-occupied house in these terms is a hybrid of money and material (Smith, 2008). Housing in capitalist societies is allocated socially and spatially in accordance with the market which dictates the relationships between its production, distribution, consumption and exchange. So for structuralists, housing has become increasingly seen as a tradable commodity and form of wealth accumulation. Speculative activity in housing therefore takes place around the possession and disposal of property with its exchange value being more prized than its use value as a form of shelter. Such speculation contributes to the booms and busts in housing and land markets that characterize market-based societies where enhancing individual status and wealth is a strongly held goal.

The degree of choice people have in this process depends on their access to resources and therefore many people are very constrained in their housing options with significant minorities excluded from mainstream housing possibilities by circumstances that are not of their choosing (Somerville, 1998). Thus a variety of government interventions take place to address the inequities that arise within the market. These form the basis of social-housing policies and affect the patterns of renting and owning and thus the relationship between where people live and the conditions under which their houses are occupied.

There are, however, other ways of thinking about housing; not all countries, for example, operate a housing market in the way touched on above. Globally there is distribution of tenure types and occupancy rights with freehold ownership being only one. In some settings, forms of customary title and collective-use rights may prevail and there may not be a reliance on the idea of ownership as conferring a right of exclusive individual possession over a piece of land. Relationships with land thus vary according to whether they are seen as exclusive or collective rights.

These preliminary reflections on housing show that residential places and spaces are constituted differently along many dimensions. Notwithstanding the important contribution of the structuralist perspective it does have the effect of glossing over the intricate and diverse relationships that shape the ways people live in and experience their 'place' and 'home'. For members of the New Zealand Māori population, for example, land has a special meaning. This was illustrated by a 2010 report of an interview with Mataamua, a member of the Ngāti Tuhoe of the Eastern North Island. When interviewed he said that he had moved back to a remote home settlement after completing a doctorate in philosophy. It was, he said, an easy choice to make:

> There are decisions you make every day in your life, such as what to have for breakfast, that sort of thing, but there are a handful of major decisions that define you as a person for the rest of your life. That [coming home] was one for me. I sacrificed income and opportunity to come home. We don't have the amenities and services here [that I could have in a city], but the rewards far outweigh anything [available elsewhere] ...
>
> Living here is fully understanding my identity. It is the core of my being. The core of who I am is here, knowing I am part and parcel of the community I come from. No matter where I am in the world, I will always be from this area. We enact our culture on a daily basis. (Cooper, 2010)

An interpretative culturally informed analysis is most appropriate to understand the meanings ascribed to land, place and home in situations such as the one illustrated above. This approach is associated with the ethnographic, social phenomenological, symbolic interactionist and post-structuralist perspectives used to interpret the connections between social experience, meaning and action discussed in Chapter 2. In our discussion in this chapter we again turn to research influenced by those perspectives and accordingly change the scale at which our analysis is conducted. Here we emphasize agency and the ways people create a sense of home in their everyday lives. This has recently become an important area of social enquiry.

Our starting point is to acknowledge that the idea of 'home' is a broad multifaceted and multilevel concept (Blunt, 2005; Blunt and Dowling,

2006). Home can refer to one's national identity, one's place of origin, which may be distant from where one presently resides. Expressions of this kind of identity are often heard from migrants who have settled in new places and still retain a connection and affection for their 'homeland'. In New Zealand in the 1950s and 1960s it was common, for example, for British migrants to speak of the United Kingdom as 'home' and for their strongest social and political ties to be with the 'old country'. In more recent decades the prevalence of this phenomenon has dropped away as ties have weakened through generational change and the population has become more culturally diverse (Thorns *et al.*, 2010). Multiple cultural ties and identities are now common and provide resources and opportunities for the construction of different understandings of the meaning of home (Gorman-Murray and Dowling, 2007; Mallet, 2004). This is also the case for well-established immigrant communities in many countries.

Home can thus be thought of in spatial and non-spatial terms, and refer to sets of relational ties and sentiments shared by individuals and social groups such as families, kinship networks and communities. The term may also be used to denote what many people would not think of as home. The street dweller's idea of home, for example, may be a rudimentary shelter that he or she moves when looking for a place to sleep for the night. Street dwellers might be 'roofless' but not necessarily think of themselves as 'homeless'. Somerville (1998) identified several key signifiers of home including: the social, hearth, heart, privacy and paradise. These ideas are about the emotional quality of home and how it links to our understanding of ourselves and others. Notwithstanding the comments about homeless people above, home is generally seen as an arrangement that provides people with a sense of permanence, continuity, routine and security (Dupuis and Thorns, 1998). Home has thus been linked with debates about social inclusion and the role that secure housing tenure plays in the formation of a stable population that can increase its social capital and form resilient communities (Levitas, 2005; Baker and Arthurson, 2007). Home is most commonly linked in some way with place, land and buildings (King, 2004; Ashton and Thorns, 2007). The important argument here is that we all live somewhere, and a place to live allows us to connect with people, the wider community and natural environment, and for many of the world's people, the source of their livelihood. The very strong connection between the experience of living in a house, whatever its form, and the creation of a home means that houses and home are frequently talked about interchangeably. People happily talk about homes when they are referring to houses and vice versa. This terminological slippage is a taken-for-granted part of social life and reinforced in a wide range of settings and situations.

With this in mind, we begin this section of our discussion with the suggestion that where people live, their house and/or home, contributes significantly to their sense of place and notions of who they are. Houses at their most basic comprise spatially organized building materials on particular sites. They become homes when and as people live in them. The physical form of housing, and the ways people turn houses into homes, vary in myriad ways. Houses differ from country to country and from region to region within countries. This reality, in part, is produced by the geographical, historical and material conditions of life in those places – climate, topography, demography, degree of urbanization, economic activity, planning/building regulations, transportation and the availability of building materials. The physical and symbolic nature of house and home is also produced by variation in cultural factors – life course trajectory, family form, gender relations, social class, consumption patterns, leisure, work, employment practices, building methods and interpretations of locally appropriate uses of land. To the degree that all of these factors can change, perhaps as a result of the application of new building technology, realigned policy settings, changes in consumption tastes, new family forms, or a major natural disaster, our houses, and homes, can also change (Shove *et al.*, 2007).

Some people own or rent more than one house, associating them-selves with first *and* second homes. Their first home is the house, apart-ment or other accommodation where household members reside for much of the time in the course of their daily lives, largely dictated by employment and family commitments. Second homes are houses, apartments, cottages, cabins and condominiums sited in the country-side or urban locations, and used more or less sporadically for recre-ational holidays and, increasingly, employment. Second homes are by definition usually owned or rented by people who are relatively well-off financially and some very wealthy people own a third or even more homes to support their recreation and employment. There has been a boom globally in the ownership of such houses and these homes are often an important driving force for social and landscape change in the settings in which they are located. We will initially discuss the first home because of its centrally important presence in everyday life. But because of the significance of second homes for some people, we will also make reference to such houses as important contributors to senses of place and identity. We will therefore discuss the phenomenon of multiple dwelling and the diverse set of physical, spatial, social, cultural and symbolic forms it encapsulates (Hall and Müller, 2004; MacIntyre *et al.*, 2006; Paris, 2010).

Interpreting the First Home

The Everyday Routines of Life: Home, Place and Dwelling

The great bulk of English-language writing on house and home is based on the everyday and largely routine experiences of people in the Western industrialized countries and therefore emphasizes the lives of individuals and families living in either publicly owned (social) or private rental or privately owned housing (Perkins *et al.*, 2002). A variety of ideas have underpinned studies of the relationships between the occupants of houses, their home-making and everyday lives in and around their homes. These perspectives have included: place-attachment, domesticity, intimacy, dwelling, shelter, privacy and ontological security (Dupuis and Thorns, 1998; King, 2004). Theoretical writing about the performance of space (Crouch, 2003; Thrift, 2003) and the centrality of 'affect' in daily life (Thrift, 2004) resonates with all of this home-related research. It reinforces the notion that connections between the social and spatial are central to understanding house and home. This notion holds regardless of whether the focus is on individual or household meanings of house and home, or on wider processes of urban and community development – global processes constituting a framework for local social worlds. Homes have multiple and transitory meanings.

In this context, and consistent with our discussion in Chapter 2 about places and their pasts (Massey, 1995), the first body of work on home we want to discuss emphasizes that houses have histories. Historical and intergenerational factors, such as the past meanings and uses of the various spaces in houses, often influence present day activities and senses of place (Greig, 2000; Hunt, 1989; Ward, 1999). At the simplest level, the physical forms of housing created in the past limit but also enable the choices made by present day residents about the use of their houses. Whereas recently built houses have sophisticated reticulation of wiring for electronic devices, people who live in older housing are continually retrofitting their houses to cope with developments in home-based communication and entertainment. On the other hand, vintage houses often have a configuration of spaces which facilitates activities that smaller new houses cannot provide.

Memories of past and uses of homes also influence the experience of current homes and self (Cooper, 1976). In New Zealand research, for example, it was found that older homeowners' interpretations of home were linked to experiences of the 1930s Depression and so owning one's home in later life contributed to a sense of ontological security (Dupuis and Thorns, 1998). But, in addition, some older British migrants to New

Zealand who had lived through the bombing of UK cities in the 1940s had a view of house and home as something fragile and easily lost due to influences beyond their control.

It is common in scholarly sources to see home interpreted nostalgically and characterized as a secure and peaceful place where individuals and families can escape the pressures of everyday life, express their individuality and autonomy, and create a secure physical base from which to venture into the wider world, whether it be for work, leisure or other social engagement. It is said to be one of the places where families engage intimately and carry out the day-to-day routines of family life (Ricci, 1980; Goldscheider and Waite, 1991). Immediate and extended family members and friends and other close associates interact with each other at home, thus developing and maintaining social and interpersonal relationships (Werner, 1988). This image is also conveyed regularly in non-fiction literature, television and film.

But there is another side to experiences of home which can be stressful and contradictory. This too has been represented in popular media. In scholarly work, feminists and those who believe that too much social science has been focused on the experience of people with a heterosexual orientation have also taken a perspective on the meaning of home. These researchers have found, for example, that for lesbian women the experience of home can be difficult because they are faced with living out lesbian identities in domestic settings that are organized culturally and spatially around heterosexual relations (Johnston and Valentine, 1995). For other women, home has been a site of abuse, neglect or exploitation. Feminist writers have also pointed out that for many women, home has been a place of unremitting drudgery lacking the intellectual stimulation and financial rewards of at least some paid employment (Winstanley, 2001).

Other researchers have underscored the relationships between home and the body, indicating that homes are important places for everyday bodily experience, maintenance, appearance and function. People engage with their houses and homes through their senses of sight, touch, smell, taste and hearing, with each sense orienting them in space and contributing to an understanding of place (Rodaway, 1994). Food consumption, and its relationship to the senses of taste, smell and sight, for example, contributes to the making of home, and as Valentine (1999) pointed out, from a feminist perspective, the experience of eating and, particularly, food preparation is gendered and therefore experienced differently by men and women. From a different perspective on the body, social gerontologists have shown that in old age physical frailty and changes in appearance influence the meaning and experiences of home (Kontos, 1998; Mansvelt, 1997a, b; Mowl *et al.*, 2000). Home thus becomes a site of resistance for older people who are facing the possibility of being institutionalized in care homes for the elderly (Kontos, 1998).

The body and privacy are also implicated in the experience and making of home. Concerns about privacy and a number of social taboos associated with bodily functions such as those to do with waste excretion and management, and sexual activities have a direct impact on the ways houses are designed and used (Gurney, 2000a, b). Moving beyond bodily concerns, but staying with privacy, some writers have argued that questions of privacy lie at the heart of interpretations of home (Munro and Madigan, 1993). In the US, for example, the right to privacy is a key determinant of whether or not a place is a home, and if the idea of home is to achieve its full potential Young (1997), writing from a feminist perspective, argued that all inhabitants should be able to experience safety, privacy and opportunities for individuation. It is in this context that the notion of 'dwelling' seems most pertinent. King (2004), in his social phenomenological analysis argued that homes (dwellings) and the ways they are used (dwelling) are significant places for the creation of transformation, tranquillity, complacency, stability, meaning, conventional behaviour, sociability and privacy. They are also at the centre of experiences of desire, fear, anxiety and loss. He illustrated this in a discussion of the loss of a loved one, arguing that such loss centres on the important idea that dwelling animates us. Such a loss may temporarily, and for varying lengths of time, interrupt dwelling, but it is re-engagement with the day-to-day routines of life at home and beyond, which enables people to overcome their pain and reanimate themselves. King argued further that the ultimate loss, in dwelling terms, is to lose one's home, to become homeless. In that situation animation becomes nigh on impossible because such people 'lack the very soul of what it is that constitutes our civilised lives: a private dwelling' (170).

Home, Consumption and Identity

Dwelling in a house involves residents in an immediate interaction with a plethora of objects purchased to make a home function. Home is thus also created in the connections between consumption and identity. Household members, sometimes cooperatively, but also in conflict, create elements of their sense of place using materials, products and services associated with interior furnishing, décor and exterior spaces such as gardens (Chapman and Hockey, 1999; Madigan and Munro, 1996). Many people also decorate their houses with objects and artworks which are sources of attachment, status and identity (Csikszentmihalyi and Rochberg-Halton, 1981; Halle, 1993).

Household members are influenced in their consumption choices by a globalized network of popular print and electronic media. These media use a wide variety of practised techniques based largely on taste-making lifestyle advertising to sell products to niche markets characterized by differences in social class and status, age and gender (Leonard *et al.*, 2004). Residents seek and receive advice from these media about the appropriate way to live and make their homes. Some media convey values and ideals associated with people who have access to considerable financial and cultural capital. The interior-design literature is aimed at this audience and plays on particular historical, exotic cultural and social class motifs. This is the realm of the architect, colour consultant, interior decorator or landscape gardener where householders are likely to have their desires made real by building professionals. Other media, often less glossy, are aimed at the less well-off, young middle-class people just starting out, or members of the working class, showing them that they too can participate in stylish home renovation, but only if they are prepared to engage in do-it-yourself (DIY) home renovation activity (Shove *et al.*, 2007).

Everywhere in these media, gender considerations are to the fore. Market research indicates that women are more likely than men to engage with home-related lifestyle media and take the role of 'project manager' in many home decoration and renovation projects. The text and images in the media reinforce longstanding home-related gender roles and differences. In an analysis of home and building magazines, for example, Shaw and Brookes (1999) showed how products and household furnishings can be linked with female appearance and conceptions of beauty, aligning the care and decoration of home spaces with women's appearance and roles. Alternatively, many DIY house renovation media emphasize the masculine role of the home handyman; although recent marketing attempts to broaden the base for DIY equipment and materials have attempted to enrol women, with one company publishing a feminine DIY supplement, with accompanying hand tools in pastel colours, known as She-IY (Mackay *et al.*, 2007).

Work and Leisure

There are strong links between consumption processes, work and leisure. In this section we will first address developments in home-related work and leisure and then make reference to the relationships between work, leisure and consumption. Work and leisure are vehicles though which homes are made physically and symbolically day-to-day and contribute to the development and shape of individual and household identity

(Hochschild, 1989; Nippert-Eng, 1996; Armstrong, 1997). This is so because much time is spent in and around the home in work and leisure and these are matters around which there is considerable negotiation. Feminine and masculine roles, subsequent gender relations and idealizations of life at home are constructed in home-based participation in work and leisure and these idealizations underpin widely held views about the family. The expression and experience of work, leisure and home varies in accordance with the social class, age distribution and education of household members and also with respect to gender.

Work

The domestic and professional lives of women and men have changed considerably over the last 40 years. The nuclear family is no longer the dominant force it once was and combined with new work practices and an increased number of women participating in the workforce, home and family life have been transformed. Changes to the nature of work including technological advancement, extended working hours and the introduction of flexitime and telework have seen paid work increasingly impinge on home life, with home offices, home workers and businesses run from home becoming more common. These have added a new dimension to the home as spatial and temporal boundaries have been renegotiated between household members to allow for the accommodation of paid work as part of home-making. Consequently, some taken-for-granted boundaries between family or household members have dissolved and there is more negotiation around household tasks, particularly in the area of domestic work (Darke, 1994; Bowlby et al., 1997; Gurney, 1997).

The 'traditional' situation of women being responsible for the domestic sphere and men the sphere beyond the home has broken down leading to shifts in home–work boundaries and new configurations of home-based activity (Hochschild, 1989; Nippert-Eng, 1996). Women, whether or not they are employed outside the home, still do more domestic work and childcare than men, but today many more men than in the past engage in domestic work and are active participants in child-rearing (Schänzel, 2009). In Western liberal societies greater interchange of caring and earning in families is now present with the choice of prime earner being determined more by capacity and earnings potential than by gender. Stigmata that existed with respect to a career and childlessness have also eased (Cameron, 1997). In contrast, among migrant groups and in more traditional societies gender roles are still much more circumscribed and can lead to intergenerational conflict over the rights and roles of household members when expectations and cultural norms clash in these areas of everyday life.

Information technologies and associated data processing have affected patterns of work for members of 'creative' and professional groups and many other workers. This work can be done at many sites and has led to more dispersed or networked forms of working. Known as telework, much of this work is routine and not especially glamorous. Increasingly this is outsourced and 'contracted' to maximize flexibility (Loveridge *et al.*, 1996; Sullivan, 2000a, b). Many of the people in this new economy work from home (Felstead *et al.*, 2001) and become 'portfolio workers' doing many jobs on a contract-by-contract basis (Felstead *et al.*, 2005; Meiksins and Whalley, 2002). Further, women largely do this work, fitting it in around other tasks. Negotiating access to the 'family' computer and Internet connections can increase domestic tensions and reserving times for work alongside the demands of other family members can be problematic. Men also engage in home-based telework and one research finding is that the physical spaces in which telework is conducted are gendered with men generally creating a 'home office' and women often doing their paid work on the kitchen table or bench when the other family members are no longer using the computer (Armstrong, 1997).

The numbers of people employed in this way are difficult to determine in the absence of systematic data and more sensitive census questions. Most teleworkers are self-employed, which differs from the workforce as a whole. Recent work on multiple job holders provides some clues and shows that there is a concentration in this activity among both highly paid professionals and among lower-income workers (Baines *et al.*, 2006). Estimates from the UK suggest that home-based workers account for about 10 per cent of the workforce. Because they are contractors and usually self-employed they are paid by results and do not have access to the same range of protection and benefits available to full-time employed workers (Stanworth, 1998). Established workplace provisions such as lunch breaks and eight-hour days no longer apply. In the UK in 2005 teleworking had risen 150 per cent from 1997. There are now 2.4 million workers in the UK who work from home and require information and communication technology to enable this to occur.

Leisure

There are strong links between leisure, identity and home (Glyptis and Chambers, 1982; Glyptis *et al.*, 1987; Cherry, 1984). Houses and immediate neighbourhoods are important sites for leisure participation and the bases from which many leisure pursuits are organized and launched. The social interaction associated with home-based leisure therefore signifi-cantly influences the ways residents become attached to their homes which in turn contributes to the development and shape of individual and household identity. As mentioned earlier in a different context, houses are also repositories for a wide range of physical objects, and many of these are resources for leisure activity (e.g., sports and arts equipment, elec-tronic gadgetry, craft tools, land and water vehicles) and others act as memorabilia (e.g., ornaments, photographs, paintings), some holding great sentimental value, reminding household members of past enjoyable activity with friends and family, in a number of cases, now deceased, or living in distant places.

The house and the land upon which it sits is also often a leisure resource in and of itself as residents create a sense of enjoyment, creativ-ity and belonging by participating in such activities as home maintenance and decoration. Gardening is very important in this regard (Bhatti and Church, 2000). It has a cross-generational aspect, providing a sense of continuity with the past, as well as providing opportunities for creativity, personal expression and achievement (Francis and Hester, 1990). Older people who garden often treat it as both work and leisure, thereby chal-lenging commonly held ideas about old age as being a period of non-productivity (Mansvelt, 1997a, b). Gardening can be significantly gendered, with men and women participating in varying ways, using different parts of the residential property and taking contrasting roles and having different reasons for engaging in the activity (Bhatti and Church, 2000).

Consistent with our earlier discussions of home, consumption and identity, the connections between leisure and DIY activity such as gardening, whether by tenants or homeowners, relate more to the direct personal involvement of household members in the achievement of dreams about their desired 'ideal' home. Their activity is underpinned by commercial supply organizations which support it and profit financially from doing so. This links to recent debates about the home, consumption and the domestic environment which are now often framed by theoreti-cal accounts of consumer culture. Featherstone (1991, 2007), for exam-ple, analysed leisure in terms of consumption processes, trends and changes that he argued have become crucial markers of culture and iden-tity in contemporary society. He showed how market principles are oper-ating within the sphere of lifestyle and cultural goods, as well as the production sphere (see also Mansvelt, 2005: 69–73).

Similarly, Miles (1998) interpreted the ways that consumption takes form in and shapes people's everyday lives and argued that the domestic dwelling is a 'privileged site for the creative display of a consumer lifestyle' (Chaney, 1990, in Miles, 1998: 53). Additionally, Thompson and Tambyah (1999) positioned consumption as a source of stability in people's everyday lives, seeing it as a means by which individuals struggle with highly mobile lives, and juggle the tensions between their transient lifestyles and an ideal of being 'at home'. Such things as gardening, home furnishing and the expression of taste in choices of clothing and food, for example, empower people as they develop a sense of place and identity in an otherwise unstable and uncertain world.

These consumption choices are also linked to the recent changes in home-based leisure that have developed around the widespread domestic deployment of digital micro-electronic information and communication technologies (Gumpert and Drucker, 1998). These technologies have diversified leisure by creating opportunities and capacities unthought of 25 years ago. Text and image-based leisure activities have been transformed by the advent of word processors, multifunctional printing/ scanning/faxing/photocopying devices, e-mail, digital cameras and MP3, CD and DVD players, allowing the rapid viewing, listening, manipulation and transfer of text, images and sounds, and linking the home to wide and distant networks. A plethora of computer games are now played by children and adults: some on stand-alone machines and others played via the Internet and in virtual worlds – arenas for players from across the globe.

Leisure at home has been transformed with the advent of e-mail, cell-phones/mobiles and Internet social-networking sites such as Facebook and Twitter. Shopping, both its functional and leisure aspects, has also been affected by Internet sites offering opportunities to purchase new and second-hand products without leaving the house. These are sold at often significantly discounted prices over those available in traditional stores. The effects on family, community and identity of these home-based information and communication technologies are not yet entirely clear and opinions lie on a continuum between those who believe they will invigorate the social life of the home and those who view these developments as another step along the road to a globalized placelessness and shallower and more fleeting social relationships.

Interpreting the Second Home

For a significant group of people around the world, holidays, and increasingly employment, are pursued in a second home so it is important to pay some attention to the experience of multiple dwelling in a discussion of house and home. In her analysis of family holidays Schänzel (2009) discussed the temporal and spatial continuities and discontinuities that exist between experience at home and on holiday. Family holidays take people away from home physically to pursue the ideal of having family time together in often novel and exotic settings but inevitably they have to deal with some of the day-to-day realities of family life typical of the home experience and getting by while on holiday. This is consistent with McCabe's (2002) finding that tourists take their everyday lives with them on holiday and in that respect holidays are not entirely a form of escape. Holidays, however, spawn experiences of places distant from one's home and are important for the creation of memories and traditions and influence individual and social identity formation at home.

Information and communication technologies have also begun to transform the experience of multiple dwelling. Until recently, there was a very clear distinction for most second-home owners and renters between the first and second home. They spent almost all of their time living in their first home and went to their second home in the peri-urban or distant countryside, or in another town or city, for brief periods, perhaps long weekends, and for longer periods in the summer or winter, depending on their recreational interests and employment schedules. With the advent of relatively inexpensive information and communication technologies it is now possible for some people to spend much longer periods at their second homes engaging in a combination of recreation and work. They may therefore travel further afield, perhaps trans-continentally or internationally, for their breaks away from their first homes. The boundaries between first home, second home and place of employment are breaking down.

What has caused the growth in second-home ownership and why do people have and use second homes? In Scandinavia, the UK, Canada, the US, Central and Southern Europe, Australia and New Zealand a number of factors are in evidence: increased mobility; higher disposable incomes; greater leisure time; the increased popularity of outdoor recreation, including the harvesting of resources; environmental awareness; and latterly, in the US, security concerns for one's person, family and finances in the light of the 9/11 events. Second-home owners seek affective, cultural and recreational experiences in areas having high amenity. They also seek many other interrelated experiences: privacy; relaxation; an inversion of everyday life involving aspects of routine and novelty; the chance to 'get back' to nature; extension of personal identity and community connections; surety with respect to territorial control; family togetherness; satisfying work of a recreational nature; elite status; and feelings of presence and absence (Hall and Müller, 2004; MacIntyre et al., 2006).

The social and back-to-nature aspects of the second home can be illustrated using a New Zealand case study. Auckland medical practitioner

Alan List has been holidaying at Mangawhai Heads, approximately two hours north of the city, since his father bought a holiday home a generation ago. His own four children have grown up sailing, swimming and playing in the estuary and sandy bar at the entrance to the harbour, and now his two young grandchildren are beginning to share the pleasures of this area. 'When they're old enough I can get back into making sandcastles again', List says with relish: 'I'm probably a bit old to be seen doing it on my own' (Smith, 2003: 84).

British and US examples are also useful. Some wealthy UK residents have bought second homes in rural France spurred by nostalgic visions of a rural Britain (Buller and Hoggart, 1994). Their preferences have been for a degree of isolation, a situation offering scenic views with access to, or location in, a local village and a house with 'character'. The second-home movement is also very strong in the US. Chanen (2000), a Chicago attorney and freelance writer, reporting on a survey of 2000 readers of the *American Bar Association Journal*, related a number of stories from US citizens who have second homes. A San Francisco lawyer, Tom Thurmond, for example:

> yearned for the peace and quiet of a weekend retreat … It's truly relaxing to spend a late summer afternoon on the deck of our house [in the Napa Valley purchased 30 years ago before the vineyard boom] with a glass of wine, watching the hawks wheel above the vines and the jackrabbits and quail scurrying along the rows. (Chanen, 2000: 80)

Ed Poll, a Los Angeles attorney, and Paula, his wife, drive for six hours to their condominium in the Sierra Mountains. As a way of overcoming the travel time problem they stay away at least for a week at a time. Ed created a second office so that he could stay for these longer periods. Getting away from urban life is clearly important for these second-home owners: 'It is the contrast from the city that makes it so much fun' argues Chanen (2000: 83). For older people, Chanen suggests, one of the attractions of a second home is to get adult children and grandchildren to visit.

Sense of Place and Community

Second-home owners and renters often experience deeply felt attachments to their homes and the localities in which they are situated. This sense of place and dwelling in part relates to the enjoyment of activities but also emerges from second-home owners' search for stability in a changing world, the possibility of creating a 'real home' and a sense of community less achievable elsewhere (Perkins and Thorns, 2006). In

Norway, for example, cabin dwelling enables a comfortable and relaxed life, a sense of control without demanding too much effort. Attractive surroundings give a feeling of belonging, while at the same time providing a framework for self-reflection, contact with one's emotions and a place to evaluate one's role in a larger context (Kaltenborn, 1997). Svenson (2002) notes that for second-home owners, belonging and a sense of responsibility to a community and a place to go together. While tourists take a vacation from commitment, travelling to be in a community without being responsible to it, cottagers return to the same place year after year, often with the same people and therefore feel they have a responsibility to that community. Multi-generational ownership and use of these houses mean that they are a place where the family and friends gathers together, where work is meaningful, where there is time for leisure and contact with nature, where community feels present.

Escape

There is a sense also in which the second home is used as a place of escape where 'escape becomes an escape for home, not just from home' (Crouch, 1994: 96, though see Quinn (2004) for a critique of the emphasis on escape). Second-home owners escape from stress, compulsive work, routine and alienating employment. They are rejecting the 'thinness' of the urban landscape where nature is reduced to pretty image and the city presents as geometric streets and high rises, and replacing it with landscapes which function at a human, and therefore accessible, level (Tuan, 1998).

First and Second Homes Bound Together

While for many second-home owners time away from the first home is enjoyable, fulfilling and a break from day-to-day routines, it is not true that the second home is free from social conflict. Tensions can arise between second-home owners and others in the same locality. These can be material, related, for example, to overtaxed local resources, or symbolic, such as disagreements over the meaning and management of activities and landscapes. Issues about building design, environmental change, access to water, and appropriate use of recreational areas are good examples. Conflicts also arise between the permanent residents of holiday destinations and second-home owners who share the same spaces, facilities and resources.

Additionally, many of the pressures and imbalances found in the first home are also worked out in the second home. First and second homes are not therefore polar opposites but rather represent a continuum of experience. They are both important sites for leisure, fulfilment and the development of a sense of place and identity. In many respects the routines of everyday life are much the same in either first or second home. Households have to cook, clean, do the laundry and complete other domestic tasks and these are often done by the same people, at the same times, whether one is in one's first or second home. In the same way, it is not possible to completely escape one's 'primary life' and the activities, worries, concerns and interpersonal relationships of day-to-day experience are carried to the second home and influence life there. For those whose second-home experience is based on a small cottage offering cramped and primitive living conditions the tensions that exist between family members in their first homes may be exacerbated. Adolescents may, for example, find the cottage boring and this can be the cause of family arguments. There is also the possibility that such conditions can create a situation where the second home is just another 'kitchen sink but with a better view', particularly for women. Observations of this type have been made by others (Rojek, 1995; Quinn, 2004). Wolfe commented in 1965 on the Canadian experience, arguing that the second-home experience is paradoxical. While rural second-home owners seek an escape from their urban first homes they often find themselves holidaying among hordes of like-minded others. In this sense they are 'not in the country, they are in the city away from city' (Wolfe, 1965: 62, quoted in Halseth, 2004). Similarly, Robertson (1977) writing of Australia, discussed how ironic it was that 'the owners of these so-called "places to get away from it all" often encounter a considerable amount of "it" when they arrive' (quoted in Quinn, 2004: 116).

The similarity of experience between the first and second home is reinforced if the second home is a new house equipped with up-to-the-minute conveniences. These houses allow a nearly seamless transition between home and away, especially for children, adolescents and adults whose recreation and/or employment is based on computer and telecommunications technology. This experience of a seamless transition may also occur when the second home has been in long-term ownership, perhaps multi-generationally. In that case the lifestyles of the first and second home are inextricably cemented together in family stories, intra-family relationships, recreational equipment (including associated activity, transport and storage) and use of time. In the situations where the second home has been built and maintained over several generations by the 'sweat of the brow' of family members themselves, stories about this productive and sometimes creative labour become an important element in the second-home experience.

Other economic and cultural similarities between the first and second home occur. For many people the meaning of the first home is in part tied closely to its role in wealth creation through capital gain. Many second homes are also held for their wealth creation potential either from rental income or capital gain. In this situation, first and second homes are capital investments. They are also material manifestations of contemporary consumption patterns, and both are connected in the ways their designers and owners are influenced by local and global dissemination of ideas about style and the appropriate aesthetic use of building materials found in a variety of print and electronic media.

Returning to the notion of the second home as a haven, a place of escape, one of the notable features of the house and home literature is that many people see the first home in terms of security. So, like the second home, the first home, too, is a place of escape for many people. In the primary home the routines of daily life are connected to, and influenced by, global events and interactions, but they are perceived to be mediated in an environment that is private and largely beyond the control of others. Second-home owners are sufficiently wealthy to be able to extend this sense of freedom, and their interpretation of what and where constitutes home, by purchasing a place in the country, at the beach, or in another town or city. Interestingly, most are happy with the idea of having two homes and most do not turn their second homes into first homes. Why? Because they wish only to have a temporary escape, knowing, as do those who have only a first home, that the wider world of work and engagement with family, friends, economy and society is a fundamentally important and necessary part of life. In this situation, escape is a two-way track. Second-home owners escape their first homes for a simpler life and once satiated, escape their second homes to have a more challenging, complex and stimulating life for the remainder of the time. In this process, first and second homes become extensions of each other – both home and a place of escape (Perkins and Thorns, 2006).

Conclusion

First and second houses and homes have multiple dimensions. From a structuralist point of view both forms of house are commodities which are both accommodation and a source of income and capital gain. The idea of 'home' is of lesser interest to such writers, or if it is accounted for, it is reduced to the standing of a factor which adds to the value of a property and reflects the social status of its owners. From an interpretative perspective, houses and homes are centrally important elements of place, identity and everyday life. Individuals and households interact with their houses and the objects in and around them, taking account of past activities and meanings and creating new ways of living. In this way the social and spatial aspects of house and home interconnect and result often in strongly felt senses of place and dwelling which influence our views of who we are and where we belong.

In the next two chapters we extend our discussion of house and home by tackling the broader development of virtual spaces and places and places of consumption. We return again to the importance of housing in Chapters 9 and 10 where we discuss its incorporation into debates about sustainable living spaces.

Further reading

Blunt, A. and R. Dowling. 2006. *Home*. London: Routledge.

Dupuis, A. and D. C. Thorns. 1998. 'Home ownership and the Search for Ontological Security'. *Sociological Review* 46, 24–47.

Felstead, A., N. Jewson and S. Walters. 2005. *Changing Places of Work*. New York: Palgrave Macmillan.

Hall, C. M and D. K. Müller. (eds.). 2004. *Tourism, Mobility and Second Homes: Between Elite Landscapes and Common Ground*. Clevedon: Channel View.

King, P. 2004. *Private Dwelling: Contemplating the Use of Housing*. London: Routledge.

MacIntyre, N., D. R. Williams and K. McHugh. (eds.). 2006. *Multiple Dwelling and Tourism: Negotiating Place, Home and Identity*. Wallingford: CABI.

Mallet, S. 2004. 'Understanding Home: A Critical Review of the Literature'. *Sociological Review* 52, 62–89.

Paris, C. 2010. *Affluence, Mobility and Second Home Ownership*. London: Routledge.

Perkins, H., D. C. Thorns and A. Winstanley. 2008. 'House and Home: Methodology and Methods for Exploring Meaning and Structure', in P. Mangin and S. Thompson (eds.), *Qualitative Urban Research*. London: Elsevier.

Smith, S. J. 2008. 'Owner-Occupation: At Home with a Hybrid of Money and Materials'. *Environment and Planning A* 40, 520–535.

CHAPTER 6

Virtual Places and Spaces

Introduction

We have already touched on aspects of the ways computers, the Internet and cellphones have become widely distributed and influenced the working out of everyday life in the last decade. In this chapter we elaborate the social and geographical effects of their development, and those of related information, communication and surveillance technologies. Some writers have argued that these technologies have the potential to destroy spatial differences and create a more flexible world. They have also suggested that these technologies are full of possibilities and risks to our well-being and represent a significant globalizing influence. In this view future social relationships are expected to span the real and the virtual; information overload will become a growing problem; and people will have greater difficulty appreciating the difference between the real and the virtual, the latter based on various forms of computerized representation, simulation and three-dimensional effects such as seen in the film *Avatar* (2009). Psychologists from Leeds University in the UK recently reported 'startling evidence that some avid net users develop compulsive habits in which they replace real life social interaction with online chat rooms and social networking sites' (*The Press*, 2010: B1).

The arrival of the Internet and the World Wide Web occurred comparatively recently but their spread and acceptance have been rapid and extensive. By 2010 there were 1,966,514,816 users representing 28.7 per cent of the world's population. It is now difficult to think of a world without these systems of communication but it was only in 1972 that the Advanced Research Projects Agency Network (ARPANET), the prototype for the Internet, was demonstrated for the first time. The Internet as we know it today became publicly available only in 1983. This innovation opened up new ways of communicating – such as email. The next major innovation, the creation of the World Wide Web occurred in 1990 and enabled the storing, retrieving and communicating of documents through hyperlinks (http) and hypertext (html) from 1992. By the mid-1990s 'browsers' were developed making the Internet easier to use, expanding access to information and communication between people across the globe. The next phase of innovation was the emergence of the cellphone (or mobile) which is relatively inexpensive and flexible, can be used to take photographs and transmit images, and send messages by voice or text. In many countries growth in cellphone usage has been phenomenal and is approaching saturation. There are now just over four billion users worldwide which means more than half the world's population is connected; unlike the spread of Internet connectivity via computers developing countries account for two-thirds of the mobile phones in use. Africa is the continent with the fastest growth. One of the reasons for this growth in developing countries has been the capacity the cellphone provides for the safer transfer of money via text messages. Vodafone, one of the global providers, for example, introduced an M-Pesa money transfer system in Kenya in 2007 (*The Guardian*, 2007) and by 2009 had five million users. One reason for the rapid adoption of cellphone technology is that it bypasses older computer-based communication technology and allows multiple functions from the same device as greater connectivity between these telephones, the Web and computer communication systems is developed.

These new technologies have therefore created the capacity for immediate and constant connectivity. For young people being constantly connected is a central part of their everyday life. This has been enhanced recently with the release of Apple's iPhone, iPod and iTouch technology that does away with the need for a keyboard. Some commentators have suggested that the iBook will one day replace the 'book'. With the development of Web 2.0, social websites have been created with *YouTube*, *Facebook* and *Twitter* being among the most prominent.

This enhanced connectivity through the presence of a growing array of media can, however, have some counter-intuitive outcomes as illustrated by Fairbairn-Dunlop's recent experience of the Tokelau Island in the South Pacific Ocean. She noted that:

> I can sit on one of the most isolated atolls in Tokelau and I will know more about [President] Obama and the riots in Bangkok than I do about what is happening on the neighbouring island ... Tokelau can now tune into CNN and that is where they get their news about life ... they can see the clothes, fashions and their English is getting better. (Thorns *et al.*, 2010: 101–102)

There are also potential downsides to these technologies. Cellphone messages can be traced as can computer email messages. Social websites can also be accessed relatively easily (see Time website at Further Reading section at the end of this chapter) endangering privacy and confidentiality. Personal computers have a unique Internet Protocol address (IP address) which is the equivalent of a street address or telephone number. IP addresses tag our computers so they can be readily identified on a network by Internet service providers (ISPs) who record computer traffic for charging purposes and to inform them about level and type of use, including the array of sites being visited. Interestingly, the current set of IP address numbers is nearing exhaustion, such has been the rapid increase in Internet users. The original number format settled on in 1969 allowed for 4.3 billion users – almost enough to provide one IP address for every man, woman and child on the planet which at the time seemed very unlikely to be a problem. Creating a solution will require a new identification system to ensure all users can have a unique ID for their connection.

There is therefore a tension in the use and management of computer networks between opportunities for openness, communication, discovery, linkages and establishing relationships, and the greater capacity they afford for surveillance, data collection about individuals and groups, and control by various agencies and organizations. Linking information about individuals, which was previously kept separate, greatly increases the threat to privacy and the possibility of inappropriate use of personal information. For many people, sharing aspects of their lives through the Web has resulted in damaging publicity and the erosion of their sense of security. The difficulty of securing information that people transmit via the Internet and then store has been shown in the extensive publishing of information through 'wikileaks' that have attracted global attention and concern. The 'leaks' have sparked an intense debate over whether this enhances freedom of speech and information and is therefore intrinsically good or that it endangers and harms governments and citizens that are exposed through these 'leaks'.

Information and Communication Technologies and Social Transformation

One of the key debates about the advent of the digital age focuses on the ways in which it might be stimulating a social transformation. So questions arise as to what the result is of these new ways of knowing and watching. Have they replaced other forms of economic and social practices and interpersonal activity or has it simply speeded things up? Do we now acquire our information and knowledge in radically different ways? Do we build our network of friends through the new 'media' and do we seek entertainment on demand rather than through the diet offered us by the 'providers' of television programmes and films? Has this reduced our degree of social connectedness or have some of the new ways we can 'connect' led to a strengthening of networks and building of social relations?

Those commentators who believe that a social transformation is occurring argue that computing power is accelerating and new communication possibilities are opening up even more rapidly than were expected just a few years ago. Information and communication technologies are therefore affecting all aspects of our lives in the twenty-first century. The Internet, in particular, has been interpreted by many analysts as a transformative technology. This is because it has changed how we access and communicate knowledge and information, shop for goods using websites with global reach, and carry out our social activities and form relationships. The suggestion is that these changes have revolutionized the ways we organize our everyday lives. Transformationalists point out that for many people, e-mail has become the most significant form of written communication which has had a notable effect on more traditional forms of communication such as telephoning from a fixed location using a landline and letter writing. E-mail is now being challenged for supremacy by social media websites and face and voice communication via such things as Skype and cellphone texting, the latter of which has created its own language of communication. Another example, *Wikipedia*, has initiated a collaborative approach to the creation of knowledge. This is based on allowing open access to its contents and the possibility that through a series of iterative contributor interventions the text of each entry is developed and becomes more accurate. *Wikipedia* has progressed from being an outlier to one of the most used and referenced sources of information. But because the stories and articles in Wikipedia are written by people having varying levels of knowledge and skill, and are not verified using the traditional norms of peer review, there is a possibility that complex issues are being presented simplistically (Carlaw *et al.*, 2006).

Commentators identifying the most significant aspect of the 'noughties' (2000–2009) have focused their attention on the impact of the Internet. A newspaper article reported that:

> The birth of *Wikipedia*, the death of *Napster*, the iPhone, *Facebook* and *Twitter* have been named by the Webby Awards as among the top 10 internet moments of the past decade. Other events singled out yesterday by the New York-based International Academy of Digital Arts and sciences which bestows the annual Webby awards was Iran's election protests, Craigslist's expansion and the launch of Google *AdWords*.

'The internet is the story of the decade because it was the catalyst for change in not just about every aspect of our everyday lives, but in everything from commerce and communication to politics and pop culture' said David-Michel Davies, executive director of Webby Awards. 'The recurring theme among all of the milestones on our list is the internet's capacity to circumvent old systems and put more power into the hands of ordinary people', he said. (*The Press* 20/11/09: B5)

The Internet has allowed a growing number of people to build or at least supplement their relationships through social media sites. Facebook has been the big winner in the popularity stakes in this regard. Launched in 2004, Facebook celebrated the achievement of 500 million users by mid-2010 and claims to be the 'Internet's biggest information network ... it has connected old friends, far flung family members, even drawing in the unwilling who join for fear of being left out' (*The Press* 22/07/2010: B7). Twitter, MySpace, Classmates and LinkedIn have also played a role but not on the same scale as Facebook. These sites provide new ways of doing everyday things from meeting people, playing games, sharing experiences, to shopping, planning holidays, catching programmes missed on television and seeking information about health and well-being. As we alluded to in Chapter 5 and reinforce in Chapter 7, the Internet and its associated technologies have changed workplaces, homes and, arguably, most significantly the ways we socialize and engage in leisure (Felstead *et al.*, 2005; Shields, 2003). In addition, these technologies have formed the basis of a huge global consumer market, and new products are awaited eagerly.

The launch of the iPad in early 2010 in the US is a case in point. New York's Mac aficionados, filled with anticipation, could inspect and buy their iPads at the Apple Cube Shop located on Fifth Avenue, by Central Park. The shop comprises a small glass cube in a plaza set beneath tall skyscrapers. Shoppers walk up to it, and are greeted by young people in blue sweatshirts, who usher them inside and down a spiral glass staircase in the middle of which there is a cylindrical glass elevator to return shoppers to the open air. At the bottom of the staircase, beneath the plaza, is a shop the size of a middling supermarket, only it doesn't look like a shop, it seems more like some sort of celebration: big tables with iPads, MacBooks, iPhones: crowded with people trying everything; a sort of funfair of computing and design. This shopping experience was worked out in similar spaces across the globe as the iPad was introduced at a later date in other countries. In each jurisdiction the launch of the product was preceded by an advertising campaign and a good deal of media discussion about the product which had the effect of informing people of its imminent arrival but also stimulating consumer anticipa-tion and desire.

It should be pointed out at this stage that the rise of electronic infor-mation and communication technologies has also created a digital divide between those who have and haven't got access to cellphones and computers. This has exacerbated feelings of exclusion among those who don't have access because of lack of income and skill or because they are not located within easy reach of appropriate equipment and services. In most developed countries high-speed Internet is still relatively expensive and it is also costly to update software and hardware constantly to make greatest use of Internet and Web services. Broadband Internet is usually well developed in urban areas but rural areas are sometimes not as well serviced. Equally, cellphone coverage and costs are variable and also affect use and availability.

The divide also operates globally. With respect to the Internet there is an ongoing inequality of access with the highest rate of coverage being in North America where 77.4 per cent of the population are Internet users. Oceania/Australia is next with 61.3 per cent, Europe sits at 58.4 per cent, Asia at 21.5 per cent and Africa 10.9 per cent (International Telecommunication Union, 2009). These global inequalities of access and coverage extend to variations in the quality and speed of connection which is very important for such uses as surfing the Web, downloading music videos and films and participating in such activities as on-line gambling and games. The spread of fast advanced networks is mainly confined to the developed world where they link the major finance and business centres and leading research clusters across North America, Europe and Asia. A 2009 report of the International Telecommunications Union stated that 'there is a clear gap between the rich and the poor world: fewer than one in 20 Africans went on line in 2007, less than 15 per cent in Asia whereas Europe and the Americas recorded penetration of 43 per cent and 44 per cent respectively' (ITU, 2009). However, if we look at absolute number of users rather than the proportion of a coun-try's population this shows that by far the greatest number of users are in Asia where the growth in computer use in India and China accounts for much of this growth. In Asia there are 825.1 million users compared with 266.2 million in North America and 110 million in Africa (Internet World Statistics, 2011). In these developing countries it is typically, wealthy, highly educated, younger males who are the dominant users and in this circumstance information and telecommunication technologies are extending the power and privilege of those who are already well posi-tioned (UNCHS, 2001b).

What Sort of Transformation?

From the perspective of a social science of everyday life it is still an open question as to whether, in the developed countries, the Internet and other information and communication technologies are having the dramatic transformative influence so often claimed by commentators. It is equally possible that these technologies are simply providing ways of extending what we usually do and changing the speed at which these things can be done (Carlaw et al., 2006). In studies of the future, and associated scenarios, attention has been paid to how information and communication technologies will influence our everyday activities (Allan and Thorns, 2009). One such scenario from a recent future focus report from the European Union (COST, 2009) provided, for example, this look into the future:

> Sarah (in 2030) mainly uses technology in order to accommodate her passion for fitness and a healthy life balance and nutrition. Every day she enters her plan of daily activities in a system located in her kitchen which creates a special menu for her according to her activities and the estimation on the needed calories. The system is connected to the house fridge and pantry and through modern sensor/classifying system that can detect if all the necessary ingredients for the meals are already available at home. If not, the system directly orders them at the nearest supermarket and Sarah can have them delivered at home. (COST Foresight, 2009)

Sarah's story highlights how new technologies will extend but not dramatically transform our everyday lives. It picks up on an increasing concern in Western societies with health and fitness and a search for ways of creating customized health and lifestyle programmes. The 'smart' approach is favoured here with new technologies being used to monitor and control intake to ensure we have a 'balanced' diet and exercise regime. Such a scenario extends people's current use of the Web as a place to seek assistance on a range of issues, a good example of which is using it to get information about illnesses. This is linked to the present use of the Web by product manufacturers and advertisers who use databases to profile sub-populations seen to be at 'risk' from diseases, and once identified, attempt to sell them 'health products'.

One area where there is clear evidence of change, if not transformation, relates to the increase in slippage between the real world and the imagined world in the construction of everyday life. This slippage began with the development of radio, film and television in the early twentieth century. As their influence spread, new ideas and experiences were introduced and these challenged taken-for-granted understandings about human behaviour, and undermined some people's senses of place and blurred the distinction between the material realities of everyday living and the depiction of fictional worlds (Baudrilliard, 1996). Television challenged people's assumptions about the behaviour of others, in their own country and across the globe. It largely depicted a controlled set of experiences chosen by television programmers and networks with the different channels having their target audiences, differentiated by age and taste.

Widespread availability of television is a post-Second World War phenomenon. In New Zealand, for example, where television was introduced relatively late, in the 1960s, families watched programmes together and these stimulated comment and discussion at home and at work. In 2010, New Zealand celebrated 50 years of television, and in reflecting upon the changes that have occurred in the intervening years Agnew (2010: E3) commented that:

> because there was only one channel, TV [in the 1970s] was a unifying force. People discussed last night's programmes on the bus. A business conference was paused for half an hour so everyone could watch *The Plane-Makers*. The Canterbury Historical Association had a TV set at one of their [*sic*] meetings so everyone could watch Glenda Jackson in *Elizabeth R*.

This involvement and identification was especially the case with the long running 'soaps' such as Britain's *Coronation Street* and *East Enders* and Australia's *Neighbours*, New Zealand's *Close to Home* and *Shortland Street* and US's *Days of Our Lives* which finally ended at the beginning of 2010 after a run of 44 years. Their replacements appear to be 'reality shows' which draw people together to be watched as they 'survive' or compete under the constant pressure of being 'on camera'. These programmes challenge our view of what is 'everyday' behaviour, of what is normal, of value and acceptable. They are promoted as 'pushing the boundaries' and creating and modifying tastes.

Like the soaps, the reality shows have a globalized dimension, being watched by people in many countries. This phenomenon is replicated in sports television. The 2010 Football World Cup was an excellent example with fans following the fate of national teams while being drawn together around the shared experiences of watching the games and socializing. This occurred in private homes but also in bars and cafés across the world. One of us was in Hong Kong, the UK, and Scandinavia during this period and saw this process being worked out in a variety of settings, most often in the afternoon, and early and late evening. In New Zealand, on the other hand, the games were televised from South Africa in the middle of the night and early hours of the morning so many sports bars stayed open well past normal closing hours to accommodate fans wanting to gather in large groups to watch. The unexpected success of New Zealand's national team, the All Whites, in the early part of the competition, had a singular unifying effect and viewing figures were at a record high.

The globalized nature of television and film also raises interesting questions around the transformation of both personal and place identities in the context of tourism. Many people identify so thoroughly with particular television programmes and films that they will travel to the sets of these productions to indulge their interests. In the late 1990s, for example, taking a bus tour in Los Angeles, one of us was intrigued by a passenger who kept up a constant dialogue about how the places being passed or visited had been part of a film of television series. His understanding of Los Angeles was as a television or filmset full of fictional characters who for him were seemingly as real if not more real that his fellow passengers. The long-running UK 'soap' *Coronation Street* has shown how people identify with the characters and their lives and how these people become 'real' to them. From 1988 until 1999 a theme park incorporating part of 'the Street' was managed by Granada Television and this for many visitors helped reinforce the overlap between fiction and reality. Similarly, in New Zealand after the filming of the *Lord of the Rings* trilogy, visitors wanted to see the places where the films were made. Many thought they would be able to see and experience Gondor and all the other mysterious and unusual places shown on the film. But most of these were pastiche or simulation created on a cluster of high speed computers located in Wellington, New Zealand's Capital City, rather than structures built physically in the landscape.

Consistent with these experiences outlined above, interconnected global television and film media, and also the Internet, have helped create a sense that spatial distance is collapsing and people are being opened up to new ways of knowing and sharing events around the world. Good examples are major cultural events and news of disasters and disruptions. We are sometimes connected to such events through both global news reporting and our own personal networks. When, for example, the ash clouds from the Icelandic volcano, Eyjafjallajokull, disrupted air traffic across Europe in April 2010, news and pictures of the clouds and closed airports were beamed regularly around the world. By the end of the six days of airport closures most middle-class Australians and New Zealanders, on the other side of the globe and as far as it was possible to be away from the actual volcano, were in fact connected to the unfolding events through multiple connections with colleagues, family, friends, or neighbours. Those people whose travel plans were affected were either delayed somewhere in Europe or North America, or were forced to stay at home where they were cooling their heels waiting for flights that could not leave.

Network Society

One way of characterizing the nature of the experiences and changes we have illustrated above is to think about social linking in terms of a network society. In this context, information and communication technologies have produced a range of new tools such as e-mail, Skype, video conferencing and social networking sites, etc., which together help produce 'a globally interrelated network society'. This society is vastly more flexible and powerful than either personal networks or the hierarchically organized institutions of the past (Castells, 2000). As a result, the configuration of everyday life is changing from being 'group centric' to 'network centric' (Wellman and Giuha, 1999). In everyday life we now find more 'networked individualism' which has a profound impact on social cohesion because people now belong to multiple partial communities. Their links are increasingly person-to-person, facilitated through new information and communication technologies rather than a shared physical locality (Ashton and Thorns, 2007). For some commentators, a logical extension of this argument is that the loss of local social connectivity leads to a loss of community; but evidence shows that while in a fluid and virtual world spatially determined relationships may decline in importance for some people, they do not disappear altogether. It is Castells' (2000) view that territorially defined community still plays a role, albeit a minor one, in the development of social relationships for the majority of the population in developed societies.

If territorial and interest-based communities are being complemented, and sometimes supplanted, by virtual communities, questions arise about how the latter are created, how trust is established between members, and the ways these communities can be identified. Researchers have sought to understand whether virtual communities replace or complement other forms of linkage and relationship building. They have found that territorial, interests-based and virtual communities have issues in common, associated with shared interests, trust and norms of behaviour. They also note that the formation and continuity of these communities depends on how well they cater for the needs of members (Hampton and Wellman, 2003). Clearly, also, there is not just one form of 'virtual' community any more than there is one form of 'real' community. Sometimes virtual and real communities overlap but this does not necessarily promote or strengthen their activities. In Malaysian research, for example, it was found that members of virtual communities had significant difficulties when they tried to meet face-to-face and socialize due to differences in everyday social practices between different ethnic (Malay, Chinese and Indian) and religious groups (Muslim, Christian and Hindu) with respect to modes of interaction, food preparation, eating, and alcohol consumption (Wan Jaffir, 2011).

There is much about the social and geographical aspects of these new networks that we only partially understand. One of the interesting aspects of information and communication technology diffusion has been that the use of cellphones has spread much faster than computer-based systems because they are smaller, easier to use and the costs of coverage extensions are less than those for the fibre-optic cables often needed for fast Internet networks. There is also an age gradient in the use of the technology. Young people, who are 'digital natives', see these forms of communication as 'normal' rather that new (Besser, 2004); whereas for older people they are most definitely novel and at times frightening innovations, hard to understand and operate, which can lead to feelings of disconnection and isolation from the rising generation. The ubiquity of cellphone usage is also very noticeable and interesting. We are increasingly struck by the fact that wherever we travel, the cellphone is present. The minute a plane lands and clears the runway, for example, the cellphones are out and people are regaining their sense of connection with others. In the taxi from the airport the driver will have a cellphone often used while driving (hopefully a hands-free variety but not always the case) while also using a Global Positioning System (GPS) device to guide the car to its destination. So in many ways keeping in touch is now almost seamless and the next generation of hand-held devices will be even more integrated and powerful and fully link our various means of communication to form a common and integrated platform.

In the network society people may also create 'other lives' for themselves. A number of options are available on the Internet with research and development proceeding in several countries including Sweden, Finland, China, US and South Korea (Keegan, 2007). Perhaps the best known is Second Life, a free, three-dimensional virtual world in which users can socialize, connect and create a myriad of virtual experiences as well as using voice and text 'chat'. Users, or residents as they are known, can create a new self, choose a body image, personality and clothing. In order to do this they need to acquire and invest 'second life dollars'. Thus Second Life mirrors much of first life in that it is shaped by acquisitiveness and status, based on achievements and possessions. Research into this new 'world' has shown that we tend to favour similar body shapes and attributes that are currently valued in our first life and that it may therefore not really be a place where we are free to explore new 'selves' or craft and explore new identities (Boellsstorff, 2008). It seems that many of the characteristics and prejudices of 'first life' are carried into 'second life' rather than people creating radically new aspirations and ambitions.

A significant criticism of these virtual worlds is that they further confuse the relationship between real and virtual lives. But despite this, some commentators see therapeutic possibilities in them, that they might be used to help people explore their psychological and emotional problems. These virtual worlds also extend the possibilities for people to be 'pro consumers', people who live, acquire, consume *and* produce in a virtual as well as in a real world. This opens up a wide range of new issues for national states and for the ways economies can work. Creating, buying and selling virtual products provides a new way of making value that uses fewer physical resources and frees people from spatial constraints or specific territories because the things that are traded are often services and information. Virtual worlds such as Second Life are not entirely aspatial and they have become places in which it is possible to buy and sell virtual spaces and buildings, and real estate companies have been formed to enable this to take place. They are not entirely crime free either, and attempts are being made in several jurisdictions, worldwide, to police this (Keegan, 2007).

In the network society, communicating globally has also created problems for national states wishing to control the flow of information to their citizens. In 2010 a dispute arose between Google and the Chinese authorities over the degree of control that they want to exercise over the information that can be accessed from Google by Chinese citizens is a case in point. A further example is the threat by the United Arab Emirates to ban Research in Motion Blackberry services. The conservative regime was concerned about the material that could be accessed by its citizens. Authorities in Saudi Arabia, Indonesia and Lebanon were in 2010 considering a similar ban (*The Globe and Mail* 06/08/2010). In Egypt in the demonstration that led to the downfall of the Mubarak presidency one of the means that was used to spread information and organize the movement was the mobile phone and the use of social networking sites to place pictures and information about the progress of the protests. This draws our attention to changing ways that information can be disseminated and to the growing need for people to ensure that personal data are secured. The new media also provide a means for surveillance which can both allay our fears when it is directed to our protection from harm or terrorism, but at the same time this intrusion can also undermine our rights to privacy and freedom.

Crisis, Conflict, Fear and Demands for Security

The network society is also at the same time a risk society characterized by a number of conflicts and crises which operate at local, national and global levels. These include ecological conflicts, global financial crises, the threats of transnational terror networks, crises of poverty, social exclusion and dislocation and associated criminal activity (Beck, 2002). As indicated in Chapter 3 the global network society is vastly more fluid and mobile than the one we knew in the past (Castells, 1998; Urry, 2000). Recently these elements of crisis and fluidity combined to punch home the significance of living in an electronically and globally connected age. The 2007 international credit crunch showed that when large financial institutions make self-interested but unsound decisions, their effects can rapidly have widespread negative impacts of great magnitude, and influence the everyday lives of many people very significantly for extended periods of time. Crises of this nature have created the conditions required to undermine trust in and between public and private institutions which was very apparent during the recent period of chaos in financial markets (Thorns, 2011b). These crises have also increased uncertainty and heightened a sense of risk for individuals and their families.

In many respects the risks of the network society have been exacerbated by a wider loss of trust in public institutions which has been brought on by the withdrawal of the state from areas of protection and the privatization of safety. Many people think that we now live in a much more dangerous world where keeping ourselves safe is an increasing problem. There are perceived threats to our personal safety by violent people in the streets of our towns and cities. Law and order has become a major political issue with parties vying over who will get tougher on crime. Dangers to young people and children from sex offenders and other predatory people are highlighted and many parents do not allow children the freedom they once had to play outside, walk and cycle to school and have the opportunities for 'urban adventure'.

Parents have become chauffeurs, driving their children to school where once they walked or took the bus. With this has come pressure on time, stress and higher use of vehicles leading to increased carbon footprints with family cars, including the ubiquitous sports utility vehicle, being used predominantly for short-distance urban travel. Government health and safety regulations have become focused on ensuring that risks to children are minimized and this has discouraged a range of school and other young people's recreational activities. These concerns are reducing the mobility of children and young people encouraging them to spend more time on the Internet and Web with the consequent impact on their health and well-being.

The social, economic and environmental complexity with which we are thus faced is compounded by information overload as we try and determine which account of our current condition carries the truth (Beck, 1992). The contradictory data around climate change, for example, and the recent revelations that some of the material used in the Report of the Intergovernmental Panel on Climate Change is based on limited evidence drawn from anecdotal reports has fuelled the debate between the various pro- and anti-climate change positions. Similar confusions are associated with global media coverage which now takes new forms. Television news, for example, may be accessed not just by watching the day's headlines but also by turning to websites which offer more in-depth information, including interviews with key participants. The visual images with which we are presented are sometimes not in fact current but drawn from video databases to fit the story and used to illustrate and enhance the presentation which further muddies our ability to see 'what happened'. The availability of multiple sources of information raises questions about what constitutes an eye witness account: which is the most reliable, which sources can we trust? The representation of crises in various parts of the world such as the Moscow hostage crisis (23/10/2002), Bali bombings (12/10/2002 and 1/10/2005), Madrid bombings (11/03/2004), London bombings (07/07/2005), Sumatra–Andaman earthquake and tsunami (26/12/2004), Haiti earthquake (12/01/2010), Canterbury/Christchurch earthquakes (04/09/2010 and 22/02/2011) and Japanese earthquake and tsunami 11/03/2011) have all highlighted this phenomenon. The multiplicity of formal media information sources has been made more complex by vernacular use of information and communication technologies to convey perspectives on events. In 2009, for example, cellphone pictures posted on the social websites Twitter and MySpace provided the most powerful and lasting images of the Iranian elections and associated demonstrations. They allowed information about violence and government intimidation of citizens to be shared both within the country and across the world. Such forms of communication are difficult for even the most restrictive regimes to control. This again raises the question about what constitutes the 'authentic' account of these events?

The increase in fear and anxiety discussed above now also surrounds the use of the Internet and Web. Social websites which are designed for sharing images, and facilitating friendships and other positive social connections can also expose people to exploitation. There is therefore a growing concern for the safety and security of the information we place on the Web and in the files we hold and share. Hacking into social websites by unwanted viewers, especially when personal material of an intimate nature is displayed, is now an integral part of the network society and an increasing source of danger for younger people. It is also difficult to control the content of websites used to distribute pornographic and violent images over the Internet and people can often get unwittingly drawn into such websites. E-mail scams and bogus websites also can persuade the unwary to give away confidential banking information so that people's account can be raided. Cyber terror and the raiding or targeting of sites by those opposed to particular social and religious groups, for example Islamic sites after 9/11, has also become an issue (Lyon, 2003). This raises important questions about security and surveillance.

Security and Surveillance

One way of thinking about security and surveillance is to draw upon the ideas of Michel Foucault (1976) who drew attention to the power of the 'gaze'. His work built on the idea of the panoptican, a prison designed by Jeremy Bentham in 1791, where the guards were located so they had the ability to see all the prisoners at the same time. The prisoners, however, never knew when they would be under scrutiny and they therefore modified their behaviour even though they were not being watched all the time. Foucault extends this idea to that of the 'disciplinary power of the normalising judgement'. The subtlety of this form of control was identified by Rheingold when he discussed the power of technologically mediated hyper-real spectacles. He suggested that hyper-reality results when the 'Panoptican evolves to a point where it can convince everyone that it doesn't exist; people continue to believe they are free, although their power has disappeared' (Rheingold, 1993: 297, quoted in Dear 2000: 214). Thus surveillance can change and modify behaviour even when we are not actually being watched because we fear we may be. This form of 'social control' is strengthened by the power of universal electronic surveillance and contemporary society becomes a version of the panoptican in which we are disciplined and encouraged to conform because we perceive that we are being observed by others – especially those with greater power (Lyon, 2003).

A perceived increase in risk and an associated growth in fear and anxiety have therefore become central attributes of late modernity and have led to greater demands for heightened security and thus more surveillance. The connection between these two activities and changing social conditions in everyday living is illustrated in Figure 6.1. These four dimensions highlight that police and related security agencies, many now

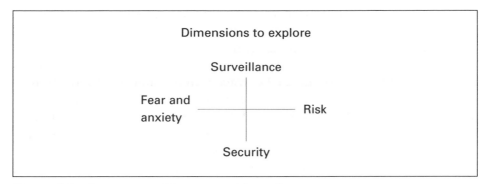

Figure 6.1 Dimensions of Security and Surveillance

private companies, use a range of surveillance techniques to increase security to allay our anxiety about the risks posed by an array of threats. Since 9/11 we have become accustomed to greater security at airports and other points of border control and on entry points to public buildings, corporate offices, private dwellings and major sporting and cultural events. Such increases have been accepted as they are believed to make us safer. They help to reduce our anxiety and risk, they keep us safe and enable us to protect our collective and individual property and ensure personal safety.

The most visual and increasingly prevalent form of surveillance is the closed circuit television (CCTV) camera which is now widely used as a deterrent in high-crime areas and to protect businesses, public buildings, thoroughfares and open space. Equally significant are cameras used on motorways and other major highways to monitor traffic flows and capture images of speeding motorists. Between April 2009 and March 2010 in the UK, for example, 188,000 motorists received fines totalling £8 million after being photographed by smart cars fitted with CCTV cameras (*The Independent* 08/07/2010: 25). X-ray machines to check our luggage at airports have also become commonplace. So one of the facts of everyday life is that we are being increasingly watched and having our activities recorded and stored for possible later analysis. One of the most recent developments in such surveillance technologies concerns the ability to scan people to see if they are concealing objects beneath their clothing. We are assured that the machines will not store the images and thus will never appear on YouTube but can anyone be sure this will be the case?

New security systems also rely on biometric scanning such as iris scanning, facial recognition software and the use of finger and palmprints which are then linked to a range of smart cards with a chip containing information about the individual. These are now mandatory for some travel and increasingly passports carry this new form of identification. But it is not just airports and government buildings that are moving to these electronic security systems. Clubs wishing to check for underage drinkers see possibilities, schools are looking at using them to check their roll and enable the absent to be traced more quickly. In the UK a Chippenham school, for example, uses fingerprinting to check up on who is at school. In another example a club in a Somerset town uses finger-printing to check people entering its premises to ensure they are members. Prisoners can now be tagged and given home detention. Tracking devices can be placed on motor vehicles so that they can be taxed for using central cities as part of congestion control, or for using toll roads, bridges and tunnels. They can be used by parents to check on the whereabouts of the family car and their teenage children. Devices can now be fitted to cars which disable them when the driver has over the permitted level of alcohol in their blood. The cellphone also provides a new way of tracking people, both the movements of individuals and their messages. This can help to solve crimes, for example, by tracking cell-phone messages it is possible to locate the place of the phone and posi-tion of the user thus placing them either at or away from the crime. The messages themselves received on both cellphones and via e-mails are stored and can be used as 'evidence' in court cases and pubic inquiries.

Alongside these mainly public surveillance measures has been a growth in private security firms specializing in the design, selling, installation and monitoring of security systems. Over a decade ago, in Australia, for exam-ple, 1,714 security services businesses were generating \$AUS1,395 million of income during the 1998–1999 financial year. These figures did not include locksmith services or the companies dealing with alarm manufacturing, wholesaling or installations (Caluya, 2007). As a result, in Australia, and many other countries, myriad products and services are available to protect businesses and houses from intruders and theft of objects and information. In the area of 'home protection' we are no longer simply dealing with security devices designed to block – such as locks, bolts and fasteners. The electronic revolution has aided the production of security devices that are increasingly more specialized and more difficult to manipulate, which paradoxically makes it more difficult for the secu-rity consumer to understand. Detection systems now include:

> continuous wiring, knock-out bars, vibration detectors, breaking glass detec-tors, pressure mats, underground pressure detectors and fibre optic signalling. Audible alarm systems have been upgraded to wire-free intruder alarms, visual alarms, telephone warning devices, access control and closed circuit television and are supported by uninterruptible power supplies and control

panels. The whole house is literally re-routed as a series of relays in an electronic grid. If the house as a security risk is defined in terms of points of vulnerability, alarm systems take these points as potential points of contact. Relays running through floors, doors and windows can be triggered by pressure, sound or dislocation. We see a proliferation of sensors: switching sensors, infra-red sensors, ultrasonic sensors, microwave radar sensors, microwave fence sensors and microphonic sensors. The increasing diversification of security products attests to the sheer scale of these architectural/engineering changes to our everyday architecture. In our fear of crime we have produced increasingly more complex security products for the home, thus complexifying the spaces we somehow inherently feel should be 'simple'. (Caluya, 2007)

Some of these products can be monitored by a company employed on contract or by using one's own laptop or other computer. Allied, sophisticated computer controlled systems are now also available which allow houses to be monitored from a distance so that access may be granted to the appropriate people. One positive aspect of this is that 'strangers' such as tradesmen and home helps may be permitted access to the house to complete tasks without the owner being at home or having to leave a key or password to override the security system. Depending on the level of sophistication, house alarm systems might also be managed at a distance to facilitate the entry of these people and they might also be monitored as they work. The perceived need for safety, and protection of this sort is one of the reasons for the growth in gated communities worldwide (Dupuis and Thorns, 2008)

Aspects of home security are now routinely measured and discussed by government statistics and policy agencies. According, for example, to the Home Security Precautions, New South Wales, October 1999 report conducted by the Australian Bureau of Statistics, 47 per cent of New South Wales dwellings were 'secure' (meaning that they either had a burglar alarm, or all entry points were secured or they were inside a security block) while only 9 per cent of New South Wales households had no home security devices. In a similar report for Western Australia conducted in October 2004, an estimated 71 per cent of Western Australian households had window security of some sort (screens, locks or shutters) while 67 per cent had deadlocks on at least one external door. An estimated 27 per cent had a security alarm installed while almost half (49 per cent) had sensor lights (Caluya, 2007)

There are a number of surveillance technologies which have both security and commercial applications. The amalgamation of digital databases to create new units of analysis are now an increasingly significant tool for social researchers and market analysts who have created such websites as

Up My Street in the UK. The ability to watch and profile behaviour as a result of building more complex databases by linking public and private information has become more prevalent. Data from public records can now be coupled with information gathered from focus groups and market research surveys, loyalty and credit card profiles and transactions. The scanning of goods at the supermarket checkout gives a much more precise understanding of what gets bought and consumed in each area of a city, region or country. Thus supermarkets can customize their stock and better plan the flows and requirements of their clients. These new data sources have significantly increased knowledge of consumer behaviour. When supermarkets link electronic information on sales with data which profiles cardholders they can alert customers to special offers and promotion via e-mail and text messages.

Big Brother Is Watching: Critiques of Surveillance

Much of what the new surveillance technology enables is positive and assists in a more efficient and responsive service to citizens and consumers. There is, however, a sinister side where those watching, without our knowledge, may be shaping our behaviour and making us conform to their wishes. Databases can be used to include and exclude groups within the population and thus can become important aspects of social control. Government databases can, for example, be amalgamated to identify clusters of 'clients' for social service provision and therefore a new way of defining the 'excluded'. Burrows and Ellison (2004) on the basis of their research into this practice observe that information systems 'are beginning to categorise and define us in ways that may be useful for commercial companies and governments but that might not be in accord with our perceptions either of ourselves or of our communities'. So the rise in what might be described as the surveillance society, where individual and social behaviour is constantly watched from a distance, has been accompanied by its own set of fears and anxieties, some of which are not new. Fears of a 'big brother' watching our every move were foreshadowed by George Orwell in his book *Nineteen Eighty-Four* (published in 1948). He saw a society emerging where we were increasingly watched by electronic media, limiting our freedoms and controlling our actions. Nineteen eighty-four has come and gone and the precise way of being controlled he suggested has not occurred but what has happened is that there is an increasing ability to track and trace us and to store, retrieve and connect data about us and thus enable greater surveillance.

A more recent critique of this phenomenon suggested that the most insidious attack on democracy and our freedom comes not from political dictators but from the marketplace. Rheingold (1993: 288, quoted in Dear, 2000) quipped that 'the assault on privacy ... takes place in the broad daylight of everyday life. The weapons e-cash registers and credit cards. When Big Brother arrives, don't be surprised if he looks like a grocery clerk'. A good recent example of privacy infringement has been the activities of Google employees collecting 'wifi information while photographing house and streets with 3D cameras for its mapping service' (*The Press* 06/06/2010). Google admitted that it had collected unprotected wifi data from accounts that it accessed as its operative passed through suburban streets, indicating the lack of security over such wireless Internet systems. In many countries, including New Zealand, this activity was a breach of statutory rights to privacy; but because Google is a company based outside New Zealand it has been difficult to manage this adequately. This raises questions about the capacity of nation states to safeguard their citizens' personal data. Facebook too was found, in 2010, to have failed to adequately protect material on its website and as with Google has received adverse publicity and decline in the trust that people can place in the integrity of these web-based systems (*The Press* 06/06/2010).

Identity theft has also become a growing problem and so there has been an erosion of confidence around the security of personal information as a consequence of high-profile leaks of sensitive data. In New Zealand a survey by the Privacy Commissioner (2006) found that 56 per cent of those responding to the survey were concerned about individual privacy. The security of their personal details on the Internet was a concern for 84 per cent. Despite these concerns it was shown in other research that people were not particularly careful with such things as passwords and other forms of security to protect access to their information (TVNZ, 2010)

Conclusion

In this chapter we have explored recent developments in digital technology and the opportunities they provide for people to connect locally and globally. We have engaged with elements of current social theory to help understand how the world is constituted and changing under the impact of new technologies and how they become incorporated into both our everyday and global worlds. These new technologies have facilitated new ways of crafting and organizing social relationships. In this process formerly very close connections to place and local community have been eroded. Place and community are still relevant but our understanding of them has to expand to incorporate real and the virtual 'spaces' in which people can meet, engage, and build ongoing relationships. This will demand ongoing changes to our everyday lives such as finding ways of dealing with the growing volume of information now contained on the Web, evaluating its veracity and usefulness, and working and playing in new real and virtual spaces. It also demands a vigorous interrogation of the growing number of means governments and private organizations have to watch us, collect data, store, retrieve and share it. Such mechanisms can be used to control and limit our freedom, shape our behaviour, or provide us with greater safety and security. Questions of trust and integrity are being raised in the hope that information is collected and stored appropriately and used only for the purposes for which it was acquired. This discussion keys into debates about the decline of the 'trust' many people now have in government and political and economic systems and in turn raises questions about how much 'social agency' we have, to what degree can we can shape our future and to what extent is this about both individual and collective engagement.

In the following chapter we extend our discussion of the bounds of and constraints on social agency in everyday life in a discussion of places of consumption.

Further reading

Castells, M. 2007. *Mobile Communication and Society: A Global Perspective.* Cambridge, MA: MIT.
2001. *The Internet Galaxy: Reflections on the Internet, Business, and Society.* New York: Oxford University Press.
Graham, S. (ed.). 2004. *The Cybercities Reader.* London: Routledge.
Lyon, D. 2003. *Surveillance After September 11.* Malden, MA: Polity, in association with Blackwell.
Shields, R. 2003. *The Virtual.* London: Routledge.
Urry, J. 2000. *Sociology Beyond Societies: Mobilities for the Twenty-first Century.* London: Routledge.

Websites

www.guardian.co.uk/money/2007/mar/20/kenya.mobilephones; accessed 30/08/2010
www.time.com/time/business/article/0,8599,1990582,00.html; accessed 03/08/2010
www.upmystreet.com; accessed 09/08/2010

CHAPTER 7

Places of Consumption

Introduction

Aspects of the relationship between leisure and consumption have been touched on in a number of ways in earlier chapters. This relationship is profoundly important in the making of everyday life and so here we elaborate that relationship and discuss the places in which it is worked out. Our starting point is the observation that a lot of effort has gone into interpreting the form and expression of leisure and associated places of consumption. People's pastimes have been scrutinized and scholars have debated whether leisure should be thought of as a particular type of time, activity and/or state of mind. Social scientists from a number of disciplines have contributed to these debates. There is general agreement that for most people who have the time and resources to engage in non-work activity, leisure is an important element of everyday life, and that individual and social leisure activity contributes to identity formation.

Early researchers in this field studied how people created their own opportunities for leisure within a broader context of cultural norms and expectations. The impetus for leisure was considered to come from within individuals and groups as they sought ways of relaxing or participating in enjoyable and sometimes challenging pursuits. Leisure was seen, at least ideally, as the freedom to be oneself and to engage in authentic and playful experience. While it was generally accepted that individuals and groups relied on products, resources and services produced by others, sometimes commercially, to support their leisure, these were not the main sources of leisure experience (Perkins and Cushman, 1998).

A transition in the form and manifestation of leisure and associated lifestyles occurred in the post-Second World War period, and worked itself out in different countries at varying times. Starting in North America in the 1950s, and among members of the upper and middle classes, a work-and-spend cycle emerged in which leisure and day-to-day life became increasingly linked to the consumption of an ever-widening range of commercial products, activities and services, often purchased on credit. The extent of these developments has led writers such as Chaplin (1999) to argue that the commercialization of leisure has been a fundamentally important part of capitalist growth in the late twentieth and early twenty-first centuries. The outcome of this process has been that shopping and related consumption have themselves become dominant leisure practices for those wealthy enough to participate, and around which individual and collective lifestyles have become established. This pattern emerged later, during the 1960s, 1970s and 1980s, in Europe, Asia, including Japan, Hong Kong and Singapore, and Australasia. More recently, in the developing economies of Asia, South America, Eastern Europe and Africa, members of the growing and aspiring middle classes have begun to purchase for pleasure and sociability. It follows that today, for many people in developed countries and the emerging economies of the developing world, leisure, identity and everyday life revolve to a significant extent around desire fulfilment by purchasing consumer products and experiences.

Where does place fit in? The answer is at a variety of levels and in myriad ways. As discussed in more detail in earlier chapters, for products to be either mass produced inexpensively for sale in distant markets or made locally to supply niche markets, new urban service and production landscapes have emerged in both developing and developed countries. Reciprocally, in those parts of the developed countries which experienced deindustrialization in the 1980s and 1990s, a response to widespread economic decline for the regions, cities and peoples involved was to create services-based economic development projects; many of them leisure and tourism oriented. The overall result of these combined processes for developed and developing countries has been restructured regional and local spatial configurations of economic opportunity and the transformation of places and ways of living in them.

In those regions which have prospered as a result of these restructuring processes relatively large proportions of local populations have sufficient discretionary income to engage in consumption-oriented leisure pursuits and related lifestyle activities. These are pursued in many places including, for example, the home, shopping malls and other retailing outlets, cafés, restaurants, bars, clubs, entertainment complexes, exercise and health centres, convention centres, sports and arts stadia, hotels, gambling venues such as casinos, and rural recreational and tourism developments such as shopping villages, wine regions, resorts and commercialized encounters with nature and adventure. As discussed in Chapters 5 and 6, increasingly important today are virtual leisure settings which may be experienced using television and the Internet, including watching televised 'food and living' and sports channels and taking advantage of web-based on-line shops and gambling, opportunities. The Internet also provides the possibility of 'visiting' exotic places and engaging in activities, and participating in social networking and discussion groups. The latter, along with websites and blogs are useful both as leisure resources and for gathering information about matters of recreational interest. These grounded and virtual activities are open to people of all ages and represent a continuum of experience ranging from the local to the global. Our focus in the remainder of this chapter will be to discuss these places and associated activities and experiences but before doing so we will outline some of the theoretical ideas required to understand them.

Leisure, Consumption, Advertising and Commodification

The desire to participate in consumption-oriented leisure pursuits and associated lifestyles is influenced by image- and taste-makers who use local and global cultural and commercial frameworks to reflect and shape taste and thus create images and ideals about what constitutes a 'good and appropriate way to live'. This shaping is done via media which direct people consciously and subliminally to give particular meanings to all aspects of their lives, including their leisure and the places they inhabit. Newspapers, popular, trade and recreational magazines, outdoor and indoor posters and billboards, radio, television, product packaging, brochures, CDs/DVDs and the Internet are all used by taste-makers to promote information, ideas, services, experiences, products and above all lifestyles to which people may aspire. The lifestyles portrayed in these media are created within a global framework, and notwithstanding some local variation, the products, services and experiences promoted in one country could be transferred to many different places with comparative ease. These media influences and their relationships with the creation of meaning, desire and consumption are well documented (Baudrillard, 1968, 1998; Veblen, 1970 [1899]; Bourdieu, 1984; Corrigan, 1997; Marcoux, 2001).

The interconnection of leisure, consumption and place is a corollary of a set of societal conditions characterized by Baudrillard (cited in Corrigan 1997: 20) as 'the need to need, the desire to desire'. This is closely related to the now pervasive culture of advertising which, as Gottdiener (2000: 4) argues, has increased a craving for all types of object and the attributes they symbolize: 'sex, success, notoriety, uniqueness, identity or a sense of self, privileged social status, and personal power'.

Baudrillard (1968: 170) suggested that we purchase objects because we feel that advertisers are interested in us, which personalizes the objects and we therefore see them as essential to our lives. Advertisers also encourage the idea of consumer choice and empowerment indicating that shoppers can meet their needs by developing their own 'solutions'. Media advertising and related journalism are therefore designed to generate desire and stimulate continuous rounds of purchasing which 'encourages the individual to maintain a cultural consistency in his/her complement of consumer goods' (McCracken, 1989: 123). Once particular products are in our lives we need to maintain a consistent aesthetic, so new objects are incorporated and the old discarded. Advertising thus underpins a condition where people identify themselves and others through the possession of objects. It helps stimulate conspicuous consumption (Veblen, 1970 [1899]) in which commodities have social meaning and form the basis of social distinction and status hierarchies (Bourdieu, 1984). Years of advertising have reinforced this situation such that the reach of objects has been extended to encompass most aspects of human life in industrialized countries. 'There is no want or need that does not already have its correlate in some object manufactured for profit' (Gottdiener, 2000: 9). It is no accident therefore that it has become common to speak of members of the public unidimensionally, as consumers. The term 'objects' in the discussion above refers to more than physical things and can indicate also services, processes, practices, cultural performances, places and lifestyles including those associated with leisure.

The process which brings objects into the market so that they can be used to generate profit, in our case objects associated with leisure and related lifestyles, is known as commodification. There are various perspectives on this process. And the ways it works and should be characterized are matters for debate (Best, 1989). Simply put, objects become commodities when they take on an exchange value and are traded in a market. So in this sense commodification refers to processes of commercialization. Debord (1983) went further, arguing that commodification represents a way of living where individuals consume a world made by others rather than producing their own. He wrote about life in capitalist societies suggesting that it was dominated by spectacle, a complex idea which refers to mass media society and the vast institutional and technical apparatus of late capitalism. In the society of the spectacle people are pacified and depoliticized because commodified forms of leisure and entertainment act as 'narcotics' and which, while they seem to meet people's needs and satisfy them, are in fact a form of deprivation. This kind of sentiment has pervaded critical popular music and literature for many years.

Baudrillard (1983a, b) took a different tack on the way commodification developed as a form of deprivation, arguing that the development of late capitalism has seen the process of profitable exchange disconnect from the actual objects traded in the market. What people are really selling and buying, he argues, are not objects, but hyperreality, the signs, images and information symbolized by the objects concerned. In such a process objects such as places designed for leisure, are able to be sold because they signify 'aestheticised spaces of entertainment and pleasure' (Meethan, 1996: 324).

Much of the discussion of spectacle and hyperreality in leisure and tourism has been linked with questions of how commodification has transformed local communities and cultures (Cohen, 1988), suggesting that commodification expropriates and exploits customs, people and objects and makes them inauthentic and meaningless. Other writers have challenged this view, and by extension the views of Debord and Baudrillard, arguing that commodification should not be viewed as a universal form of deprivation but simply as the commercialization of cultural performance and objects, and the places in which they occur. It is a reality that is negotiated by people in particular places to meet particular situations and requirements and therefore differs in form and content from place to place (Stymeist, 1996; Watson and Kopachevsky, 1994: 652). Whichever position one takes on the meaning of commodification it is a process which generates considerable fluidity in social and economic life as people seek to bring new services, processes, practices, cultural performances, places and lifestyles into the market. It is also a process, which while for many people is taken for granted, is also contested and resisted in a variety of settings (Goss, 1995).

Leisure, Home, Shopping and Entertainment

National leisure participation surveys from various countries have shown that the home is a fundamentally important leisure space (Cushman *et al.*, 2005). In Chapter 5 we discussed how the home is a place to participate in individual and social leisure, plan activities beyond the home and use as a leisure object in and of itself. It too is an aestheticized space of entertainment and pleasure for many people. Leisure therefore sits at the nexus of home; self, family and household identity; senses of place and dwelling; *and* consumption. These same national leisure surveys have also shown that home-based leisure is today closely connected to other spaces which are not of the home but which are extensions of it: places to shop,

Figure 7.1   Eat, Shop, Unwind: World Square, Sydney, Australia

eat and relax such as the shopping precinct or mall, another space of aestheticized entertainment and pleasure.

The connection is well illustrated in Figure 7.1, an advertising billboard and part of the branding of a 90-speciality store shopping, entertainment and office complex in downtown Sydney, New South Wales, Australia, known as World Square. The message of the billboard, elaborated on the World Square website, is clear enough: this is a good place to come to eat, shop and unwind – a direct appeal to consume and relax; and the illustrations on the sign and on the website suggest that these activities can be conducted in this place in a stylish way by engaging with part or all of the full range of activity supported by World Square: 'fashion and accessories, restaurants and bars, cafés and fast food, lifestyle, supermarkets'.

A more detailed examination of the World Square website is revealing. Using the heading 'COME OUT THIS MARDI GRAS ...' the shopping and entertainment opportunities at World Square, located away from home and requiring one to 'come out' to enjoy them, are linked playfully to the 'coming out' associated with a major Sydney cultural, leisure and consumption event: the Gay and Lesbian Mardi Gras. The website indicates that shoppers can 'Save and be inspired during the World Square 3 Day Mardi Gras Sale ...'. And that they may 'Enjoy the LiveSite slideshow during the festival period, and pick up ... [their] exclusive, limited edition "Anthems for Mardi Gras" CD (of which there are limited quantities and for which $US100 must be spent in a single transaction)'.

In another section of the website under the heading 'FEVER ...' shoppers at World Square are invited to 'Bloom into spring and feel the fever with the latest fashion at World Square – exotic, bold and sizzling! Be inspired and escape on a colourful adventure with hints of floral and tribal patterns. From statement dresses, to neutral tailored office wear and bright accessories – the heat of summer starts here'.

The website also announced the opening of a new restaurant on the World Square site known as 'TASTE OF SHANGHAI' which 'offers

World Square customers a mix of casual and takeaway dining options. The restaurant offers a unique selection of authentic Asian cuisine, specializing in a variety of dumplings, pork buns and stir fries'.

The commodities or objects on offer at World Square are numerous and are presented in such a way as to signify many of the things one thinks of when seeking a leisure experience. They include relaxation, inspiration, enjoyment, escape, adventure, and exotic and authentic experience, and all are available to those who can afford to participate.

Places such as World Square exist within a broader urban infrastructure of leisure related consumption. An examination of the lifestyles of any significant prosperous city reinforces this view. One is immediately struck by the ubiquity of the signs of consumption. Transport hubs are often co-located with shops and food outlets and are replete with advertising for a range of products and experiences, many associated with leisure lifestyles. A good example is airport duty-free shops with their brightly lit interiors and dazzling display of wares for sale. Advertising for these and similar products abounds both within the airport and on billboards on the roads leaving for the city. Urban shopping and entertainment precincts display similar signs. The most obvious is crowds of people sampling a wide range of sites, sights, products and activities, sometimes located near gentrified inner-city landscapes.

On a summer Saturday afternoon we visited such a place, which combined a 'traditional' shopping street with a street market located beside a major urban park and a short drive to a shopping mall owned by a transnational corporation. We were struck by the intensity of consumption activity. The street was lined with shops which housed both local and global brand retailers. Advertisements encouraging people to purchase all manner of products and services were in abundance. Expensive, stylish motor cars were common. People, 'consumers', were cruising the market and shops; buying and looking at products; walking their pets; eating, drinking, chatting, face to face and on cellphones, while walking or sitting in cafés, pubs and restaurants; and standing in queues at money machines. The crowds were swelled by a steady stream of adolescents and young adults passing down the street to attend an annual music festival in the local park.

In the nearby mall, comprising five stories of shops, the elevators were packed, and, as we sat and observed, the overall impression was of purposeful activity: people, many stylishly dressed in obviously branded clothing, talking, walking, drinking coffee and chatting, some staring into space, teenagers in groups, families, children with helium-filled balloons, babies in carriages, purchases carried in bags, groceries pushed in shopping carts, flowers on sale for Valentine's day and for taking home and decorating the house, people queuing to purchase movie tickets at the multiplex cinema, advertising everywhere.

This for many prosperous urban residents is a typical summer's Saturday afternoon. No doubt some of this shopping involves the purchase of necessities, but it is an inescapable fact that much of the social interaction we observed was organized around the twin poles of leisure and consumption. This interaction is facilitated by the existence of easily accessible credit, although we acknowledge that in the current recessionary environment there has been a consequent rise in the use of debit cards. In the shopping mall mentioned above we noted that outside the supermarket there was a large advertisement for the American Express credit card which read: ' "It's not just for big things": supermarkets welcome American Express'. Those people identified by American Express as potentially interested in having such a credit card are sent unsolicited offers in the mail encouraging them to sign up. As a further encouragement to participate, the people contacted about the American Express® Gold Credit Card are told about an associated rewards programme, so that for every dollar spent using the card the shopper can earn one membership reward point. These points can be redeemed, the potential cardholder is told, for 'fantastic rewards' including those ranging from 'flights, luxury accommodation, electronics, vouchers, wine, quality homewares and so much more'. The connections between using the card, consumption and leisure are clear enough.

Easily available credit and debit cards are integrally tied to the rise of on-line shopping. For those who have such a card and are able to afford a home computer the high-street shopping experience is now linked to Internet use. At the simplest level, and returning to the World Square example above, shoppers are able to use the Internet to examine and evaluate the websites of such retailers, look at their catalogues and inventories and see if they are selling any products or services of interest. But shopping directly over the Internet for new or second-hand products is a more significant marker of the influence of the World Wide Web on leisure. Over the last decade the rise in on-line shopping opportunities has been considerable. A wide range of products is available and sophisticated global distribution networks exist to display, process and transport goods purchased in this way. Those searching for a particular item to contribute to their leisure activities are able to seek out reviews of products and make evaluative comparisons. On-line product discussion groups may be used to gather further information and advice, and if necessary, e-mails may be sent to clarify particular points about the products or services under discussion. The leisure, and business, travel industries have been greatly affected by the rise of the Internet. It is now possible to view images of travel destinations, examine recreational opportunities, construct itineraries, book rental cars, rail and air tickets, reserve accommodation and organize travel insurance over the net before leaving home or while travelling. An increasing number of travellers use e-mail and websites to post stories about, and pictures of, their travel activities and experiences, thus allowing family, friends and colleagues at home to keep up with travelling progress, and experience the trip vicariously (German Moltz, 2006; Sheller and Urry, 2006).

The Car, Motorcycle, Mobility and Identity

The private motor vehicle is such an important leisure-related consumption object that it deserves a chapter section all of its own. The motor car has been a central element in the development of suburban family life, and essential for the pursuit of many activities, but the motor vehicle's obvious importance in transportation should not distract us from understanding it also as a universal marker of status and distinction (Urry, 2000; Sheller and Urry, 2006). This can first be understood by examining its role in youth culture. Since the 1950s, cars and motorcycles have been associated with growing up and gaining the freedom to move; they have been linked to the development of social relationships in adolescence and early adulthood and gaining credibility among peers. Cars and young people have also proved a volatile mix. Death or injury by car accident is highest among young people under 25 years of age and in some cities motor vehicles and young people have been at the centre of clashes with residents, authorities and police. Antisocial use of the car by young men, so-called 'boy racers', has, for example, seen residential and commercial city streets turned into drag-racing tracks at night and at weekends. The onset of a moral panic about boy racers has seen heavy penalties and the threat to crush their cars being applied in New Zealand and Australia but these have not had a significant impact on this activity (Sachdeva, 2010: A10). Similarly, the emergence in a number of countries, in the 1960s and 1970s, of 'biker gangs' who wore what was perceived by some to be threatening insignia and often drove around in convoys was another vehicle-related phenomenon which raised public concern.

In many respects there is nothing particularly new about these activity patterns. The behaviour of adolescents has always worried their elders. In New Zealand, as in many other countries, there has been a series of moral panics over the years (Soler, 1989). Similarly, in the 1950s and 1960s youth culture flourished in the UK, centred on new musical forms and particular subcultural activities and often flamboyant, representational styles. In the 1960s, for example, a noticeable number of British youths aligned themselves with preferences for particular forms of motor vehicle and popular musical styles. These included the mods and rockers, with the mods preferring motor scooters and rhythm and blues, mainly British music, and rockers riding motorbikes and preferring US rock and roll. These weren't just riding clubs but manifested in intense and often violent rivalries.

Cars and motorcycles have also been an obvious element of popular culture for those over the age of 25 and have been celebrated in pictures and song. The road-movie genre is a good example. The love affair with the car continues unabated today. It is a vital part of the identity of many people in developed countries who see cars as an integral part of their lives. For a very significant minority, all things to do with cars as both machine and as a cultural symbol are well illustrated by the high popularity of motor racing and television programmes such as *Top Gear*.

The celebration of the 'Mother Road: Route 66' which runs between two of America's most significant cities, Chicago in Illinois and Los Angeles in California and its continuing popularity as a tourist route for motorcycle enthusiasts is a testimony to the significance of the machine as a cultural icon. On Route 66, retro images associated with the experience of biking and driving across the US are clearly demonstrated on the streetscape in Seligman, Arizona, a town near the western end of the road (Figure 7.2). The quintessential touring motorcycle, the US-made

Figure 7.2   Route 66 California, USA

Harley-Davidson, has become a cult symbol, particularly among older riders, and is linked in the popular mind to roads such as Route 66 (see Figure 7.2). This and similar brands of motorcycle are currently seeing a revival in popularity in a number of countries, including Japan where in 2008 15,698 Harley-Davidson bikes were sold. Forty per cent of those buying them were aged on average between 40 and 41, with 30 per cent in their thirties, 25 per cent in their fifties and the rest (5 per cent) in their twenties. Women accounted for 7 to 8 per cent of customers. The purchase of large and powerful motorcycles by baby-boomers is having its corollary in road accidents in a number of countries with older people increasingly being represented in death and injury statistics.

Leisure and Consumption in the Countryside

Whatever their mode of transport, a person does not have to travel far beyond the edges of the city to see that the connection between leisure, consumption and place is also working itself out in the countryside. The city and countryside are linked in important ways in this process. Informal, largely uncommercialized outdoor recreation, for example, is conducted in the countryside but largely resourced from the city. All the paraphernalia required for fun in the forest and on hills, rivers and lakes, at the coast or on the sea are available for sale in urban shops and over the Internet. The list of available gear is too long to itemize here but important categories include: recreational on- and off-road motor vehicles, boats, other activity-oriented equipment, and clothing and footwear. As is the case for leisure products purchased for use in the city, countryside recreational gear is subject to the vagaries of fashion. It is important for many outdoor recreationists to be seen using stylish and up-to-date equipment and wearing fashionably appropriate clothing. There is also an interesting cross-over from the countryside to the city with respect to current fashions in four-wheel drive recreational motor vehicles and casual outdoor recreational clothing and footwear. It is now common in many countries to see urban residents who never, or hardly ever, engage in outdoor recreation in the countryside, driving these vehicles and wearing branded outdoor clothing and footwear as they traverse the city.

Another link between the countryside and the city are sites and sights which stimulate rural day tripping and longer holiday breaks by both domestic and international recreational tourists (Cloke, 1993). These places are commodified and can be identified by their markers which are information or any representation that labels a sight or recreational setting as a sight or setting. These markers may include brochures, guide books, on-site plaques, websites, reproductions (photographs, art prints, souvenirs), educational material, television programmes, feature films, reviews in lifestyle magazines, or the incorporation of recreational and tourism sights into cultural symbols or national marketing strategies (Britton, 1991: 463; Corkery and Bailey, 1994; Pawson and Swaffield, 1998, Perkins, 2006).

Markers and the places and activities which they represent are created in three ways (Britton, 1991): first by using existing non-commercialized places or attractions for the purpose of commodified recreation or tourism. Good rural examples include opportunities for boating, rafting, cycling, fishing, horse riding and walking. In their newly commodified forms they may have technology added to them, therefore making them more attractive. Jet boating, rafting and kayaking on white water, four-wheel drive vehicle adventures, mountain biking, some eco-tourism activities and walking tours where participants stay in comfortable back country lodges are all examples of technologically based commodified rural recreational activities catering for local and international visitors on a fee paying basis (Cloke and Perkins, 1998, 2002). The second type of marker/place/activity is produced by building new, purpose-built attractions such as resorts, shops, and facilities from which previously unavailable activities are run. The third category is produced by engaging in the rehabilitation of socially and economically depressed regions and may incorporate combinations of the first two categories. The search for new forms of leisure commodity has meant that the meaning of some rural spaces has been remade to the extent that completely new ways of thinking about and managing places have been established (Cloke and Perkins, 1998).

The rural attractions (their specific sites and their surrounding regions) that are produced are commodified first as the recreation industry works to connect its products, and thereby enhance their meaning, to already existing, often attractive public goods (e.g., rural landscapes, national parks and other areas reserved for nature and heritage conservation); and second by assimilating originally non-recreational ventures into the recreation and tourism system (e.g., retail outlets) thereby imparting new meanings to specific places. The primary mechanism for imparting these meanings (apart from the effect of propinquity) is advertising, packaging and market positioning, that is, by selling places; and in the process by suggesting that the recreationist or tourist will get more than in reality the place can offer (Britton, 1991; Gold and Ward, 1994; Kearns and Philo, 1993).

Shopping Villages, Wine Regions and Opportunities for Adventure

Sociologist John Urry argues that the changes and processes mentioned above in the context of rural recreation and tourism have occurred in conjunction with the rise of post-mass tourism or post-tourism (Cloke and Perkins, 1998, 2002; Perkins and Thorns, 2001; Urry, 1990/2002, 1992, 1995). Unlike mass-tourists, who purchase packaged holidays, post-tourists search for and consume the signs and symbols of niche recreational experience. To a much greater degree than mass-tourists they prefer to make their own travel arrangements, find their own accommodation, eat local foods and try to use the local language when obtaining goods and services. Most importantly, rather than just sightseeing or playing in the bars or on the beaches of tourism resorts, post-tourists attempt to participate in local cultures and places. This often includes purchasing local cultural products and/or doing active and physically challenging things in the outdoors (Hall, 1992). In the following section our purpose is to illustrate examples of the niche recreational experiences domestic recreationists and international tourists are searching for and consuming in the countryside.

The Heritage Shopping Village

The first example is of heritage shopping villages in North America which are created by entrepreneurs and supported by local governments wishing to increase economic growth in their jurisdictions (Mitchell, 1998; Kneafsey, 2001; Harvey 1989b). These villages are located within an easy drive of metropolitan urban areas and trade on anti-urban sentiment among city dwellers who idealize the countryside, partly as a reaction to the chaotic nature of urbanization and also because of a nostalgia for a simpler and mythical rural life. Entrepreneurs, recognizing the potential for profit, have attempted to satisfy visitors' desires for this imagined countryside by recreating pre-industrial village landscapes and reproducing pre-industrial commodities. These landscapes visually represent the ideal, and the commodities give the ideal its material form (Mitchell, 1998: 275). Heritage shopping villages therefore comprise restored or reconstructed vernacular buildings or streetscapes upon which tourists can gaze and perform. These purposefully constructed landscapes present a visual experience consistent with the imagined landscape: one devoid of 'jarring elements' that would detract from the symbolic experience being presented and sought (Dorst, 1989: 29, quoted in Mitchell, 1998: 275). So in these villages visitors spend their time walking, gazing, eating and drinking and buying products which are reproductions that symbolize the 'idealised [pre-industrial] mode of production' (Dorst, 1989: 64, quoted in Mitchell, 1998: 275). The consumer purchases both an object (e.g., a quilt), and the ideal of the object (quiltness) with all its attendant associations (Dorst, 1989).

There are multiple variations on this shopping village theme in many developed countries. Rather than all being *heritage* villages, many have their economic bases in economic activities such as rural primary and secondary production, or small-scale industrial manufacturing, and perhaps also act as dormitory towns for larger cities nearby. Recreational consumption opportunities supplement these activities and offer urban day trippers, overnight domestic tourists and rural second-home owners the chance to take a break from the city and to drive in the countryside with family or friends and eat, drink and shop, perhaps at a farmers' market, artists' studios or giftshops.

Peri-Urban Wine Regions

Another example of commodified niche recreational experience occurs where peri-urban areas support grape growing and winemaking such as those in the Napa and Sonoma Valleys near San Francisco in California, USA. Relatively wealthy domestic urban residents and international tourists who are interested in wine take such areas very seriously and entrepreneurs are able to profit from the sale of wine, food, accommodation, wine-tasting tours (Figure 7.3) and wine-related souvenirs such as books, corkscrews, posters, DVDs and other representations of viticulture, winemaking and tasting. While what is being sought by visitors to wine regions and settlements has much in common with that desired by people who visit rural shopping villages, wine entrepreneurs trade specifically on the perception that the tasting and appreciation of wine requires knowledge, skill and discernment, that is, a particular kind of high-status cultural capital (Bourdieu, 1984). So wine tourists are consuming not just the wine and wine region but also what that consumption signifies about them.

In some cases these regions are visited mainly by residents of nearby cities such as the vineyards on Waiheke Island, a 35-minute ferry ride from downtown Auckland in New Zealand. Approximately 700,000 people visit each year and are drawn to the island's 'unique combination of the harbour crossing, beautiful beaches and scenery, as well as its cultural diversity – relaxed island charm, a diverse and varied community, sculpture, world-class food and internationally acclaimed wine' (Baragwanath and Lewis, 2010: 1). Other wine regions are promoted to

Figure 7.3 Wine Tours

attract international as well as local visitors, as places to visit, enjoy, relax and consume. A good example is the Hurunui District, also in New Zealand. Its marketing byline is:

> Welcome to Hurunui
> One of New Zealand's most stunning and spectacular regions located on the rugged east coast of the South Island, just north of Christchurch.
>
> Experience the irresistible charm of our towns and villages, superb wine and food at our cafes, restaurants and wineries, and a huge range of activities and attractions – there's plenty to do.
>
> In Hurunui we live the lives others only dream of – come visit, and travel well.

So the wine consumption experience is packaged and sold alongside a range of complementary activities and landscapes.

Commodified Adventure

Our final example of a niche rural consumption experience is less dependent on peri-urban areas, but also sometimes associated with them (Schöllmann *et al.*, 2000). These are rural sites and sights where adventure has been commodified so that typically young adult visitors can purchase the opportunity to engage in a range of adventurous outdoor recreational activities ranging on a continuum from 'soft' to 'hard' adventure (Cloke and Perkins, 1998, 2002). Soft adventurers are often newcomers to outdoor activities who want to experience low-risk physical activity but also have the comforts of home, good meals and accommodation. They may be people who in many respects would be classified as mass-tourists except that they participate in an occasional physically adventurous activity (e.g., jet-boating, bungee-jumping, river rafting or hot-air ballooning) while staying in a well-established destination area. Hard adventurers are willing to travel to remote, little-known locations, particularly areas of outstanding natural beauty and participate in activities which are very challenging and risky such as mountaineering.

Commercial adventure recreation set along this soft-to-hard continuum is now available in North America, Europe, Asia, South America, Africa and Australasia with several very diverse places promoting themselves as the 'Adventure Capital of the World' including: South Africa (in this case the whole country); but also particular towns and cities such as Moab, Utah; Queenstown, New Zealand; Rio de Janeiro, Brazil; and Victoria Falls on the borders of Zambia and Zimbabwe. In answer to the question 'What to do in Victoria Falls' an enquirer is told:

> No one is going to complain of being bored in Victoria Falls. Frequently and affectionately coined the adventure capital of the world, there are lots of things to see and do in Victoria Falls. Activities on offer include: Bungee Jumping, White Water Rafting, Helicopter Flips, Boat Cruises, Canoeing, Elephant Back Safaris … Walking with Lions, Adrenaline Days, Bridge Swings, Jet Boats, Skydiving, Microlighting, Walks and Game Drives.

Adventure tourism promotion literature and websites present potential visitors with images and ideas about spectacle, desirability, novelty, having thrilling experiences and attaining cultural capital. Consequently, they anticipate having an adventurous time when on holiday and plan travel itineraries accordingly. The tourism destinations being promoted are managed so that their symbolic identities and physical forms remain as consistent as possible thus ensuring that adventure tourists' anticipations are fulfilled. The visitors therefore pay for and consume the recreational experience and associated place-meanings, and additionally, purchase memorabilia such as digital recordings and tee shirts which they take home to remind them of the experience and display to others. All of these factors combine to help elaborate their senses of personal identity.

Resisting Consumption

On returning either from the urban or rural shopping or commercial recreation activities discussed above the people in question integrate their purchases or memorabilia into their everyday lives, often at home. In this context an interesting literature has emerged which takes a critical perspective on the connections between leisure, consumption, happiness and waste (Hamilton and Denniss, 2005). In Australia, for example, where incomes are three times higher than they were in 1950 many people feel that they still don't earn enough to buy all the things they need. This is the case despite some of what is purchased day to day, such as food and other consumables, being thrown out unused, or not completely used. For many people who earn good incomes, increasing levels of wealth and consumption do not seem to make them happier. They are often financially indebted, emotionally stressed, physically unfit, overweight and unwell, and their lives are filled with objects, the storage of which requires bigger and bigger houses. But even these bigger houses are not large enough to store all that has been purchased, and in a number of countries there has been a proliferation of commercially provided small-scale storage facilities to take the overflow of possessions that houses and their surrounding land cannot hold. There is also a dawning concern that current consumption patterns cannot be sustained because of the impacts they are having on the natural environment. Similarly, commentators on the implications of peak oil production question whether current consumption patterns are sustainable. Furthermore, there is an increasing concern about the social and environmental impacts of commercial recreation and tourism growth in some rural areas. This is illustrated, for example, by the controversy over scenic flights into an important international tourism destination, Milford Sound in New Zealand's Fiordland National Park. These flights create 'noise pollution' which affects the peace and serenity of the Sound's coastal rainforest landscape.

As a result of these factors, some people are questioning whether current consumption lifestyles are worth pursuing and are embracing new ways of life and making a living that are centred on downshifting. They are resisting the blandishments of the consumption-oriented image- and taste-makers in the advertising industry and seeking a better quality of life and environment which incorporates earning and consuming less, living in stronger local communities while attempting to enhance their health and strengthen social connections (Hamilton and Denniss, 2005). But currently there is little sign that the majority are engaging with such practices.

Conclusion

In this chapter we have showed how leisure and consumption are integrally linked. They are influenced by globalizing aspects of product manufacture, advertising and retailing and the working out of an array of experiences set in homes, neighbourhoods, regional or central city retail precincts, and in urban and rural routes and tourism destinations. Increasingly, these experiences are being supplemented and sometimes replaced by the opportunities for consumption provided by the proliferation of information and communication technologies. In the short to medium term it seems highly likely therefore that a globalized culture of leisure-oriented shopping and related consumption will continue to be integrally important in the creation of people's senses place and identity in the working out of their everyday lives.

We pointed out in the last section of the chapter that there are a growing number of people wondering whether this consumption trajectory is socially, economically and environmentally sustainable and it is to these issues that we turn in the next chapter.

Further reading

Bourdieu, P. 1984. *Distinction: A Social Critique of the Judgement of Taste.* Cambridge, MA: Harvard University Press.

Cloke, P. and H. C. Perkins. 2002. 'Commodification and Adventure in New Zealand Tourism'. *Current Issues in Tourism* 5, 521–549.

Corrigan, P. 1997. *The Sociology of Consumption: An Introduction.* London: Sage.

Gottdiener, M. (ed.). 2000. *New Forms of Consumption: Consumers, Culture and Commodification.* Lanham, MD: Rowman & Littlefield.

Hamilton, C. and R. Denniss. 2005. *Affluenza: When Too Much is Never Enough.* Crows Nest, NSW: Allen & Unwin.

Meethan, K. 1996. 'Consuming (in) the Civilized City'. *Annals of Tourism Research* 23, 322–340.

Urry, J. 1995. *Consuming Places.* London: Routledge.

Zukin, S. 1995. *The Culture of Cities.* Cambridge, MA: Blackwell.

Websites

http://worldsquare.com.au; accessed 10/03/2010
http://news.bbc.co.uk/2/hi/business/7432643.stm; accessed 10/03/2010
http://worldsquare.com.au; accessed 10/03/2010
www.americanexpress.com/newzealand/campaigns; accessed 12/03/2010
www.historic66.com; accessed 26/05/2010

www.japantoday.com/category/executive-impact/view/harley-davidson-gains-popularity-in-japan; accessed 27/05/2010
www.mardigras.org.au; accessed 10/03/2010
www.rhinoafrica.com/destinations/vic_falls/victoria_falls_facts/victoria_falls_activities; accessed 23/03/2010
www.visithurunui.co.nz; accessed 22/03/2010

PART III

A Finite World?

The last part of the book takes up the issue of how everyday life might be reshaped and affected by the recognition that we are living in a world of finite rather than unlimited and abundant resources. The debates around these issues are complex and shaped by both global and local understandings. Chapter 8 explores some of the more global-level debates that have grown out of a reappraisal of the relationship between the natural and social world. This debate has been informed by the growth of both environmental studies and the debates around sustainability. Chapter 9 views the debates from a more grounded approach which returns to thinking about the construction of our dwellings and homes, communities and neighbourhoods and how these are being changed by ideas and practices emerging from the wider global debates and being worked out in accordance with the needs and priorities of people and organizations in local areas. These manifest in community activities, local government planning schemes and private sector design approaches to managing human settlements. The argument developed in Chapters 8 and 9 is based on an appreciation that modifications in everyday understanding and living are not just about individual behaviour change but also require analysis of our social and institutional practices and structures as well as how we live out and experience local environmental change in conjunction with those people who are significant to us.

CHAPTER 8

Sustaining the Places in Which We Live

Introduction

The end of Chapter 7 touched on the environmental consequences of and concerns about current high rates of consumption. This has created the paradoxical situation that at a time when demand for consumption goods and services is soaring we are also in the middle of a global debate about how to live more sustainably and justly on planet earth. Reconciling these divergent trends is proving to be a gargantuan challenge. This reconciliation demands the overhaul of the enlightenment idea that nature and society are polar opposites (Macnaghten and Urry, 1998). It also requires the development of a set of social and economic practices that will sustain nature–society in the long term (Therborn, 2000; Vallance *et al.*, 2011). This chapter therefore addresses current debates about economic growth, global environmental change and sustainability.

Economic Development and Global Environmental Change

During the period after the end of the Second World War, the goals of economic growth and increasing domestic consumption were prized politically. In the US, Europe and the remainder of the developed world there was a strong belief in 'progress, material abundance and the goodness of growth, faith in the efficacy of science and technology; and a view of nature as something to be subdued' (Dunlap, 2008: 5). These beliefs encouraged the growth of a carbon-intensive economy and an industrial system based around mass production, lowered unit costs and an increase in number and range of consumers. The post-1945

Western economies recovered from war and economic depression by increasing the production of new commodities, many developed using new techniques. The restructuring of the global economy which began in the late 1960s saw this patterns of production and resource use being replicated in a wider range of countries in Asia, Central and South America. Consequently, in the second half of the twentieth century an ever-growing collection of commodities was created, leading to the rise of the sophisticated and widespread consumer culture discussed in Chapter 7.

As alluded to in Chapter 6, these commodities have recently included television, personal computers, the Internet, cellphones, compact discs, DVDs, electronic game stations and social websites which have revolutionized how we work, play and shop. Widespread motor car ownership and inexpensive fares on wide-bodied jet aircraft have also increased first-hand experience of regional and international travel. Domestic life has been improved by the advent of central heating, electric and gas stoves, vacuum cleaners, refrigerators, freezers and washing machines. Many commodities are linked to processes and services which have changed people's lives dramatically and irrevocably. Good examples include modern dental products and techniques which have saved teeth; drugs including antibiotics which have transformed the management of disease; sophisticated surgical procedures such as organ repairs and replacements; safer births which have improved survival rates for babies; greater control of fertility which has reduced the number of unplanned births; fertility treatments that have enabled people to have children who were previously unable, and cosmetic surgery for people who have suffered accidents or who want to look 'better'. Possessing many of these commodities and having access to these services is a sign of success; they are the contemporary symbols of status and position, hence their desirability and sometimes high price.

Just as individuals measure their success by comparing their commodity consumption with that of other people, governments have also measured their nation's progress by constantly comparing their own country with that of others through the use of such measures as gross national or domestic product (GNP or GDP). Data on standard indicators of GNP/GDP are collected by international organizations such as the OECD and World Bank and form the basis of the league tables that pervade political consciousness and the aspirations of nation states (Oxley *et al.*, 2008). One way of seeing the global distribution of these differences in wealth is by using a world map derived from Worldmapper, a collection of world maps which resizes territories on each map according to the subject of interest. Figure 8.1 represents

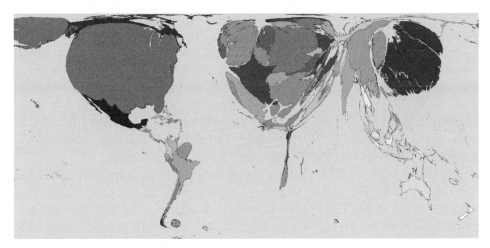

Source: Worldmapper (www.worldmapper.org). Copyright SASI Group (University of Sheffield) and Mark Newman (University of Michigan). Data for the Worldmapper maps are derived from various agencies of the UN, the US CIA, the World Bank and allied organizations

Figure 8.1 GDP Wealth (territory size shows the proportion of worldwide wealth, that is, GDP based on exchange rates with the $US)

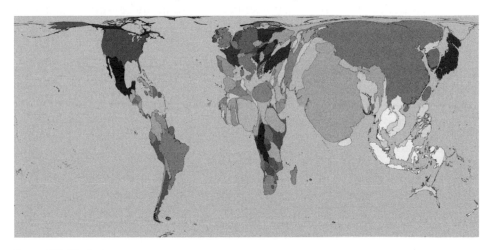

Source: Worldmapper

Figure 8.2 World Population Map (size of each territory shows the relative proportion of the world's population living there)

GDP wealth expressed in terms of the size of national territories. This figure, and the other figures from Worldmapper in this chapter, should be compared with Figure 8.2 which shows global population distribution. In this map, India, China and Japan appear large on the map because they have large populations while countries with small populations are barely visible.

A comparison between Figures 8.1 and 8.2 clearly demonstrates the global inequalities in wealth distribution (as measured by GDP), its concentration in the countries of the 'north' and the significance of North America, Europe and Japan compared with Africa and South America. Taking one country in particular, the USA, and comparing its population with its GDP wealth makes this point particularly well. While not indicated in Figure 8.1, on the GDP per person measure the wealthiest countries are Luxembourg, Norway and Switzerland and the poorest are Ethiopia, Burundi and the Democratic Republic of Congo.

Measures such as GDP have a significant normative influence and set the benchmarks for global and local policy making. In those countries which have a high GDP the question of whether or not commodity production can be constantly expanded was not until recently generally addressed in such analyses of growth. Nor was the question of whether quality of life is necessarily improved by people having more things to buy. People living at the beginning of the twenty-first century experienced measured real consumption that was over ten times that of those living at the beginning of the twentieth (Lipsey *et al.*, 2005). It is debatable, however, whether they have experienced a similar increase in quality of life over that period. As an illustration of this it is not at all clear whether the advent of the domestic appliances discussed above have liberated us from 'housework' or just made domestic life more complex (Winstanley, 2001; Hayden, 1980; Watson and Gibson, 1995; McDowell, 1999).

In the cities of developed countries the dramatic increase in commodity production was accompanied by the growth of very large low-density car-dependent suburbs providing a ready market for 'consumer durables' and places to build shopping precincts, later malls, to which people could easily drive and park their cars while shopping (Gans, 1967; Berger, 1960). In these new suburbs, individual ownership of houses and land, and the display and use of commodities, both indoors and in gardens areas, became a mark of social and economic progress. Car ownership was also important in this regard. For many people these attributes became synonymous with a desired lifestyle and the development of a 'modern society'. In part, the desire to consume commodities, and a sense of choice that accompanied it, was a reaction to the 1920s and 1930s economic depression and shortages resulting from wartime rationing and restrictions. Post-war growth created a sense of 'affluence' and encouraged acquisition and display to demonstrate and signify individual and family success (Packard, 1957).

This rising affluence and urban growth came at a price. From the 1960s there was a growing realization that the earth's natural environment was under increasing pressure. Calls for a greater recognition of the earth's limits were made (Meadows *et al.*, 1972). Concerns about human population growth emerged at approximately the same time (Ehrlich, 1968; Ehrlich and Ehrlich 1970). In 1968 Hardin, a biologist, brought attention to his thesis about the 'tragedy of the commons' in which he argued that human beings had developed individualist solutions to the use of land and resources rather ones in which resources were managed in the interests of all of us, thus leading to the degradation of the environment. The impact of all of this work was to raise new questions about the capacity of the earth's systems to cope with human use of resources. Warnings were issued about the human health and ecological impacts of industrialization and intensive agriculture, the latter based on the use of pesticides and fertilizers to encourage higher yields and greater productivity (Carson, 1962). These critiques of continued economic growth were reiterated during the energy crisis in 1973–1974, when oil supplies were cut and prices climbed rapidly threatening the world economy with an economic slump.

Research attention on the effects of energy shortage and environmental constraints on society, politics and everyday social practices grew and a new environmental paradigm was formulated (Catton and Dunlap, 1978) underpinning the establishment of an 'environmental sociology' to challenge mainstream social research which was built around ideas of 'human exceptionalism' and of human progress based around growth without limits, including our capacity to solve social problems using technological and scientific advances. Known as the 'new environmental paradigm' its proponents argued that the world is 'finite and that there were potent biological limits constraining growth, social progress and other societal phenomena' (Catton and Dunplap, 1978: 45). The new paradigm was used to interpret the rise of environmental concerns and has also examined political resistance to calls for environmental change such as when some powerful groups and politicians have sought to undermine the legitimacy of the science of global environmental change (Schulmman, 2006).

At the global level environmental and population concerns relative to economic growth were raised in debates about the pace of growth and need for economic development to address issues of poverty and low income. The first formal global meeting to discuss these issues was held in Stockholm, Sweden, in 1972 at the United Nations Conference on the Human Environment. The dangers posed by development were canvassed and a call for a more 'sustainable' approach made (Satterthwaite, 1999). Also in 1972, the Club of Rome warned of the planetary dangers stemming from economic growth and excessive resource exploitation. These stirrings began to challenge the assumption that unlimited growth and wealth creation were possible. They also challenged the view that distributional and environmental issues could be addressed using mainly technological rather than political solutions.

In the 1980s, further international attention was drawn to the issues of environment, growth and development. Discussions were centred on the idea of sustainable development as articulated by the World Commission on Environment and Development (WCED, 1987). Its report, entitled *Our Common Future*, focused on ways in which the basic needs of the world's population, now and in the future, could be secured while at the same time protecting the life-giving attributes of the biophysical environment. When it was originally formulated, sustainable development incorporated a number of dimensions of 'sustainability'. These included biophysical environmental sustainability, predicated on the idea that there are environmental limits to human activity; social sustainability drawing attention to the need for a greater degree of equity in resource use across the planet, and economic sustainability, emphasizing the importance of quality rather than the quantity of economic growth.

This new way of thinking was designed to ensure that we don't create wealth today by depleting resources and options that will be needed by future generations (Redclift, 1987; Stoker and Young, 1993). Subsequently the idea of sustainable development was extended to include cultural sustainability and the preservation of threatened languages and the protection of heritage and customary practices – seen by some as obstacles to modernization and development. In elaborated form sustainable development then relies on a large set of ideas that attempt to address how it might be possible to create growth in developing countries; change the quality of growth in the developed economies; provide jobs, food, energy, water and sanitation; ensure a sustainable level of population; conserve and enhance resources; reorient technology and manage risk; and merge environmental and economic concerns with a benign distribution of power and influence in decision-making (Vallance *et al.*, 2011).

More recently, the concern with intergenerational responsibility and equity has been reinforced by the climate change debate and how the present generation can change its behaviour to enable future generations to have tolerable lives. Climate change is, however, only 'one component of a much bigger problem, that is, the unsustainable and inequitable use of nature by growing numbers of human consumers' (Spellerberg and McNeely, 2010: A15). Many writers see the world as facing a perfect storm comprising 'runaway climate change, huge water, goods and energy shortages and enormous population growth' (Urry, 2010; Gluckman, 2010). They argue for creating a low-carbon society requiring not just individual behavioural changes but the dismantling of the carbon–military–industrial complex with its reliance on fossil fuel and a high degree of human mobility. These writers point to the ever-increasing demand for cars, suburban housing, commodity consumption, commodified leisure and global travel as a major determinant of global environmental deterioration. Debates about these issues has been fuelled by significant media attention, a series of reports and predictions from the International Panel on Climate Change (IPCC), Al Gore's *Inconvenient Truth*, intergovernmental meetings and shifting political rhetoric about the need for action. These issues and their connections to the sustainable development programme have been debated at a number of international conferences but getting agreement at the meetings and then adequate action afterwards has proven difficult.

Debates about Urban Sustainability

Living within our environment in safe, fair, efficient and environmentally responsible ways, lie at the heart of debates about sustainable development (Vallance and Perkins, 2010). More than half of the world's population live in cities and many live in very big urban concentrations known as mega-cities. Between 1975 and 2015 it was expected that the proportion of all city dwellers living in cities of over one million would have lifted from approximately one-third to around 43 per cent (UNCHS, 2001b: 23). By 2015 it is further expected that nearly 10 per cent of all cities will contain more than ten million people; a further 6.5 per cent will be populated by between five and ten million residents; and 26.3 per cent of cities will be home to between one and five million people. The majority of these cities will be in the developing world (Figure 8.3).

Using the same form of presentation as for GDP in Figure 8.1 and population in Figure 8.2, Figure 8.3 helps us to understand the changing distribution of the world's urban population. Unlike the concentration in GDP, with North America, Europe and Japan predominating, this map shows the significant growth of the Asian urban population with substantial dominance, and therefore mapped territory size, emerging from India, China, Indonesia and the Philippines. The comparison between GDP and the location of these rapidly growing urban populations suggests that there will be more people living in cities in countries with a lower GDP which will create pressure to increase economic growth to raise the overall standard of living. This will likely increase the consumption of energy and the emission of greenhouse gases because much of the

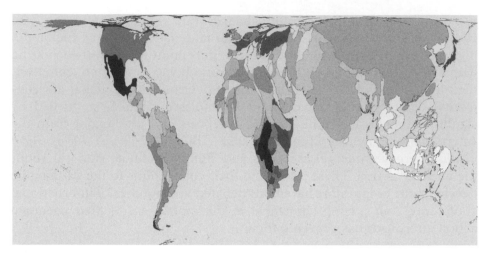

Source: Worldmapper

Figure 8.3 City Growth (territory size shows proportion of all extra people that will start living in urban areas in 2002–2015 in each territory)

required energy is likely to be met through burning fossils fuels. The data here and in Figure 8.1 show how closely the issues of wealth and poverty and urban and rural population growth are linked to questions of sustainable futures.

In the developing countries of the 'south', such as India, China, Indonesia and the Philippines, cities are growing and changing as young people migrate to them in search of economic opportunities and also because of high fertility rates. Together these create enormous pressures on housing and urban services. Unplanned squatter and other unregulated forms of settlement have proliferated on the edges of many world cities. These settlements typically provide insecure tenure and inadequate housing, infrastructure and services. In addition to those living in squatter settlements there are 20 to 40 million homeless households with no permanent roof over their heads. This emphasizes the important links between housing, poverty, poor health and access to many of the services and activities taken for granted by the developed world's population such as electricity, street lighting, clean drinking water and adequate sanitation. Without these both the quality of everyday living is compromised and survivability rates are lowered.

The obvious injustice and urgency of this situation unpins a number of programmes to ameliorate and improve the everyday lives of those affected in this way. Local and central governments have created partnerships with communities to assist them in self development *in situ*, thus legitimizing informal settlements. This is seen by many commentators as being a much better solution than schemes for squatter clearance and rehousing. In Latin America and the Caribbean these schemes have led to a reduction in evictions and negotiation to improve security of tenure and the upgrading of settlements. The United Nations points out, however, that much new construction is focused on growing middle-class markets rather than providing affordable housing to those in the lowest-income groups (UNCHS, 2001b).

The cities of the developed countries display a different but overlapping set of difficulties and challenges. There too, homelessness is an urgent issue (Cloke *et al.*, 2010) and so too is poverty and inadequate housing, but these are usually limited to smaller sectors of society. A more general problem involves the ageing of populations, rather than an explosion of growth driven by younger cohorts. Policy makers and politicians are being confronted by questions about how older populations might be supported economically and socially as their proportion rises and increases the 'dependency' ratio which reflects the proportion in the working population and those not earning (Thorns, 2002). In Japan, for example, this raises critical issues about the future requirement for both wealth generation and support for elderly family members. Here a change is occurring as younger people can no longer afford housing and are looking to find secure long-term work in an economy which has not been growing. Women are looking for careers, for more independence, and are becoming less willing and able to provide the support for their parents that would have been normal in the past. Delay in moving into housing and finding a partner has reduced the fertility rate to below replacement in urban areas. Some analysts have described the emergence in Japan of a 'lost generation' faced with a very different set of circumstances to that of their parents leading to a radical change in how they live their everyday lives. Homeownership looks likely to decline and thus connections to, and configurations of space and place will change (Hirayama and Ronald, 2008).

Living with the Motor Car

Urban areas, and particularly those in the developed world, also create enormous demands for services and infrastructure. These include health services and an expanding range of social and community services to meet the needs of growing and diverse populations. Water reticulation and waste disposal are of very great importance as are energy and transport infrastructure. In the context of the latter, the car-dependent cities created in the twentieth century, such as Los Angeles in California, were predicated on the easy movement of people in their private cars fuelled by the plentiful supply of cheap oil and other petroleum products. Low-density sprawling cities are, however, very energy inefficient because they require considerable investment to link residents to services and it is difficult to provide adequate transport alternatives to the use of the private car. Los Angeles has thus been created as a network of freeways that stretches across the coastal region between the Pacific Ocean and the Sierra Mountains at a very low density. The city's nearly 15 million inhabitants spend much of their life on the freeway! As Banham (2009 [1971]: 213) observed 'The Freeway system in its totality is now a single comprehensible place, a coherent state of mind, a complete way of life'. The resulting traffic congestion and pollution from private and commercial vehicles, exacerbated by Los Angeles' topography and weather patterns, has led to significant pollution and a deterioration in air quality. Many other cities now have similar combustion engine-induced air quality degradation, high levels of traffic congestion and an urban form built around the motor car.

Christchurch, New Zealand, for example, a very much smaller city with a population of 350,000 people, shares some of the Los Angeles' characteristics. It is a highly dispersed city built since the 1850s with a dominance of single-family housing on separate lots. A recent survey of 500 Christchurch residents sought their views about future transport issues. Most thought their travel patterns would not change much in the next ten years (*The Press* 25/02/2010: A15). Beyond 2020 they thought that there would be greater change but they attributed this largely to lifestyle reasons rather than because of resource shortages or external factors such as those associated with energy or environmental concerns. Cars were still expected to be the dominant mode of transport. No alternatives were envisaged and they had a strong faith in technological solutions which would make vehicles more energy efficient. Christchurch has one of the highest vehicle ownership rates in the world and around 70 per cent of trips made in the city are by car or van and fewer than 5 per cent are by public transport. The enduring significance of the car is that it offers freedom, mobility and speed yet as Giddens (2009: 159) observes the 'proliferation of cars negates these very qualities'.

In the opinion of some analysts, urban transport systems based around the car have proved unsustainable and are delivering a declining level of service despite increasing investments. They note also that many of these negative impacts fall disproportionately on the social groups who are least likely to own and drive cars. Despite the current domination of the private car, one of the questions for the twenty first century is how personal mobility will be maintained or changed as the 'peak oil' point of maximum global petroleum extraction is reached, after which reserves of oil that are recoverable will begin depleting (Newman *et al.*, 2009). Also part of this equation is the increasing cost of extraction. Finding new sources is possible but they are likely to be expensive to recover and present a number of risks. Great risks are now taken to extract oil from places that were once considered inaccessible. The major environmental disaster in the Gulf of Mexico in 2010 is an excellent example of what can happen when risks become reality. The long-term consequences of the oil spill for marine life and the economic viability of local employment is still unknown but they are likely to be long lasting. Deep-water drilling is still continuing in a variety of locations internationally and clearly poses high risks to both people and the environment.

To help solve this problem a new focus on renewable energy has appeared. But the possible rate of substitution is a contentious issue as demand for energy is still growing, particularly from both India and China because of their burgeoning economies. It is likely that a more 'sustainable' solution will demand quite significant changes in everyday lifestyles and in urban form. The degree of disruption that might be caused in this process will depend on the speed with which the impacts of peak oil and climate change impinge on our lives. Assuming a manageable rate of transition, urban form could be made more compact. Such a change could result in patterns of circulation and use which shift the balance from a high level of dependence on private modes of transport to greater use of public/mass transit systems. But given the fascination and enthusiasm for automobiles, the political influence of car makers and road transport and construction interests, shifting current patterns will not be simple (Bradsheer, 2002). Car manufacturing and servicing are significant components of many economies (Table 8.1). This also

Table 8.1 World's Top Car Makers (ranked by vehicle sales (millions), in first half of 2008)

1	Toyota	4.818
2	General Motors	4.540
3	Volkswagen	3.266
4	Ford	3.217
5	Hyundai	2.187
6	Honda	2.022
7	Nissan	2.014
8	PSA/Peugeot/Citroën	1.697
9	Renault	1.326
10	Suzuki	1.283

Source: As reported on Wheels24.co.za

includes, for example, product merchandising, such as designer clothing to be sold to the owners of expensive cars such as Jaguar, BMW and Porsche. This kind of merchandise emphasizes the connection between car ownership, lifestyle, status and markers of distinction (Bourdieu, 1984; Urry, 1995).

In 2007, a total of 79.9 million new automobiles were sold worldwide: 22.9 million in Europe, 21.4 million in Asia Pacific, 19.4 million in USA and Canada, 4.4 million in Latin America, 2.4 million in the Middle East and 1.4 million in Africa. The markets in North America and Japan were stagnant, however, reflecting the downturn in these economies, while those in South America and other parts of Asia grew strongly. Of the major global markets, China, Russia, Brazil and India saw the most rapid growth. About 250 million vehicles are in use in the United States and approximately one billion have been produced since manufacturing began. Globally, there were approximately 806 million cars and light trucks on the road in 2007; they consumed over 260 billion US gallons (984 billion litres) of gasoline and diesel fuel.

Again, using territory size, Figure 8.4 shows the dominance of North America, Western Europe and Japan relative to South America, much of Asia, Eastern Europe, Russia and particularly the countries of Africa in terms of the number of passenger cars found in each territory in 2002. In the world as a whole there is now one car for every ten people. This, however, varies between countries. New Zealand is at the top of the list

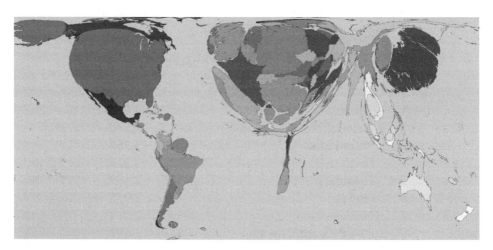

Source: Worldmapper

Figure 8.4 Passenger Cars (territory size shows the proportion of all cars in the world that are found there)

with 61 cars per 100 people, followed closely by the Western European countries. The countries with the fewest cars per population are the Central African Republic, Bangladesh and Tajikistan having one car for every 2,000+ people.

The situation in some developing countries is changing, something that is not captured in Figure 8.4. India and China, countries with very large populations, are good examples. In these countries a growing middle class has an appetite for commodities such as cars and housing which will inevitably increase energy consumption and the spread of both the benefits and costs of growth. Recognizing this demand, and the huge market it might potentially serve, in 2008 the Indian car maker Tata Motors launched the world's cheapest car selling for around $US2,500. The car is about 10 feet (3.048 metres) long and five feet (1.524 metres) wide and accommodates four adults. Tata claim a 50mpg (21.25kpl) fuel efficiency and lower emission levels than scooters now produced in India. The locally produced car is being manufactured in a new plant costing $US220 million in West Bengal and is seeking to take a share of India's growing market.

India produces 1.3 million cars a year. With the market growing at 10 to 12 per cent per year, this could reach three million a year by 2018. This potential for growth has attracted the attention of the major players so Suzuki, Toyota, Ford and General Motors are also seeking to enter this market with a lower-cost car. Tata motors see opportunities to sell their new low-cost vehicle globally. This is set to expand the market and place more pressure on an already overstressed Indian and global urban infrastructure.

China too is experiencing a growth in car ownership and the need to build roads and manage urban traffic congestion. Again this is linked to the growth of the middle class. Also in China a new group of young people has emerged who dream of being financially successful and commodity rich. It has become clear that a great many of them will not achieve their dream. Nevertheless, they are attracted to the cities to study, gain qualifications and seek work. Rising numbers of these young people are living on the edge of cities in suburban locations which means that travel to work is costly and time consuming. These new entrants to China's 'growing economy sleep in boxy rooms crammed in dingy low rises, and spend hours commuting to work on crowded buses as part of a trend of poorer white collar workers being forced to the fringes of China's wealthiest cities' (*The Press* 25/02/2010: B5). This example highlights the conflict between growth and quality of life and illustrates the complexity inherent in looking for sustainable solutions to urban development.

The motor vehicle then is the greatest single user of environmental resources on the face of the planet when one factors in the materials from which they are made, the space they occupy, including parking buildings and surface parking, the energy used in their manufacture, roads and fuel. Added to these should be the cost of degraded air quality, health impacts and costs including those associated with accidents, and respiratory and heart-related problems arising from reduced physical activity. Perhaps most important is the costly connection between the car and climate change (Satterthwaite, 2008). US car manufacturing and use, for example, accounts for 60 per cent of all its carbon dioxide emissions and 45 per cent of all emissions by cars worldwide (Giddens 2009: 159) (Figure 8.5). Transport, in all its forms, accounts for one-third of global carbon dioxide emissions.

The emissions of carbon are clearly not distributed evenly across the countries of the world. Figure 8.5 provides us with a map of this distribution. The dominance, as measured by territory size, of North America is very obvious as against the contribution of Africa and South America which are small by comparison. Within Africa a high proportion of total carbon emissions is derived from the more highly industrialized South Africa. In 2000, of the almost 23 billion tonnes of carbon dioxide released 28 per cent was from North America and 0.09 per cent was emitted by Central African countries. The emphasis here on global trends is therefore very important as cities and regions across the world

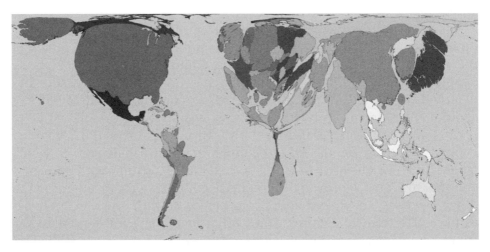

Source: Worldmapper

Figure 8.5 Carbon Dioxide Emissions, 2000 (territory size shows proportion of emissions that were directly from each country)

display very different patterns of land use and modes of transport circulation.

Moving Beyond Environmentalism – Degrees of Sustainability

In the 1990s the way that 'sustainability' was taken into national debates was often through improved environmental management rather than through the adoption of a broader sustainable development agenda. In New Zealand, for example, the longstanding Town and Country Planning Act regime was reformed in 1991 and replaced with a Resource Management Act aimed at achieving 'sustainable management of resources' (Memon and Gleeson, 1995; Memon and Perkins, 2000; Perkins and Thorns, 2002). The Act encouraged a greater degree of social and environmental impact assessment for planned new development but this relied heavily on a legal process of interpretation through the Environment Court. Such processes were an advance on previous practices but still failed to create a shift toward thinking about ways of achieving a sustainable steady state with respect to resource use and distribution.

In an assessment of this situation, the New Zealand Parliamentary Commissioner for the Environment (PCE, 2002) argued strongly that environmentalism, a movement against pollution, habitat degradation and loss of biodiversity, should not be confused with sustainable development, which is about redesigning the economy and society more generally. This approach would require integration of knowledge developed within the social *and* natural science and a much stronger focus on the integration of bio-physical environmental concerns with issues of social justice, income generation and poverty eradication (Perkins and Thorns, 1999; Satterthwaite, 1999, PCE, 2002).

Debates around the nature of sustainability have therefore led to the identification of different 'degrees' of sustainability ranging from a 'weak' version which is largely about taking on some of the rhetoric of sustainable development and focusing action mainly on the management of the biophysical environment and natural resources and a strong version which fully embraces a multidimensional and extensive elaboration of the idea. The weak and strong versions are illustrated in Figures 8.6 and 8.7. In Figure 8.6 sustainability is characterized as a political process which attempts to manage elements of society, economy and environment in ways which are efficient and effective in the present but which don't undermine opportunities for development in the future. In many respects this approach represents a modified version of 'business as usual' but also

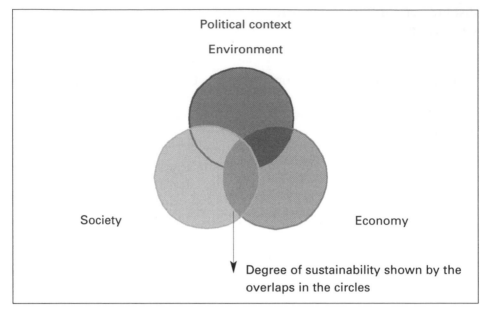

Figure 8.6   Weak Sustainability

incorporates attempts to integrate overlapping environmental, economic and social concerns in decision-making.

By contrast, Figure 8.7 represents a much more radical view of how things should be done, and accords more closely with the view expressed by the New Zealand Parliamentary Commissioner for the Environment. Again sustainability is characterized as a political process, but this time, one which demands that economic, cultural and social activity are integrated closely with concerns for biophysical environmental protection.

This approach would demand very significant changes to the economic activities and ways of life of many people in industrialized countries. As a result, internationally, there is resistance from politicians other than those from green parties to adopt a version of sustainability that challenges economic management models based on growth and the expansion of commodity production.

In 2002 a global forum was held in Johannesburg to review progress on the sustainable development agenda made since 1992. Many participants indicated that over this period the language of debate had changed but they were less certain that social, economic, political and environmental practices had improved. While the rhetoric of sustainable development had flourished, the same could not be said for effective action (Memon, 2003). In these terms, as Becker *et al.* (1991: 1) noted, the arena of sustainability is a 'contested, discursive field that allows for the articulation of political

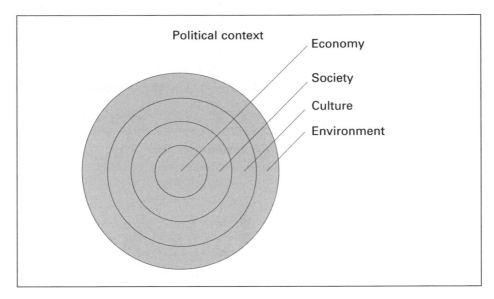

Figure 8.7 Strong Sustainability

and economic differences between North and South and introduces environmental issues and concerns with social justice and political participation' and is thus likely to be characterized by myriad responses and ongoing political debate. This was clearly demonstrated at the 2009 Copenhagen Climate Change Conference that failed to reach any binding outcomes to reduce significantly the levels of greenhouse gas emission into the atmosphere.

Prospects for the Future

Political debate surrounds the veracity of the science underlying the prescriptions for sustainability and environmental change. Some people argue that the science is flawed and that there is no need to take radical action. This position operates at two levels. Many laypeople are suspicious of scientific claims about the need to act and as the recent debates around climate change have shown, scientists themselves do not agree completely about the quality of the evidence (Stehr and von Storch, 2010). The majority view as expressed by the Intergovernmental Panel on Climate Change (IPCC) is that global temperatures are rising, due in part, at least, to human action emitting greenhouse gases into the earth's atmosphere. The Stern Report (2008: iv), for example, stated that 'the scientific evidence is now overwhelming: climate change is a serious global threat, and it demands an urgent response'. With no solution in sight the balance of scientific opinion is that the planet will heat up at a rate that will fundamentally change the climatic conditions of regions around the world affecting crop and food production and radically transforming the everyday lives of millions of people (IPCC, 2007). The climate change sceptics do not deny climate change but rather argue against human causation. Their view is that it is natural process, part of the normal cycle of global warming and cooling.

Stehr and von Storch (2010) attempt to interpret the current confusion by drawing a distinction between weather which is something we experience each day, and influences our attitudes to climate and its variation, and climate science which is based on data and modelling from 30 years of observation and scenario building based on the best estimates that are available from our current knowledge of global change. As weather is the immediate experience for laypeople, what has been occurring over the past few days tends to count more than the long-run averages and scenarios built through the work of the climate scientists. This difference assists in creating a gap in understanding between climate scientists and many members of the lay public.

Additionally, data from attitude and public opinion surveys suggest that support for action on a range of environmental issues has reached a plateau despite a general acknowledgment that problems are getting worse. This can result in a conservative politics. As we showed earlier with our Christchurch urban transport example, people do recognize environmental change but they feel that their everyday lives will carry on as at present; some changes will be needed but the problems encountered will be solved using technological solutions. In part this perspective has arisen because the environmental movement has changed, becoming more differentiated, and its many messages are therefore harder to incorporate into everyday concerns (Macnaghten, 2003). Seen in this way, it seems likely that most people will be only spurred into action when environmental issues impinge directly on their everyday experiences and expectations of nature through such activities as 'gardening, therapy, walking, fishing, climbing, boating and even motoring' (Macnaghten, 2003: 69). Jacobs further suggests that one reason why there has been a diminution in lay support for action is that current global environmental arguments fail to link to their experiences of transformative social and economic processes associated with 'globalization, information technologies, increasing individualism and rising inequalities' (1999: 14). Environmental prescriptions are perceived by many people as essentially normative, saying what the world should be like, rather than explaining how a desired future state can be achieved.

Thinking about Solutions

In the face of these challenges what are the solutions being examined? These now include everything from the 'do nothing' position through to a variety of interventions, some of which are technological and others which demand significantly different ways of living, encompassing social and economic changes. Increasingly, doing nothing is not a viable option as a 2010 UK report notes: 'Looking ahead just 20 years there could be substantial changes affecting the country and by 2060, the world is likely to be a very different place' (Foresight Land Project, 2010: 6). The report identifies six factors of importance: population change, economic growth and changing global conditions, climate change, new technologies, societal preferences and attitudes, and the policy and regulatory environment. We think a seventh factor is also important, political will, because change will be affected by the degree to which politicians are willing to make unpopular decisions about modifying current practices. The report suggests that even with change there will still be a high degree of likelihood that significant relocation of population and economic activities will need to take place both to accommodate the projected growth of population and to counter the changes likely from climate change which would render lower-lying parts of the UK uninhabitable.

Technological Solutions

Technological solutions to provide a sustainable future might include currently emergent forms of electricity production not based on fossil fuels such as wind and wave power. Older technologies could be more widely distributed such as hydro, nuclear and geothermal power generation. Other technologies being advanced include the greater use of bio-fuels and purified coal and in the area of road transport, dual-fuel and electric cars. Solar energy technologies are also attracting interest. Given the climate change scenarios currently in place, technological solutions are also being advanced which will reflect the sun's rays away from the earth and reduce heat absorption. These together with the use of various carbon sinks and other techniques to sequester and contain emissions will help to limit global warming. Many of these technologies are still experimental and their precise effects are difficult to assess. The two which have the greatest support are nuclear and solar power, but although new generation nuclear energy generation is claimed to be safe, the technology comes with risks, not least of which are those surrounding residual waste and its disposal and the possibility of accidental leakages of radioactive material as occurred in Japan in 2011 after a large earthquake and Tsunami (Giddens, 2009).

The application of some of these technologies can be at the household level or in larger commercial systems, although there are also many commercial opportunities for making houses more energy efficient. At the household level, insulation, multiple glazing of windows, monitoring use of power through smart meters, solar panels and domestic wind generation are part of the solution advocated to shift away from dependency on unsustainable and resource limited forms of power generation. New designs which are environmentally friendly and conserve energy are now finding more government support; although retrofitting existing houses and other buildings is costly. Larger activities such as wind farming and finding new ways to power motor cars will depend on commercial responses to technological development. These kinds of technologies appeal to the public, politicians, industrialists, unions and investors because they are interpreted as allowing current practices to be largely maintained. This is particularly the case with technologies which allow the reliance on the private car to continue, and contrast with other technologies which will demand more stringent conservation activities and lifestyle changes (Rahmstorf, 2010).

A further aspect of technological change relates to the ways that many people now live with the aid of computers, cellphones and related electronic information and communication devices. This provides the possibility of living away from congested cities while maintaining social and economic connectivity (Perkins and Thorns, 2006). The new vision is of working, shopping and playing using the new super highway of fibre optic and satellite links that provides an alternative to the congested, inefficient, slow and rigid physical urban world of clogged roads. In contrast, the new world of cyberspace is interpreted as being more flexible and open and where we can communicate at the touch of a button from wherever we are located. This vision is not without its problems, however. Researchers have found that although improved virtual working and connecting exists many people prefer to work and find their leisure in the real relationships that require physical presence (Graham, 2004). In part this is because communication is about more than speech and text. The subtleties of gesture and body language which are very important for everyday social life are still not easily transmitted and received through a computer monitor or cellphone. A combination of the virtual and the real is necessary for building trust and establishing lasting relationships (Allan and Thorns, 2009).

Social Solutions Including Market Solutions

This suggests that *only* implementing technological solutions is unlikely to create the progress hoped for. Significant changes to social practices and ways of living and working are also required. Good examples of local schemes to change everyday behaviour are those developed around recycling and reusing material rather than filling landfill sites. These are now widely adopted and include such activities as kerb-side collection with bins for organic compostable material, recyclable paper, plastics and glass and for materials that still have to go to landfills. Waste disposal is also now a major international industry with global players assuming greater shares of the market for this activity. A much more extreme example of behaviour change is the banning of private cars from some areas of cities at specified times, such as those of peak traffic demand. Park-and-ride schemes and car pooling have grown in popularity often associated with higher charges for parking private cars in central city areas.

The use of charges and incentives to encourage new ways of thinking and interacting brings us immediately to debates about the usefulness of market mechanisms such as road user and congestion charges that are designed to discourage people from taking their private cars into congested areas. One of the most significant recent examples emerged from the Kyoto protocol, an international agreement linked to the United Nations Framework Convention on Climate Change. The major feature of the Kyoto protocol is that it set binding targets for 37 industrialized countries and the European Union, who initially signed up, for reducing greenhouse gas emissions. These planned reductions amount to an average of five per cent against 1990 levels over the four-year period 2008–2012. The protocol was eventually ratified by 184 countries and came into force in 2005. However, this did not include the United States which was and continues to be the country that emits the largest amount of carbon per head of the population. One of the mechanisms favoured in the Kyoto protocol to assist in changing the behaviour needed to reduce carbon emission levels is a carbon-trading market. The idea behind this is that industrial emitters who create an excess of carbon over their limits have to find a partner in the market whom they pay to sequester that level of carbon. These are people or companies who, for example, grow trees. The theory is that this financial 'tax' will encourage the emitters to reduce their emissions to save expenditure and improve profitability. In line with this approach, a number of countries have introduced emissions-trading schemes, including the multination scheme in the European Union and the arrangements introduced in New Zealand in 2010. Other countries have been slower to act because market mechanisms such as these are complex, add to production costs and are perceived to be unfair, because high emitters who are not headquartered in countries with a carbon-trading scheme or equivalent carbon emissions taxation regime have lower costs and therefore greater market advantage than those who have to pay for their emissions.

Another example of a similar carbon-related market mechanism at work involves UK and New Zealand partners. In Christchurch, New Zealand, the city council is capturing methane gas, one of the most damaging greenhouse gases, from a closed landfill and using it to provide energy to heat and power Queen Elizabeth II Park, a major sports and swimming-pool complex. The scheme will save the equivalent of 200,000 tonnes of carbon dioxide from being released into the atmosphere over the first five years of its operation. In that time the scheme will generate approximately 200,000 Kyoto carbon credits. These are being on-sold to British Gas, an emitter of carbon, to help meet its commitments under the European Trading Scheme. This will earn the city council $NZ3 million covering a substantial part of the $NZ4.2 million capital cost of this project. In addition, the scheme will save the council $NZ900,000 for the 1.5 million litres of liquid petroleum gas it would otherwise have had to purchase to power the complex. The landfill can produce methane for more than 20 years and the quantity being harvested will not only supply the sports complex but has sufficient potential to provide power for other civic buildings. The New Zealand prime minister, when opening the scheme in 2007, described it as innovative and a 'triple-win' as it reduced greenhouse gas emissions, saved money and generated cash from the sale of carbon credits (Clarke, 2007).

Planning and Design Solutions

Other attempts to change ways of living are associated with urban planning and design. In line with the urban sustainability agenda, planners have advocated building more compact cities designed to reduce the inefficiencies of sprawl and create more social interaction (Vallance *et al.*, 2009). This has mainly involved the construction of medium and high-density housing (Crookston *et al.*, 1996; Dupuis and Dickson, 2002; Vallance *et al.*, 2005). This new housing has produced a dramatic negative reaction from many urban residents, particularly in countries which have a long history of low-rise urban form (Perkins, 1988a; Troy, 1996; Lewis, 1999; Vallance *et al.*, 2005).

One of the challenges facing those who want to build sustainable housing, whether it be built in high- or low-density settlements, is that it is hard to do so without incurring more costs, thus undermining another desirable criterion of sustainable development: affordability. Housing affordability is normally measured as a proportion of income required to buy or rent. These costs will be higher if houses are built, for example, using increased insulation, double or triple glazing and include the use of grey-water and solar energy systems. Land prices are also an issue in this regard and while spreading into greenfield or brownfield sites may reduce the land cost proportion of sustainable housing other costs will be incurred associated with infrastructure such as roads, schools, drainage and water supply and transport, thus violating other sustainability criteria. Additionally, while new integrated developments combining home, work and recreation to ensure high-quality environments can be built, there is the possibility they will not suit today's highly mobile households (Urry, 2000). This high mobility reflects the increased level of individualism that is now prevalent in late modernity (Bauman, 1998).

Ethical Challenges and Adaptive Strategies

As highlighted in discussions of housing affordability, the question of ethical practice is never far from the surface in discussions about solutions to current environmental predicaments. This is nowhere better exemplified than in the climate change debate. It is important to understand that climate change is not just an area of natural scientific enquiry but also crucially an arena for the social sciences and humanities as it raises ethical and political issues. For some it is all about politics because of the classic difficulty of apportioning the cost of collective action and trusting all parties to take their share of responsibility (Sané, 2009). Sané argues further that it is necessary to rediscover the ethical foundations of our decision-making if we are to find a solution to this problem. An ethical approach it is suggested would 'provide a perspective from which questions of responsibility, equity, knowledge sharing and global dissemination of ethical practices can be assessed' (2009: 6).

Such an approach will be crucial in attempts to deal with climate change. Pressure is now growing for governments to consider adaptive and preventive strategies. Regions and communities will have to change their ways of living with Stehr and von Storch (2010) arguing that proactive strategies are better than reactive tactics which means shifting the attention to planning for the future of cities and regions. Adaptive strategies can include technological solutions and economic and social changes, and the possible relocation of populations from areas that are likely to be affected by changes in sea level. In considering such policies, detailed knowledge of local conditions as well as global trends is required so that both the benefits, where they exist, and costs, are understood. The Stern Report (2006) also advocates action now and argues this would allow the world to offset the worst effects of climate change. It suggests that one per cent of GDP should be invested currently and that this would avoid having to invest upwards of 20 per cent of GDP later. Stern (2006: ii) suggests that waiting could risk 'major disruptions to economic and social activity ... on a scale similar to those associated with the great wars and economic depression of the twentieth century' (Stern, 2006: ii).

Conclusion

In this chapter we have addressed questions associated with economic growth, global environmental change and sustainability. Creating a sustainable future has become a major issue, demanding local and global attention, and presents a huge challenge to those responsible for policy and planning, in all sectors. It is becoming increasingly clear that the route to success will require politicians and planners to connect with the 'planned for' in ways that have in the past often not been pursued. Dear (2000: 117) notes in his discussion of planning in Los Angeles that:

> at one point ... the principles of 'new urbanism' were being applied to the downtown industrial eastside (of Los Angeles) – an unimaginable mix of skid row, clothing, electrical, wholesale food markets, and toy importers. After a morning of plonking down schools, open spaces, and other undoubtedly desirable icons of civic amenity in totally infeasible locations, I suggested that we could actually leave the office in order to go and look at the sites in question. This crudely utilitarian advice was immediately rejected because the intrusion of urban actualities would, so my colleagues said, hinder the visionary process.

To some extent this is because the planners had started with a 'vision of the future' rather than the reality of everyday living in the diverse environments and circumstances that make up contemporary human settlements. In Chapter 9 we examine some of these environments in a discussion of sustainable housing, communities and neighbourhoods.

Further reading

Catton, W. R. Jr. and Riley E. Dunlap. 1978. 'Environmental Sociology: A New Paradigm'. *American Sociologist* 13(1), 41–49.

Ehrlich, P. R. and A. H. Ehrlich. 1970. *Population, Resources, Environment.* San Francisco, CA: W. H. Freeman.

Giddens, A. 2009. *The Politics of Climate Change.* Cambridge: Polity.

Meadows, D. H., D. L. Meadows, J. Randers and W.W. Behrens. 1972. *The Limits to Growth.* New York, NY: Universe Books.

Satterthwaite, D. 1999. *The Earthscan Reader in Sustainable Cities.* London: Earthscan.

Stehr, N. H. and H. von Storch. 2010. *Climate and Society*. New Jersey, NJ: World Scientific.

Urry, J. 2010. 'Sociology Facing Climate Change'. *Sociological Research Online* 15(3), 1–3.

Websites

http://articles.moneycentral.msn.com/Investing/Extra/IndiaReadiesWorlds CheapestCar.aspx; accessed 13/09/2010

http://en.wikipedia.org/wiki/Automobile; accessed 09/09/2010

www.npr.org/templates/story/story.php?storyId=17984516; accessed 13/09/2010

www.worldmapper.org/index.html; accessed 07/09/2010

CHAPTER 9

Sustainable Housing, Communities and Neighbourhoods

Introduction

This chapter extends the discussion in Chapter 8 and shows, using as examples sustainable housing and recent developments in the management of human settlements, how concerns about sustainable futures are worked out in people's everyday lives. The chapter highlights the challenges being faced in this regard as plans to create sustainable practices run up against complementary and counter-trends such as economic globalization and the rise of neo-liberalism, the effects of the global financial crisis and the rise of new ideas about spatial planning. In shifting to this level it is clear that a complex set of relationships and settings is being dealt with. In Chapter 5 the centrality of the house–home relationship in interpretations of everyday life and for the creation of individual and collective identity was argued for. We will further elaborate these connections and relationships by examining how house and home are being reconstituted through a combination of global and local processes and how communities and neighbourhoods are being recreated socially and physically paying attention to the ways global and local influences intersect. This returns us to our theme of exploring this complex set of interactions and interconnections which operate at many levels, influencing housing markets, the design and building of sustainable housing and the creation of new settlements.

Sustainable Development and Neo-liberalism

We think that it is useful at this stage to revisit some of the central ideas associated with the rise of the sustainable development agenda in the late twentieth century and the emergence of various forms of neo-liberalism in many developed countries. This political philosophy encouraged individualism, market-based solutions to economic and social development and therefore less direct government intervention in economic allocation decisions. So at the time when an increasingly globalized approach to planning and finding solutions to a variety of social, economic and environmental problems was emerging the political will to engage in planning was weakened by the rise of a philosophy that supported the view that government should not intervene in citizens' lives and that market and individual decision-making should prevail. Governments thus retreated from much national, regional and local planning, leaving it to the private sector. This approach reinforced the characterization of citizens as consumers and rational actors making choices informed by the best possible information. The consequence was a diminution of national and regional government strategies to manage urban and regional development. Those charged with implementation of various elements of the sustainability agenda were therefore put in the contradictory position of advocating for public intervention in planning without having the tools and resources necessary to effectively turn advocacy into action. One commentator noted that:

> A substantial impediment [to a broad policy on sustainability] that has existed for much of the past decade [the 1990s] has been an ideological commitment to let market solutions and non intervention by government resolve a wide range of environmental decisions on a case by case basis. (PCE, 2002: 16)

A slight modification to this neo-liberal approach occurred in the early twenty-first century when a significant number of governments began to rethink aspects of their market-led approach as a consequence of the market failures created by the global financial crisis that started at the end of 2007 with the collapse of the subprime housing market in the USA. Trying to stave off and then recover from the recession that then took place many governments intervened to stabilize their economies by borrowing funds to shore up failing financial institutions, thus accruing large debts. For a time there was considerable discussion about the need for a new economic order to ensure greater stability and prevent such failures in the future. However by 2010 a reversion to austerity measures took place to overcome the 'debt crisis' that was hindering recovery. A series of governments adopted the prescription of cutting expenditure, encouraging savings, paying off debt and adopting market-led 'growth strategies'. The bailout of EU members, for example Greece and Ireland, required the adoption of austerity measures as a condition of receiving financial assistance. In both cases these have created significant local resistance with strikes and social unrest and political conflict. In France a series of anti-austerity strikes against raising the age of entitlement for pensions across a range of government jobs disrupted the transport and energy sectors.

Tension continues to exist between the goals of the sustainability agenda and that of the economic recovery which is still predominantly guided by a neo-liberal agenda. On the one hand, the focus of activity within conservation and sustainability projects, often spurred on by dire predictions about climate change, peak oil and continuing underdevelopment in many countries has been maintained strongest at the local community level. Here the impetus for ongoing action around sustainable development has come from some local governments and non-governmental organizations (NGOs). Such groups have been active in projects to create transition towns, green the city by introducing more open spaces, develop alternative transport systems and encourage walking and cycling, initiate recycling schemes, and organize community produce gardens.

On the other hand, central and most local governments have mainly emphasized reviving economic growth and developing business-friendly policies ahead of concerns for sustainable development. Resurgent markets have been seen as essential. This has reinforced a now well-developed trend for cities to compete with each other for economic opportunities and spectacular and high-status events such as the Olympic Games and other major sporting and cultural events (Friedmann, 2006). Under these circumstances city politicians and managers, and allied business elites, have viewed cities primarily as 'containers of investment' which has led to a focus on place promotion and city branding rather than developing the city's 'human, cultural, intellectual, and environmental assets' (Friedmann, 2006: 4–6).

This chapter now turns to consider how these competing trends have worked themselves out in housing and the development of human settlements and especially as they have affected the everyday lives of the people involved.

Impact of Marketization in Housing

As we discussed in Chapter 5, it is undisturbed and largely taken-for-granted day-to-day occupation of housing that creates the sense of security required to make a house a home, whatever the form of tenure in which it is held. In some countries many people from across the social spectrum rent their housing. This is certainly the case for people on moderate to low incomes who often live in private rental or government-provided social housing. In other countries, however, owner-occupation predominates. While it is possible that renting housing can provide secure tenure there is a widespread view that a sense of security is reinforced by owner-occupation of housing. It was this view that underpinned policies designed to encourage the rise of homeownership in a number of countries, for example the US, Canada, the UK, Australia, New Zealand and Japan, in the middle years of the twentieth century. Home ownership was seen as part of a nation and community-building project, a way of generating a connected and engaged citizenry, and as a bulwark against extremism on the political left and right. It was thought by politicians and other community leaders that home ownership linked people to place and thus encouraged local communities to form. Schemes were developed that initially increased the number of middle-income homeowners and then later these were extended to include lower-income groups, usually through government grants, tax concessions and savings schemes. Such schemes encouraged the process of housing marketization which had up until that time been the purview of wealthy people and organizations. In this process housing increased its role as a market commodity and became one of the key ways to hold wealth. But despite this, houses still remained primarily shelter; places to live and develop a sense of belonging and attachment to community (Forrest and Murie, 1995; Forrest and Yip, 2011).

In the industrialized countries of the West, the focus on home ownership as a community-building project was replaced in the 1980s with a neo-liberal programme of housing marketization which included the transfer of social/public housing from rental to home ownership (Forrest and Murie 1988). It was not thought appropriate that governments should be landlords. This role was to be reserved for individuals and companies in the private sector. Houses came to be seen as *primarily* marketable commodities, held for profit rather than as a social asset.

In other settings, such as in Eastern Europe, housing markets re-emerged after the collapse of socialism in 1989, and became an increasingly important part of the economy. Prior to 1939, high levels of home ownership had existed in these countries, but was associated with rural real estate ownership and were mostly transferred as part of family inheritance rather than through market operation. Under socialist governments the period from 1945 to the late 1980s was dominated by the building of public rental housing which has now, in many cases, been sold creating a different pattern of ownership and leading to the emergence of the same market cycles of growth and decline prevalent in Western market societies (Hegedus, 2011). These cycles favour people who can afford to enter the market and particularly those who have sufficiently high incomes to allow them to lower their debt (Marja and Roland, 2011; Forrest and Yip, 2011).

A good example of this marketization process took place in the UK, encouraged by the Thatcher government. State-owned housing stock was sold to tenants in residence so that they could enjoy the benefits of home ownership. This was designed to create a property-owning democracy (Murie and Forrest, 1988). The pronounced booms and busts in the housing market through the 1980s, 1990s and 2000s, and the consequent creation of wealth and its transfer within and across generations, meant that housing became valued more for its wealth accumulation capacities than its role as shelter and home (Hamnett, 1999; Hamnett *et al.*, 1991). Nigel Lawson, the UK chancellor of the exchequer, in 1987, referred to home ownership as creating a new 'inheritance economy' and had a vision of this wealth 'cascading down the generations' (Forrest, 2011). This proved to be an over-optimistic view, not taking cognizance of the changing patterns of household formation and dissolution, the increased longevity of the population and costs of retirement, and fluctuations in the housing market. The view that wealth would be created, was however reiterated and reinforced by other politicians, financial advisers and real estate investors, developers and sales consultants, and served to consolidate the idea that housing was a marketable asset and a 'safe bet' when it came to accumulating wealth. Transfers did occur within and between generations but they did little to reduce either intra or intergenerational inequality as some analysts expected (Badcock and Beer, 2000; Hamnett, 1999).

The wealth-generating aspects of housing were influenced considerably by the crisis in the global financial system which began in 2007 and arose out of the collapse of housing markets. The ensuing crisis involved a combination of housing overproduction driven by a boom in housing prices, liberal lending policies by banks and financial institutions, and by the refinancing and extraction of money from housing for consumption by homeowners. The boom in prices was fuelled by investors making very significant profits from speculating on future house price rises which encouraged more speculation and thus leveraged up the price of housing still further, to unrealistic levels. Many homeowners used the equity in their houses created by rising 'value' on a surging market to refinance their mortgages and spent the proceeds on consumer commodities rather than saving the added value of the property (Stone, 2009; Case, 2009; Stiglitz, 2009; Forrest and Yip, 2011; Duncan and Constantino, 2011). This increased their risks of being exposed to financial loss. The refinancing was encouraged by mortgage brokers, many of them newly appointed, and largely unregulated, who received their income and bonuses from signing people up to new loans. Homeowners were encouraged to refinance and spend the proceeds by the use of targeted lifestyle advertising. Once the crisis occurred, housing prices declined rapidly, quickly eroding many of the notional capital gains made during the boom years and left people in negative equity and facing the possibility of losing their homes through mortgagee sales as lending institutions sought to recover their money.

In the US, this process had a considerable impact on the everyday lives of US citizens, and also their relationships with a range of institutions. As indicated in Figure 9.1, the year 2003 saw the rate of refinancing in the United States decline. Brokers therefore attempted to draw in new participants to encourage the housing boom to continue. These were people who earned low or relatively low incomes, known collectively and technically as the subprime market, and who had little prospect of reducing their debt principal because they paid interest only on their loans, hoping to increase equity via capital growth. These borrowers were issued with 'low document or even no document' loans. The effect of this new lending activity dramatically increased the demand for housing and therefore also house prices. Four states led the way with California (incorporating 25 per cent

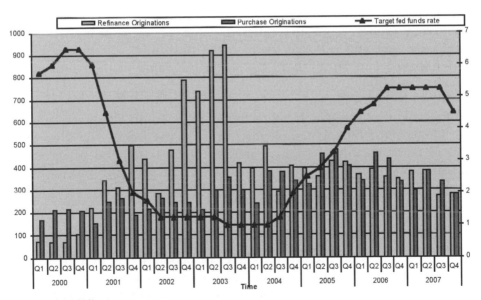

Source: Case (2009)

Updated estimates provided by Jim Kennedy of the mortgage system presented in 'Estimates of Home Mortgages Originations, Repayments, and Debt On One-to-Four-Family Residences,' Alan Greenspan and James Kennedy, Federal Reserve Board FEDS working paper no. 2005-41.

Figure 9.1 Refinancing and New Loans 2000–2007 in the USA

of the total US market), Florida, Nevada and Arizona sustaining increases of around 54 per cent in the lowest house price band (Case, 2009). The lending institutions assumed risk to be low as prices were expected to keep rising – 'the boom was not ending any time soon' – and this optimism prevailed until the collapse in 2007. In this process, many loans became 'toxic' and the subprime market dissolved leaving financial institutions, investors and homeowners with considerable debt. Very significant damage was also done to the credibility of banks and other finance institutions. Additionally, the liberality of bank lending had weakened the ties between lenders and borrowers as local sources of finance were replaced increasingly by national and global ones. This helped to lessen any sense of commitment or responsibility bankers may have held toward members of local populations. The erosion of public trust in financial institutions was boosted still further when the large size of banks' profits and bankers' salaries were revealed as the crisis took effect and major financial institutions of longstanding collapsed.

Other countries had similar experiences. In the UK, for example, the expansion of credit and inexpensive refinancing of mortgages allowed housing wealth to be used like an ATM machine! (Williams, 2011). Young people in particular drew out money for a variety of consumption-related activities. In Australia a similar pattern of withdrawal occurred with around 43 per cent of households between 2001 and 2005 extracting money from the inflated value of their properties. This increased debt and exposed them to the possibility of negative equity and financial and family hardship when the value of their houses fell (Berry *et al.*, 2009).

The collapse of housing markets and the ensuing financial crisis set off a global reaction which led to the worst economic depression since the 1920s and 1930s. Unemployment rose in the US to over 9 per cent and in some hard-hit regions, particularly those dependent upon car production, more than double that level. In the European Union, unemployment rose to an average rate of 9 per cent. Financial institutions in the US and Europe were bailed out by governments which hastily developed depositor guarantees to save a run on the banking system and to restore liquidity. Many investors lost money. The combined effects on the everyday lives of people living in a great variety of urban and rural localities included increases in housing stress and the unaffordability of shelter. Despite this experience, there remains a strong belief that property ownership and speculation are still good ways to increase wealth. The very recent revival in the housing market of many countries has encouraged these beliefs (Thorns, 2011b; Duncan and Constantino, 2011).

Market Models and Sustainable Housing

In general terms, then, an overemphasis on the economic value of housing devalues its other social, psychological and environmental attributes. This poses a considerable threat to the achievement of a more sustainable living environment. Relatively rapid turnover of ownership in pursuit of profit means residents are often not strongly connected to neighbourhoods and this affects the strength of local social relationships. Using houses to create capital gain and generate wealth through constant upward mobility over a lifetime also limits commitment to long-term housing maintenance in favour of short-term 'makeovers', often conducted prior to sale (Winstanley *et al.*, 2002). These titivation exercises and associated real estate sales advice are encouraged in highly rated television programmes of the *Changing Rooms, The Block* and *Location, Location, Location* variety (Perkins *et al.*, 2008a). Such approaches are at odds with the requirement for more sustainable houses that are durable and fit for long-term occupancy.

Sustainable Housing: 1

Sustainable housing derives its impetus from two separate traditions. The first of these is concerned with the notion of the green or natural house. These houses are considered to be healthy because they minimize the use of products which damage the environment while being manufactured. Advocates of this position also like indigenous designs and using traditional materials which 'fit' with the local environment. They also focus on energy efficiency: increasing insulation, reducing the need for additional heating or cooling and make greater use of solar energy. The use of natural ventilation in housing design is not new, having been used for many centuries. What is new is the now almost mandatory incorporation into contemporary designs of building techniques which reduce or prevent the need for air conditioning in winter and summer. Prior to these developments, air conditioning was seen by many as the only solution for creating a liveable internal space and owed its origin and popularity to the great impact it had on the comfort of housing in very hot and cold regions. Mindful of the profits to be made the industry that emerged around its manufacture, distribution, installation and energy supply understandably worked hard to promote its use (Shove, 2010). In addition, proponents of sustainable housing also use design techniques to limit the environmental impacts of housing (such as grey-water storage and recycling) and building to ensure a long house life (Mobbs, 1998).

Some of these techniques have the benefit of lowering building costs, but this is not always the case and sometimes attempts to be 'environmentally friendly' go awry. In places such as New Zealand, California and British Columbia, for example, which are earthquake prone, much housing is built using timber frames because these can stand a good deal of tectonic movement. For many years in New Zealand framing timber was chemically treated to prevent insect and fungal attack but a decision was made to discontinue this practice as a way of lowering costs, speeding up the building process and preventing the leaching of treatment chemicals into the environment (Hunn et al., 2002). This practice was predicated on the notion that wooden frames would remain dry, sealed from the elements by effective roofing and cladding and surrounded by moving air as walls 'breathed'. In the 1990s 'Mediterranean' building styles became popular which proved far from resistant to wind-driven rain and a major problem developed around rotting frames. Known as the 'leaky homes syndrome', and mirrored in California and Vancouver by the 'leaky condo problem', this had very serious negative impacts on the well-being of occupants (Dupuis and Thorns, 2008).

Estimates of the number of leaky dwellings in New Zealand have varied from 8,000 to 30,000 and the cost of repairs was estimated in 2005 to be $NZ1 billion (Rehm, 2008). More recently, figures disclosed in a confidential report to the government put the full cost at $NZ11.5 billion (Laxon, 2009) and the number of affected dwellings could rise to as many as 50,000 (Rudman, 2009). While these figures are bad enough, much more difficult to estimate are the costs of emotional stress and ill health experienced by homeowners whose houses collapsed from within. The leaky building problem was recognized by Justice Arnold of the New Zealand Court of Appeal when in a recent legal judgement he wrote that: 'The leaky-home problem is the result of what can fairly be described as systemic failure, occurring at all levels within the building industry, in both the public and private sectors'.

Many commentators agree, viewing this as a systemic *technological* failure within the building industry, but others argue that it represents a wider failure of neo-liberalism and represents a lack of trust between people and organizations. They point to a story which compounded a longstanding house building culture based around speculation and short-term thinking. Housing construction regulators were unable to stand in the way of a consumer preference for a stylish Mediterranean aesthetic and could not insist that only weathertight buildings be constructed. This situation also resulted in difficulties in fixing the problems and in determining accountability (Dupuis and Thorns, 2009).

Sustainability advocates also argue that environmentally friendly houses are a good long-term investment as they minimize energy costs;

but, interestingly, the *private* market and *public* providers have shown little interest in such housing, in part because both sectors are driven by the marginal cost of construction and the question of affordability. Despite this, governments in a number of countries have shown signs of wanting to encourage the building of sustainable housing by offering subsidies for such things as insulation because it is considered to assist in reducing energy use and in improving liveability and health outcomes. For example in Australia the 2007 financial crisis economic stimulation package contained measures that provided grants to homeowners and landlords for improving home insulation. This policy served to stimulate the depressed building trades which struggled with a decline in housing starts and a consequent reduction in new housing construction.

Sustainable Housing: 2

The second sustainable housing tradition emphasizes social well-being because people who live in affordable housing which is in good condition typically have better physical and mental health than those who do not (Howden-Chapman *et al.*, 2009). One aspect of the mass housing programmes of the 1950s and 1960s, as in earlier times, was directed at dealing with such issues, and also homelessness. These programmes increased the supply of public rental housing or provided state subsidies to facilitate owner-occupation. But living in suburban mass rental housing and speculatively built suburban owner-occupied housing often had the effect of divorcing people from their former inner-city communities and day-to-day participation in long-established neighbourhood life of which self-help housebuilding and maintenance were part. International debate has thus shifted attention back to emphasizing the benefits of involving householders in these aspects of their housing. As Daly (1996) has noted 'self-help housing represents far more than shelter; it is an attempt to reclaim the commons and develop a sense of community, a sense of place, a place called home'.

This second approach to sustainable housing draws on a complex interpretation of the relationship between physical spaces and everyday living. It begins with social and cultural understandings that draw attention to human needs as well as market ambitions and rests on the idea of 'ontological security' and its importance to people who are experiencing increasing uncertainty, greater perceived risks to their personal safety and security, and a decline of trust in public institutions which in past times could have been relied upon to provide support to individuals and households. Ontological security was originally conceptualized by Laing (1969), and in his psychological and therapeutic terms, refers to an individual's sense of safety and well-being, a feeling of reassurance in an uncertain world. Giddens (1990) applied a sociological lens to the concept adding that it refers to an individual's sense of certainty and continuity with regard to his/her social and material worlds. Dupuis and Thorns (1998) used the idea to interpret home ownership and the strong sentimental feelings with which it is associated. For many people, owning a house confers a sense of place and security. In property-owning countries this sense of security is invariably linked with ownership of land and a house and reflects a sentiment that one's home is one's castle. We note, however, as per the discussion in Chapter 5, that some feminist research has challenged the assumption that homeowning is necessarily linked to security and safety. These writers point out that house and home, whether or not owner-occupied can be a place of abuse and violence, and where freedom is severely limited (Oakley, 1976; Gavron, 1983; Winstanley, 2001).

Writers from the perspectives of ontological security and feminism therefore both suggest that people often engage with housing at an emotional level. This is particularly noticeable when they are looking to purchase or rent a house. Research into real estate agency and sales methods documents the way people enter a house, surrounding property and neighbourhood and express the view that it feels right, has good feng shui, is auspicious in some way, or alternatively, just isn't them. People buy or rent houses using such emotional criteria, but supplemented by functional and price considerations (Perkins *et al.*, 2008a). This focus on the connections between houses and social and psychological fulfilment relates to conceptualizations of human needs. The most famous of these is Maslow's (1943) hierarchy of needs. At the first, basic, level these needs are physiological such as those associated with breathing, food, water, reproductive sex, sleep, homeostasis and excretion which lie at the core of everyday living as without which human life would not be possible. At the second level, Maslow identified needs associated with safety: security of the body, employment, resources such as an income or other capacities to exchange goods, morality, the family, health and property. It is at this level that housing as 'shelter' is seen to meet the need to have a secure place where we can eat and sleep, keep ourselves warm and attend to our bodily functions. The third level of needs is associated with love and belonging and thus relate to friendship, family and sexual intimacy. This is the level of relationship building and where the idea of creating home is relevant, as satisfying these needs is often achieved in this way. Once these needs are met then the fourth level of Maslow's hierarchy, associated with esteem, come into play. These are associated with self-esteem, confidence, achievement, respect of others, respect by others. Finally, in this schema,

self-actualization becomes possible drawing our attention to needs associated with morality, creativity, spontaneity, problem solving, lack of prej-
udice and acceptance of facts. It is clear from this hierarchy of needs that
house and home are one of the key constituents of everyday existence
because they provide the context for, and are created in, the meeting of
our needs. At the higher levels these are linked to the creation social capital built around trusting relationships which also contribute to the meeting of individual and collective needs (Putnam 2000).

A focus on needs and satisfying them raises issues about housing rights
and provision. Globally, the right to shelter has been taken up by UN
Habitat (UN Second Conference on Human Settlements, 1996) and
included in various declarations as a basic human right that national
governments should meet for their citizens. This poses questions about
what constitutes homelessness or rooflessness (Daly, 1996). In many
jurisdictions public policy centres on those who have been made homeless 'involuntarily' thus making a distinction between people who have
brought this condition on themselves, and who are therefore not considered as deserving of public support, and those who can be supported
because they have been made homeless through no fault of their own.
Such distinctions in practice are hard to administer and can be manipu-
lated by local and national authorities to limit their liability. Becoming
homeless can be triggered by many factors including eviction, unemployment, relationship breakdown, psychiatric illness, alcoholism and drug
dependency (Culhane and Fried, 2000; Somerville, 1992; Daly, 1995).
For many people, homelessness results from multiple events that create a
downward spiral in their lives. Stopping this decline can be very difficult
because without a place to live homeless people become 'non-persons'
unable to access the rights and benefits of citizenship including participation in the wider community and the capacity to seek paid employment.

So sustainable housing requires the integration of the physiological,
social, psychological, economic and environmental attributes of 'residence'. It rests on the experience of having a place to live and belong and
where identity can be created and maintained. Its critical attribute is that
it has sufficient permanency to allow everyday living to flourish
(Friedmann, 2006). Putting house and home at the centre of settlement
planning and development allows its significance to be clearly seen. It is
from this base that people can move into building wider relationships
within the neighbourhood, city and wider world, the elements of which
are outlined in Figure 9.2.

Keeping with our focus in this chapter, we now turn to a brief discussion of community and neighbourhood, important contexts for the working out of everyday life and the making of sustainable settlements.

Community

The wider context in which the house and home is set has been seen either in terms of community or neighbourhood. Both have connections with the idea of a spatially delimited area. However this is stronger in the idea of neighbourhood than community which derives from their intellectual histories. Ideas about community derive from sources that are more anthropological and sociological and traditions that emphasize 'ideal' ways of living together often shaped by utopian ideologies whereas the idea of the neighbourhood is grounded in planning and design disciplines and relates to how new housing and living spaces could be 'improved' by design. This section first considers the idea of community and then turns to neighbourhood in the context of looking at some new ideas around settlement design.

Community is generally associated with ideas of belonging to a group which may or may not be spatially fixed. One of the early sociological writers Tönnies (1956) identified community in terms of intimate social relationships built around reciprocity and underpinned by kinship ties. Another writer, Schamalenbach (1961), extended this idea by drawing of the notion of 'communion' seen as the affective ties and emotional bonds bringing people together to forge a sense of belonging. This we can see in

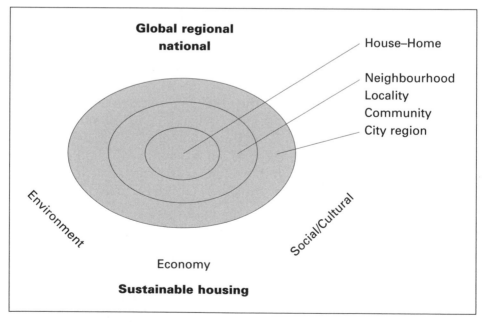

Figure 9.2   Building Relationships from House–Home to the Globe

the outpourings of emotion around such events as local sporting contests which encourage a sense of in-group solidarity set against those from outside, 'others', which enforces a sense of place and identity. This is reflected in the way that 'entering' many communities is not easy for 'strangers' because they are treated with suspicion until they become 'locals' – this can take many years to accomplish depending on the local situation. In many such communities there is a shared history that has been established around place-based family and friendship interaction and the ties associated with it can be maintained even when people move away, as long as there are still local members of the family remaining and with whom connections can be maintained. Increasing mobility is interpreted by some writers as threatening these expressions of community. They see community as something we have lost; and others see it as something that needs to be retrieved through the rediscovery of our roots in stories and our relationships to the land (Ashton and Thorns 2007; Lash 2002).

One of the tools promoted for the retrieval of community is paradoxically one of the things that some see as a threat to its continuance, namely the rise of the virtual technologies. The Internet, cellphone and social websites are, for some writers, potential destroyers of institutions such as the family and the local community because as relationships can now span the globe they can so easily become ephemeral and transitory. One such critic suggests that 'under the illusion of allowing us to communicate better, it actually isolates us from real human interaction, a cyber-reality that is a poor imitation of the real world' (Turkle, quoted in Harris, 2011).

Seen differently, these tools can help maintain relationships and re-establish connections and so counteract the strains imposed on relationship by physical mobility. Thus in contrast to Turkle's view, other researchers have claimed that the 'web is not killing family: if anything it is saving it' (Krottoski, 2011). Their argument is that in our mobile world, where people are constantly on the move, many families and friendship networks are very dispersed; they no longer exist in the same village, town or city or even country, so without the web, e-mail, cellphones and related communication systems such as Skype families and friends would be less connected as they move to pursue work, relationships and meet the opportunities and challenges of living in a more global age. Interpretations of community and sustainable housing should therefore recognize the dynamic of people moving iteratively between local place-based settings and those in the wider region, city or nation and to the globe (as displayed in Figure 9.2). However, this is a three-dimensional model as it is constantly moving as people move through different spaces and times to maintain and build their relationships and for this they use both the new and the old tools of communication and relationship building as they seek to satisfy the five dimensions of human need. One of the challenges when we consider how living places are likely to be configured is that they are relatively permanent features of the landscape and fulfil multiple functions and enshrine different ideas about both how people 'should live' and how people do live out their everyday lives.

Neighbourhood, Urban Planning and Housing Provision

Turning now to the idea of neighbourhood: for the planning and design professions, and for many local and national governments, the building of sustainable housing requires effective urban planning, an endeavour which sought to shape the city and local areas for much of the twentieth century. It grew out of reactions to the rapid growth and industrialization of cities from the late eighteenth to the nineteenth centuries and was infused with a variety of moral imperatives to make better places for everyday living that were healthier, safer and where a higher quality of life could be enjoyed. This was to be achieved by regulating and improving the quality of buildings and the layout and design of streets, and building infrastructure to deliver clean water and remove waste. Land use zoning was introduced to separate conflicting activities. These early planning attempts had a marked effect on the physical health and well-being of city dwellers and as a result infrastructure planning is currently a dominant ingredient of urban management strategies in developing countries (UNCHS, 2001a, b).

As cities improved their physical infrastructure, planners turned to wider concerns about the role of urban design in shaping social and psychological relations and behaviour. In the late nineteenth century Ebenezer Howard (1898), for example, promoted the garden city, a combination of the best of rural and urban living. In this utopian vision of the ideal city, green spaces were important to allow the city to 'breathe' and limit sprawl. The garden city was also seen as a solution to urban deprivation (Thorns, 2002).

Howard's vision reappeared in the 1950s and 1960s in the new town movement and in the idea of the neighbourhood as a balanced development that would encourage the social mixing of the population. It was also in these decades that high-rise apartment blocks were built to replace accommodation lost during the Second World War and house the growing urban populations of the time (Coleman, 1985; Power, 1993). The idea of socially mixed residential developments was again promoted in the urban renewal polices pursued by New Labour in the United Kingdom in the late 1990s and 2000s and more recently in Australia after the 2007 election of the Australian Labor Party. In the Australian case it was a concern to enhance social inclusion and address social disadvantage that spurred a renewed interest in social mix and balance (Levitas, 2005). The policy makers wanted to overcome problems arising from a combination of poor and unaffordable housing which had led to overcrowding, homelessness and, at the extreme, persistent illness and disablement. Typically, the residents of this housing also earned inadequate incomes, pushing the resident individuals or households below the poverty line. It was hoped that being able to provide affordable housing was one way of breaking the cycle of disadvantage and creating stronger communities that could in turn provide mutual support. Various types of housing assistance were offered including state rental accommodation, third-sector not-for-profit rental housing and assistance for home purchase and rent-to-buy schemes in cases for those who were occupying public rental housing. This mix of accommodation was designed to increase population diversity and the capacity to build more resilient and stronger local communities (Stone and Hulse, 2007).

The desire of planners to create mixed and balanced communities has to be considered against a substantial research literature which documents cities as places of segregation and separation where neighbourhoods have been divided by 'walls' between hostile groups. Good examples include the sectarian separation of Northern Ireland's urban communities, the racially divided cities of the United States (Marcuse, 1995) and the rise, from the 1980s, of gated communities in which populations secure themselves against 'others' to enhance property values and protect a favoured lifestyle. The growing popularity of gated communities secured via gates, fencing and monitored by security personnel shows that there is a heightened sense of anxiety in many countries about everyday living, that life is now full of hazards and dangers (Dupuis and Thorns, 2008). Gated communities represent attempts to create place-based community, albeit for those who can afford to pay.

New Urbanism – Designing New Spaces for Living

This final section discusses and critiques a market-led response to sustainable housing: new urbanism. This is an approach to residential development that is designed to be socially inclusive and environmentally benign. It draws on ideas from the garden city movement as applied to neighbourhood planning. It is therefore a form of neo-traditionalism emphasizing a return to older, established values and ways of living. New urbanism has its origins in architecture and planning in the US and arose as a rejection of modern functionalism and suburban development that had contributed to the sprawling nature of the American city. Its founders argued that suburban landscapes militated against sociability and civility (Duany *et al.*, 2000; Calthorpe, 1993). They rejected the sterile streetscapes in which 'snout houses' faced the streets dominated by garages and automatic-entry systems and in which living areas were turned away from the street and hidden behind privately fenced plots screening occupants from neighbours. Instead, they advocated compact cities, intensified housing and designs for streets and houses that encouraged residents to meet and interact. Removing barriers to social contact and recreating the village green as a place of social engagement became a key principle of the new design (Katz *et al.*, 1994; Southworth, 1997). These ideas had wide appeal and were adopted in many countries. In a 1990s New Zealand development based around these ideas the real estate marketing indicated that:

> Our design objectives [for Tumara Park] include set-back garaging, *low shrub divisions between berm and front yard areas, and verandah areas,* all of which contribute to a private yet warm and friendly neighbourhood. (Winstanley *et al.*, 2003, emphasis added)

Proponents of new urbanism thus claim that housing produced in this way will create 'community'; combining high-quality lifestyles and relationships set within well-established spatial boundaries. Talen (1999) noted, however, that there is no empirical evidence of a direct link between neighbourhood form and sense of community because there are too many intervening variables determining the influence of design on acquiring a sense of place or stimulating social interaction. New urban projects and residential developments may promote opportunities for communality through design of the built environment but they cannot 'build community' despite marketing claims to the contrary (Winstanley *et al.*, 2003). This has been borne out in some new urban settlements where the designers of these settings could not guarantee that residents would use these neighbourhoods in the ways hoped for. In Seaside, Florida, for example, residents allowed their garden shrubs to grow higher than was intended by the designers to shield their front porches and provide increased privacy from their neighbours and other 'community' members. They actively used physical barriers to prevent social interaction rather than maintain the original design and embrace the opportunity for community.

Other criticisms of new urbanism and the neighbourhoods produced in accordance with its principles have been made. One relates to the extent to which new urban communities, even if they are designed to be self-contained, will in fact remain self-contained and thus reduce sprawl. Another notes that simply requiring new housing to include work and leisure services, including fast Internet connections to enable working from home, does not ensure that it will happen. This is due to the many and varied patterns of work and leisure which generate complex travel requirements within cities and regions, many predicated on personal transport encouraged by the high levels of car ownership (Wellam and Giuha, 1999; Urry, 2000; Robbins, 1998).

Additionally, while the rhetoric of new urbanism promotes the idea of housing developments which are home to diverse populations in terms of age, income and ethnicity (Langdon, 1994), this has been difficult to achieve and is perhaps the most telling critique of the new urban concept. It suggests that new urbanism reflects a nostalgic and idealized view of small-town life that contradicts many of the findings of urban researchers which highlight the very great level of social, racial and income segregation of urban populations (Berry and Kasarda, 1977; Soja, 2000; Marcuse and van Kempen, 2000). Critics, such as Bitar *et al.* (2000), claim that new urban neighbourhoods are not accessible to people of different incomes and backgrounds, and furthermore they liken new urban neighbourhoods to 'theme parks' where truly democratic culture cannot flourish. They suggest that there are irreconcilable contradictions between the concept of 'collective good' as espoused by new urbanism and the economic practices associated with the production of, and residence in, privately developed neighbourhoods and based around private property ownership, the value of which rests on uniform investment and housing maintenance by neighbours. This suggests therefore that attempting to manufacture senses of community and place through such strategies as new urbanism are not at all straightforward.

Conclusion

This chapter has explored the day-to-day working out of sustainable urban development using housing, community and neighbourhood as exemplars. Into this has been integrated a discussion of the influence of neo-liberalism and its consequences for social life and urban form. The chapter therefore concentrated discussion on the marketization of housing, market models and sustainable housing, and urban planning and attempts to create new types of housing such as those associated with gated communities and new urbanism. This approach has brought together a diverse array of ideas about places of residence, market processes, consumption, planning, mobility, individualization, personal choice, autonomy, poverty, uncertainty, risk, insecurity, anxiety, social stratification, global and local interconnections and complexity. The chapter's purpose has been to show that while discussions about sustainable urban development are of very great importance, the implementation of the concept in the everyday lives of urban residents is fraught with contradictions, difficulties and challenges.

Further reading

Delanty, G. 2003. *Community*. London: Routledge.

Forrest R. and N. Yip. 2011. *Housing Markets and Global Financial Crisis*. London: Edward Elgar.

Putnam, R. 2000. *Bowling Alone: The Collapse and Revival of American Communities*. New York, NY: Simon & Schuster.

Shove, E., M. Watson, M. Hand and J. Ingram. 2007. *The Design of Everyday Life*. London: Berg.

Stiglitz, J. 2009. 'The Anatomy of Murder: Who Killed America's Economy'. *Critical Review* 21, 329–339.

Talen, E. 1999. 'Sense of Community and Neighbourhood Form: An Assessment of the Social Doctrine of New Urbanism'. *Urban Studies* 36, 1361–1379.

Wellman, B. 2001. 'Community Question'. *Canadian Journal of Sociology* 26, 1203–1228.

CHAPTER 10

Conclusion: Urban and Rural Futures

Introduction

The purpose in this final chapter is to examine two broad theoretical and methodological themes that have arisen from the book's discussion and which are relevant for the development of research agendas in urban and rural studies. The themes on which this chapter concentrates both link to questions of identity and everyday life and incorporate ideas about globalization, transformation, place, and urban and rural futures.

Transformation, Place and Everyday Life

We see globalization as an ongoing process of transformation. It operates at a number of scales and intersects with the regional, national and local places that make up the contexts through which we live out our everyday social practices and craft our sense of who we are as individuals. Globalization is a set of linked processes so it is not mono-causal in nature. Rather it is shaped by the engagement of people and social groups including families, households, communities, social networks and organizations in and through their everyday living in the many places where they are located. The experience of, and attachment to, place remains one of the anchors of our human experience and thus remains strong even in a more globalized world where mobility has increased and our sense of being part of a global community has been strengthened through the expansion of new ways of communicating, knowing and engaging with people across the globe in real time.

At the local level, people's need for shelter contributes to senses of place and identity because having physical shelter connects many of the world's people to land and heritage as expressed through language, culture, ancestral connection, kin, family and occupation. Shelter is also vital for social inclusion and personal well-being so the creation of secure tenure has been a significant political goal, globally. It follows that home is therefore a central element of individual and collective identity in most cultures. Homes are imbued with memories, stories, narratives and experiences and are the places which link residents to the past and where plans for the future are laid out. The idea of home is therefore multidimensional and multi-scalar, being both about our immediate location and also about our wider connection with our kin, clan and our ethnic group. This is seen strongly in some of the global diasporas such as the those of the Chinese, Indian and Irish and the spread of their cultures in the form of cuisine, music, dance and festivals. What this shows is that all people look to 'belong' somewhere; putting down roots is important. Even street dwellers have a sense of belonging albeit one that has little permanence or security.

But while being grounded in place, those people who have access to adequate resources also reach out to family, friends, colleagues and others across the globe using landline telephones, the Internet, social networking sites and cellphones to communicate and engage in a range of activities. In addition, residents of all but the most remote communities are influenced directly and subliminally by global media, especially those associated with product advertising and popular culture. So, there is a sense in which people are experiencing change in some aspects of their lives while in other respects their day-to-day existence is patterned along familiar lines. Set alongside these experiences are a set of resistances to change.

The challenge for social scientists has been to find ways of characterizing these simultaneous experiences and expressions of change, stasis and resistance. Many commentators working from a structuralist perspective have emphasized a top-down analysis which characterizes individual and collective agency as being constrained by economic forces and allied technological developments. In these terms it is new forms of technology and economic activity which have been responsible for changing people, places and cultural processes. The social, cultural and biophysical landscapes of urban and rural areas are shaped, for example, by technologies such as those associated with transport, energy, telecommunications, the position of products in national and global markets, and the manifestation of these technologies and economic outputs in the form of fixed and durable capital in the built environment such as houses, offices, factories, roads, farms, tourism facilities, etc. Such structures are said to change *and* constrain how everyday life can be expressed.

Other social scientists, working from a range of interpretative perspectives and, latterly, using poststructuralist analysis, have in contrast emphasized the role of human agency and cultural activity in discussions of change and stasis. This approach encourages an appreciation of the role of social actors, social movements, social groups, classes and individuals in the construction of everyday life. It also points to the risks of reductionism, partial explanation and flawed analysis inherent in explanations of change and stasis based on structural technological or economic analyses. In their recent economic research, therefore, these interpretative and poststructuralist social scientists have focused on the role of individuals such as entrepreneurs and innovators as the early adopters and opinion leaders in new economic activities and also drawn on behavioural psychology to explain market failures (Elster, 2010). In the area of cultural changes they have acknowledged the importance of shifts in ideas and ways of living, arguing that these are shaped by a search for identity and the revival of ways to maintain culturally distinct practices, which, rather than being expunged by globalization, have been rekindled. In part this is a reflection of increasing mobility and the added ability, provided by new communication tools, to resist change and maintain cultural and linguistic connections.

Going further, these social scientists have argued that enhanced communication, tourism and mass-migration have, on a grand scale, increased people's knowledge and appreciation of cultural diversity and highlighted, for a great many of them, the need to preserve rather than destroy differences. The same globalized influences that have been interpreted as creating cultural conformity have also aided the revival of threatened cultures and languages. The greatest cultural diversity is to be found among the populations of global and other large cities because they are constituted through a mix of migration streams involving people from many ethnic backgrounds. Global cities thus face the challenges of social inclusion and exclusion, of maintaining social cohesion and building social capital within local and national communities. Notwithstanding the argument that urban population diversity can lead to an appreciation of difference, this process can also create anxiety and a fear of 'strangers in our midst', of people who speak different languages and have unfamiliar ways of living. This can also foster various forms of urban segregation and nationalist anti-immigration politics. Thus the consequences of global change are far from uniform with globalizing influences being mediated, blended and adapted as new technological, economic and cultural practices are incorporated by the residents of cities, towns and rural areas into their everyday lives.

Having noted this, the effects of information and communication technologies should not be underestimated. The computer, the Internet, and the cellphone have helped reconfigure spatial differences and remade the ways people connect with each other. For young people across the globe the emergence of social websites such as Facebook and Twitter and such sites as Second Life where the exploration of new identities is a possibility has been both rapid and potentially transformative with many experimenting, discovering new things and testing themselves through these media. The boundaries between the real, virtual and the imagined have been reconstituted. This began in the late nineteenth century with the emergence of radio and film, followed in the twentieth century by television, and more recently web-based digital technologies. These new media expand our possibilities, open up new horizons and allow us to connect across the globe with like-minded people and discover that there are more ways of living than those with which we are familiar in our 'own backyard'. They are also a source of considerable commercial gain. These same technologies also have the potential to enable new forms of surveillance which can control and exercise power over us in subtle and pervasive ways, ranging from the acquisition and storage of personal data by governments through to data storage and manipulation by commercial enterprises who use it to market their products and influence our activities. These forms of surveillance threaten our individual freedoms.

We are wary of much of the overgeneralized commentary which privileges the nature and effects of mobility in current processes of transformation and points to a world in which all is movement and time–space compression. In this perspective, people, money and ideas are purported to be moving at increasing speed, whether this be global financial transactions or web searches for sports results, accommodation bookings or make contacts with friends or family members on the other side of the world. Migration is said to be ubiquitous, displaying many variants: permanent or temporary, education based, exploratory, touristic and virtual. While we agree that there is evidence that there are many streams of movement and forms of mobility, at the other end of the scale there are many people in all countries who live out their lives within a local place, some by choice and others through necessity. Arguments about mobility need to account better for this diversity of experience.

So the theoretical position we adhere to with respect to the study of everyday life emphasizes multi-causal pathways, co-determinism, complexity and a subtle and nuanced understanding of the changing interplay between local and global influences. This approach suggests that we need to be careful of aggregation and generalizing statements about the effects of either globalism or localism as the determinant of everyday life. Further, the quantitative analysis of trends derived from national or regional or global-level data, although useful for seeing broad trends, does not assist in understanding change in the everyday experience of living in a variety of urban and rural settings. For this a more qualitative method of approach is required (Perkins *et al.*, 2008b; Thorns, 2010).

A broad research agenda is also required. It demands an understanding of the increasing complexity of the places in which people live and how they make and interact with their homes and communities, cities and regions. Again, the use of qualitative social and ethnographic methods has grown as researchers have grappled to understand the dynamics of urban and rural change and the shifting basis of the meaning of a variety of places across societies. At a broader scale it is useful to use comparative contextual analysis to interpret the ways meaning is created, studying social interaction and mediation around the development of human settlement in a variety of settings. This allows for the recognition of the influence of larger-scale cultural, social, economic, environmental and spatial relationships and changes.

Research into everyday life needs also to interpret the variable influences of a range of social, economic and cultural factors and processes characteristic of the people under study. These may include their age, stage in the life course/cycle, gender, social class, occupation, ethnicity and their experience of and connection to service provision, reciprocities and social capital. Such relationships may be the product of mutual agreement or they may be arrived at through a mixture of agreement and domination and exploitation.

Urban and Rural Futures and Everyday Life

The study of everyday life and the contexts in which it is worked out also requires some consideration of the future. Much of contemporary discussion about the future of the city and countryside, the quality of the environments of those places, and the lives of the people who reside there, is couched within a discourse of 'sustainability'. Davidson (2010: 391) observed, for example, that 'the concept of sustainability ... has replaced others, such as equality and/or social justice, which have previously been the ideological pivot for ... planners'. One of the unresolved issues in this growing debate is what precisely should be 'sustained'. Is it all that we have currently within the world? Is it the level of development that has been attained by the richest and most advanced countries? If this is to be the case are the 'rich nations' going to stand still and let the other 'catch up'? The resource implications of raising the overall standard to that of those living at the current highest standard alone would require a huge increase in the consumption of energy and resources that would place further stress upon the environment and climate (Catterall, 2010: 481). So, as has been shown in the latter chapters of this book, in many respects sustainability is a 'fuzzy concept' that encourages political debate and rhetoric about the need for change but which is sufficiently vague to allow a variety of actual political and planning responses. Despite this, or perhaps because of it, sustainability has become a widely adopted mantra, focusing on the needs of present and future generations but meaning different things in different contexts. For some it is about global imbalances and inequalities. For these people the most pressing issues are the differential development of the 'north and the south' and the alleviation of poverty and disease to improve life expectancy and to increase social inclusion in societies that are highly uneven in their wealth distribution and access to basic resources. For yet others the key issues surround the approaching energy problems as we reach 'peak oil' as this source of energy begins to decline and affects of cost and availability of energy to power industrial and agricultural production and create the commodities upon which much of everyday life in the 'north' is based. For still others it is about technological and scientific solutions that can somehow enable most of what we do currently to be preserved and perhaps even enhanced through measures that are less damaging to the environment.

The majority of analysts now see sustainability as a very complex and systemic issue, comprising social, economic, environmental, cultural and political dimensions. For some this makes it a 'wicked problem' that is very difficult to solve because it requires a new 'joined-up' form of political practice which so far has not evolved at national or global level. As the experience with the Kyoto carbon reduction targets and the 2009 Copenhagen Climate Change summit have demonstrated any global action plan and agreement is still some distance away. Indices and solutions which target just one dimension of the issue are not helpful as it is the interconnections and dynamics between the dimensions and their overall configuration that are important in considering how sustainable or unsustainable any particular urban or rural setting might be.

Climate change, energy supply and water security are key issues for any future urban or regional strategy that seeks to develop an adaptive approach to the future that might include resettlement, for example. Action in these areas is often not easy, however, because there is a good deal of uncertainty about the future and a good deal of scepticism from a number of quarters about the veracity of scientific predictions. In the context of climate change, this is despite the recent extreme weather conditions which have (in 2010) led to record temperatures across Russia and Northern Europe, a large proportion of Pakistan flooded and up to 14 million people displaced by the exceptionally heavy monsoon rains and flooding in north-west China resulting in deaths of more than 1,100 people and more than 600 missing, and wildfires in Portugal, Canada and California – all events predicted by the IPCC 2007 Report (*The Press* 14/08/2010: B6). It is also invariably the case that these disasters affect the poorest populations most severely. The question facing planners and decision-makers at all levels from the local to the global is can we wait for further information or should we act now and start to take precautionary action based on the best available information for local areas to aid their process of adaptation? Not all areas in a future scenario will be devastated, but many areas will have to change economic and social practices to survive (Giddens, 2009; Stehr and van Storch, 2010).

It is our view that it will be necessary to develop a strong relationship between sustainable practices, social well-being and social inclusion so that alternative goals and agendas can be formed that can link the global with the local to effect change. As the City of Vancouver's statement on social sustainability suggests:

> For a community to function and be sustainable, the basic needs of its residents must be met. A socially sustainable community must have the ability to maintain and build on its own resources and have the resiliency to prevent and or address problems in the future. (Davidson, 2010: 397–398)

This reinforces our view that top-down solutions to meeting the challenges of global environmental change are insufficient, and that a renewed focus on the local is required as this is where people experience the effects of these global changes and meet the disruption caused by extreme events and attempt to rebuild social and communal relationships. In such recovery the rebuilding is about the strengthening and reforming of both the physical and social structures and patterns of everyday living and it is at this level that changes need to be made.

For many people at the level of everyday experience there is a credibility gap that needs bridging. While scientific and government reports may say that the natural environment is under threat, this is often difficult to see and comprehend from the perspective of daily life in which connections with nature are brief and fleeting for many people. The potential for damaging climate change might be well documented, but for many people there is a disconnection between scientists' predictions and the reality of everyday living. Members of the public do not trust experts and representatives of public institutions in a way that they once did. One of the reasons for this is the increased level of pressure upon individuals to assess and take action to address their own risks largely shaped by global economic and social policy making and political thinking that for the last

40 years has been influenced by neo-liberal ideas. These ideas have emphasized individual choice, less sate intervention and bureaucracy, and a greater reliance on markets for the distribution of goods and services to achieve greater efficiency. While this may appear empowering, it is by no means easy for people to calculate their risks and make choices because their calculations are made in a highly complex, interconnected and shifting world where choices are constantly subjected to intense advertising and taste-making (Lupton, 2006).

The other disconnection between global predictions about environmental change and local experience, which is so clearly expressed in everyday life, is between the demands of sustainable living and the desire to expand consumerism to maintain economic growth. So much of current economic thinking is based around encouraging and catering for a relentless commodification and diversification of activities, experiences and places to cater for frenetic consumption. These processes have created myriad new urban and rural leisure and consumption landscapes ranging from the global super mall to the peri-urban shopping village, developed at the expense of traditional streetscapes, shopping precincts and country towns. The impulse to consume is also linked to the widespread love affair with the car, its central place in contemporary society, in our leisure activities, and our assumption of personalized mobility as a necessary component of daily living. Spatial planning in the majority of countries is still strongly influenced by the growth of demand for individual mobility and privatized transport, despite the well-documented costs of this approach.

Market expansion has not only produced consumption objects but also created and reinforced a set of values and desires. Happiness has become linked to a lifestyle based around continual consumption underpinned by the easy availability of credit (Catterall, 2010: 481). The global economic recession that began in 2007, despite an initial burst of enthusiasm for reform of the economic system and the creation of more 'sustainable' economic practices, has followed a path to recovery that has been largely created around a well-established set of economic imperatives. Consumer spending and the growth of credit and marketing have again been used to persuade people to begin the cycle again through purchasing goods including housing, one of the key speculative commodities in the 2007 financial crash. The move to a more sustainable and green future for energy and consumption and use of resources has so far been stronger at the level of rhetoric than in practical actions initiated by the global leaders of nation states. Innovation, in this area, by contrast, has been much stronger at the grass-roots level where local solutions have been sought and experimentation has taken place stimulated by a mix of social and environmental concerns and the recognition of changes affecting local places. The people involved realize that the search for solutions is by no means easy or straightforward but their actions illustrate that one part of the approach to these issues lies with an incorporation of the sustainability agenda into the everyday lives of urban and rural residents (Vallance and Perkins, 2010: 449).

References

Aglietta, M. 2000. *A Theory of Capitalist Regulation: The US Experience*. London: Verso.

Agnew, T. 2010. 'TV once a unifying force'. *The Press*: Christchurch.

Allan, M. and D. C. Thorns. 2009. 'Being Face to Face – A State of Mind or Technological Design'. In *Handbook of Research on Socio Technical Designing and Social Networking Systems* (eds.), B. Whitworth and A. (de) Moor. Hershey PA: IGI Global Publications.

Amin, A. 2004. 'Regions Unbound: Towards a New Politics of Place'. *Geografiska Annaler* 86, 33–44.

Appadurai, A. 1996. *Modernity at Large: Cultural Dimensions of Globalization*. Minneapolis, MN: University of Minnesota Press.

(ed.) 2003. *The Social Life of Things*. Cambridge University Press.

Armstrong, N. 1997. 'Flexible work and disciplined selves: telework, gender and discourses of subjectivity', Ph.D. thesis, Department of Sociology, Massey University, Palmerston North, New Zealand.

Ashton, H. and D. C. Thorns. 2007. 'The Role of Information Technology in Retrieving Local Community'. *City and Community* 6, 211–229

Aupetit, S. D. 2010. 'From Brain Drain to Brain Circulation'. In *Knowledge Divides* World Social Science Report. Paris UNESCO, pp 122–3.

Badcock, B. and A. Beer. 2000. *Home Truths: Property Ownership and Housing Wealth in Australia*. Carlton, Vic.: Melbourne University Press.

Baines, J., J. Newell, N. Taylor. 2006. Multiple Job Holding: Comparison of Data from the Household Labour Force Survey and the Census. Working Paper no. 12 Christchurch: Taylor Baines and Associates.

Baker, E. and K. Arthurson. 2007. 'Housing, Place or Social Networks: What's More Important for Relocating Tenants?'. *Australian Planner* 44, 4, 29–35.

Banham, R. 2009 [1971]. *Los Angeles: The Architecture of Four Ecologies*. Berkeley and Los Angeles, CA: University of California Press.

Baragwanath, L. and N. Lewis. 2010. 'Waiheke typical of what super city must protect'. *New Zealand Herald* (www.nzherald.co.nz/; accessed 23/03/2010).

Baudrillard, J. 1968 [1996]. *The System of Object*. London: Verso.

1983a. *Simulations*. New York, NY: Semiotext.

1983b. *In The Shadow Of The Silent Majority*. New York, NY: Semiotext.

1998. *The Consumner Society: Myths and Structures*. London: Sage.

Bauman, Z. 1992. *Intimations of Postmodernity*. London: Routledge.

1998. *Work, Consumerism and the New Poor*. Buckingham, Philadelphia: Open University Press.

Beck, U. 1992. *Risk Society: Towards a New Modernity*. London: Sage.

1996. 'World Risk Society as a Cosmopolitan Society? Ecological Questions in a Framework of Manufactured Uncertainties'. *Theory, Culture and Society* 14, 4, 1–32.

2002. 'The Terrorist Threat: World Risk Society Revisited'. *Theory, Culture & Society* 19, 39–55.

Becker, E., T. Jahn and E. Stiess. 1999. 'Exploring Uncommon Ground: Sustainability and the Social Sciences'. In *Sustainability and the Social Sciences* (eds.), Becker E and T. Jahn London: Zed Books.

Bell, D. 1973. *The Coming of Post-industrial Society: A Venture in Social Forecasting*. New York, NY: Basic Books.

Berg, L. D. and R. A. Kearns. 1996. 'Naming as Norming: "Race", Gender, and the Identity Politics of Naming Places in Aotearoa/New Zealand'. *Environment and Planning D: Society and Space* 14, 99–122.

Berger, B. 1960. *Working-Class Suburb*. Berkeley, California, CA: University of California Press.

Berry, B. J. L. and J. D. K. Kasarda. 1977. *Contemporary Urban Ecology*. New York, NY: Macmillan.

Berry, M., T. Dalton and A. Nelson. 2009. *Mortgage Default in Australia: Nature, Causes and Social and Economic Impacts*. Positioning Paper No. 114, Australian Housing and Urban Research Institute, Melbourne.

Besser, H. 2004. *The Next Digital Divide*. (www.tcla.gseis.ucla.edu/divide/politics/besser.html; accessed 4/05/2010).

Best, S. 1989. 'The Commodification of Reality and the Reality of Commodification: Jean Baudrillard and Post-Modernism'. *Current Perspectives in Social Theory* 19, 23–45.

Bhatti, M. and A. Church. 2000. '"I Never Promised You a Rose Garden": Gender, Leisure and Home-Making'. *Leisure Studies* 19, 183–197.

Bhatti, M. 2006. 'When I'm in the Garden Can Create My Own Paradise': Homes and Gardens in Later Life. *Sociological Review* 54, 318–341.

Birdwell-Pheasant, D. and D. Lawrence-Zuniga (eds.). 1999. *House Life: Space, Place and Family in Europe*. Oxford: Berg.

Bitar J., A. Deguchi and S. Hagishima. 2000. 'The needs of contemporary urbanism and the missing principles in controlling smart growth'. Conference Paper, ENHR, Gavle, Sweden.

Blowers, A. 1997. 'Environmental Policy: Ecological Modernization or Risk Society?'. *Urban Studies* 34, 5/6, 845–871.

Bluestone, B. and B. Harrison. 1986. *The Great American Job Machine: The Proliferation of Low-Wage Employment in the US Economy*. Washington, DC: United States Congressional Joint Committee.

Blumer, H., 1969. *Symbolic Interactionism: Perspective and Method*. Englewood Cliffs, NJ: Prentice-Hall.

Blunt, A. 2005. 'Cultural Geography: Cultural Geography of Home'. *Progress in Human Geography*. 29, 505–515.

Blunt, A. and R. Dowling. 2006. *Home*. London: Routledge.

Boellsstorff, T. 2008. *Coming of Age in Second Life: An Anthropologist Explores the Virtually Human*. Princeton University Press.

Booth, C. 1903. *Life and Labour of the People of London*. London: Macmillan.

Bourdieu, P. 1984. *Distinction: A Social Critique of the Judgement of Taste*. Cambridge, MA: Harvard University Press.

Bowlby, S., S. Gregory and L. McKie. 1997. '"Doing Home": Patriarchy, Caring, and Space'. *Women's Studies International Forum* 20, 343–350.

Boston, J. and Dalziel, P. (eds.). 1992. *The Decent Society*. Auckland, Oxford University Press.

Bradsher, K. 2002. *High and Mighty*. New York, NY: Public Affairs.

Brah, A. 1996. *Cartographies of Diaspora: Contesting Identities*. London: Routledge.

Britton, S. 1991. 'Tourism, Capital, and Place: Towards a Critical Geography of Tourism'. *Environment and Planning D: Society and Space* 9, 451–478.

Bryman, A. 2004. *The Disneyization of Society*. London: Sage.

Buller, H. and K. Hoggart, K. 1994. 'The Social Integration of British Home Owners into French Rural Communities'. *Journal of Rural Studies* 10, 197–210.

Burgess, E. W. 1967. 'The Growth of the City'. In *The City* (eds.), R.E. Park, E.W. Burgess and R. D. McKenzie. Chicago University Press.

Burgess, E. W and Bogue, D. J. 1964. *Contributions to Urban Sociology*. University of Chicago Press.

Burrows, R. and N. Ellison. 2004. 'Towards a social politics of neighbourhood informatization'. Paper presented to the *British Sociological Association Conference*. York University, March.

Burrows R., N. Ellison and B. Wood. 2005. *Neighbourhoods on the Net: The Nature and Impact Of Internet-Based Neighbourhood Information Systems*. Joseph Rowntree Foundation, Bristol: Policy Press.

Buttimer, A. 1980. 'Home, Reach, and the Sense of Place'. In *The Human Experience of Space and Place* (eds.), A. Buttimer and D. Seamon. New York, NY: St Martin's Press.

Calthorpe, P. 1993. *The Next American Metropolis: Ecology, Community, and the American Dream*. New York, NY: Princeton Architectural Press.

Calthorpe, P. and W. B. Fulton. 2001. *The Regional City: Planning for the End of Sprawl*. Washington, DC: Island Press.

Caluya, G., 2007. 'The Architectural Nervous System'. *Media and Culture Journal* 10, 4 August (http//Journal Media and Culture.org.au).

Cameron, J. 1997. *Without Issue: New Zealanders Who Choose Not to Have Children*. Christchurch: Canterbury University Press.

Carlaw, K., L. Oxley, P. Walker, D. Thorns, and M. Nuth. 2006. 'Beyond the Hype: Intellectual Property and the Knowledge Society/ Knowledge Economy'. *Journal of Economic Surveys* 20, 633–691.

Carson, R. 1962. *The Silent Spring*. London: Heinemann.

Case, K. E. 2009. 'What are house prices telling us?', paper presented at the *Housing Mortgages and Financial Turmoil* Seminar. Melbourne: RMIT, February.

Casey, E. S. 1993. *Getting Back into Place: Towards a Renewed Understanding of the Place-World*. Bloomington, IL: University of Indiana Press.

1998. *The Fate of Place: A Philosophical History*. Berkeley, CA: University of California Press.

Castells, M. 1977. *The Urban Question*. London: Edward Arnold.

1983. *The City and the Grassroots*. London: Edward Arnold.

1998. *Information Age: Economy, Society, and Culture; V.3*. Malden, MA: Blackwell.

2000. 'Materials for an Exploratory Theory of the Network Society'. *British Journal of Sociology* 51, 5–24.

2001. *The Internet Galaxy*. Oxford University Press.

2007. *Mobile Communication and Society: A Global Perspective*. Cambridge, MA: MIT Press.

Catterall, B. 2010. 'Is it All Coming Together? Thoughts on Urban Studies in the Present Crisis'. *City* 14, 476–485.

Catton W. R. Jr. and Dunlap R. E. 1978. 'Environmental Sociology a New Paradigm'. *American Sociologist* 13, 1, 41–49.

Chamie, J. 2010. 'Foreseeing Future Population Challenges'. In *World Social Science Report*. Paris: UNESCO Publishing.

Chanen, J. 2000. 'Oh Give Me a Second Home'. *American Bar Association Journal* 86, 80–83.

Chancy, D. 2002. *Cultural Change and Everyday Life*. Houndmills, Basingstoke: Palgrave.

Chaplin, D. 1999. 'Consuming Work–Productive Leisure: The Consumption Patterns of Second Home Environments'. *Leisure Studies* 18, 41–55.

Chapman, R., P. Howden-Chapman, H. Viggers, D. O'Dea, M. Kennedy. 2009. 'Retrofitting Houses with Insulation: A Cost–Benefit Analysis of a Randomised Community Trial. *Journal of Epidemiological and Community Health* 63, 271–277.

Chapman, T. and J. Hockey (eds.), 1999. *Ideal Homes: Social Change and Domestic Life*. London: Routledge.

Cherry, G. E. 1984. 'Leisure and the Home. A Review of Changing Relationships'. *Leisure Studies* 3, 35–52.

Clarke, H. 2007. Christchurch City Biogas Project (www.beehive.govt.nz/node/ 29835; accessed: 7/07/2010).

Cloke, P. 1993. 'The Countryside as Commodity: New Rural Spaces for Leisure'. In *Leisure and the Environment* (ed.) S. Glyptis. London: Belhaven Press.

Cloke, P., J. May and S. Johnsen. 2010. *Swept Up Lives? Re-envisioning the Homeless City*. Oxford: Wiley-Blackwell.

Cloke, P. and O. Jones. 2001. 'Dwelling, Place and Landscape: An Orchard in Somerset'. *Environment and Planning A* 33, 649–666.

Cloke, P. and H. C. Perkins. 1998. 'Cracking the Canyon with the Awesome Foursome: Representations of Adventure Tourism in New Zealand'. *Environment and Planning D: Society and Space* 16, 185–218.
  2002. 'Commodification and Adventure in New Zealand Tourism'. *Current Issues in Tourism* 5, 521–549.
Cohen, E. 1988. 'Authenticity and Commodification in Tourism'. *Annals of Tourism Research* 15, 371–386.
Collins, J. 1988. *Migrant Hands in a Distant Land.* Sydney: Pluto.
Coleman, A. 1985. *Utopia on Trial: Vision and Reality in Planned Housing.* London: Shipman.
Cooper, C. 1976. 'The House as Symbol of Self'. In H. Proshansky, W. Ittelson and L. Rivlin (eds.), *Environmental Psychology.* New York, NY: Holt, Rinehart & Winston.
Cooper, T. 2010. 'Heart of the Tuhoe Nation'. *Waikato Times* (www.stuff. co.nz/waikato-times/features/3759199/Heart-of-the-Tuhoe-Nation; accessed 19/10/2010).
Corkery, C. and A. Bailey. 1994. 'Lobster is Big Business in Boston: Postcards, Place Commodification and Tourism'. *GeoJournal* 34, 491–498.
Corrigan, P. 1997. *The Sociology Of Consumption: An Introduction.* London: Sage.
COST. 2009. *Living the Digital Revolution Foresight 2030.* Brussels: COST European Cooperation in Science and Technology.
Crookston, M., P. Clarke, and J. Averley. 1996. 'The Compact City and Quality of Life'. In *The Compact City: A Sustainable Urban Form?* (eds.), M. Jenks, E. Burton and K. Williams. London: E & FN Spon.
Crouch, D. 1994. 'Home, Escape and Identity: Rural Cultures and Sustainable Tourism'. In B. Bramwell and B. Lane (eds.), *Rural Tourism and Sustainable Development.* Clevedon: Channel View.
  2003. 'Spacing, Performing and Becoming: Tangles in the Mundane'. *Environment and Planning A* 35, 1945–1960.
Csikszentmihalyi, M. and E. Rochberg-Halton 1981. *The Meaning of Things: Domestic Symbols and the Self.* New York, NY: Cambridge University Press.
Culhane, D. and M. Fried. 1988. 'Paths in Homelessness: A View from the Street'. In J. Friedrichs (ed.), *Affordable Housing and Homelessness.* Berlin: Walter de Gruyter.
Cushman. G., A. J. Veal and J. Zuzanek (eds.). 2005. *Free Time and Leisure Participation: International Perspectives.* 2nd edn, Wallingford, Oxon. UK: CABI Publishing.
Daly, G. 1996. *Homelessness.* London: Routledge.
Damer, S. 1974. 'Wine Alley: The Sociology of a Dreadful Enclosure', *Sociological Review* 22, 221–248.
Darke, J. 1994. 'Women and the Meaning of Home'. In R. Gilroy and R. Woods (eds.), *Housing Women.* London and New York, NY: Routledge.
Davey, S. 2004. *Unforgettable Places to See Before You Die.* London: BBC Books.
Davidson, M. 2010. 'Sustainability as Ideological Praxis: The Acting out of Planning's Master-Signifier'. *City* 14, 390–405.

Dear, M. 2000. *The Postmodern Urban Condition*. Oxford and Malden, MA: Blackwell.

Debord, G. 1983. *Society of the Spectacle*. Detroit, MI: Red and Black.

Delanty, G. 2003. *Community*. London: Routledge.

Dorst, J. D. 1989. *The Written Suburb*. Philadelphia, PA: University of Pennsylvania Press.

Drucker, P. 1969. *The Age of Discontinuity: Guidelines to Our Changing Society*. London: Heinemann.

Duany, A., E. Plater-Zyberk, and J. Speck. 2000. *Suburban Nation: The Rise of Sprawl and the Decline of the American Dream*. New York, NY: North Point Press.

Duncan, D. and C. Costantino. 2011. 'Effects of the Recent Credit Cycle on Homeownership Rates across Households: What We Know and What We Expect'. In R. Forrest and N. Yip (eds.), *Housing Markets and Global Financial Crisis*. London: Edward Elgar.

Duncan, J. 1978. 'The Social Construction of Unreality: An Interactionist Approach to the Tourist's Cognition of Environment'. In D. Ley and M. S. Samuels (eds.), *Humanistic Geography: Prospects and Problems*. Chicago, IL: Maaroufa Press.

Dunlap, R. 2008. 'The New Environmental Paradigm Scale: From Marginality to Worldwide Use'. *Journal of Environmental Education* autumn, 40, 3–18.

Dupuis, A. and J. Dixon. 2002. 'Intensification in Auckland: Issues and Policy Implications'. *Urban Policy and Research* 20, 415–428.

Dupuis, A. and D. C. Thorns. 1998. 'Home Ownership and the Search for Ontological Security'. *Sociological Review* 46, 24–47.

    2008. 'Gated Communities as Exemplars of "Forting Up" Practices in a Risk Society'. *Urban Policy and Research* 26, 145–157.

    2009. 'Living with risk, living in risk: an analysis of the leaky building syndrome in New Zealand'. Paper presented at the Australasian Housing Conference Sydney.

Durkheim, E. 1960. *The Division of Labour in Society*. New York, NY: Macmillan.

Durrschmidt, J. and Taylor, G. 2007. *Globalization, Modernity and Social Change*. London: Palgrave Macmillan.

Egoz, S. J. 2000. 'Clean and Green But Messy: The Contested Landscape of New Zealand's Organic Farms'. *Oral History* 28, 63–74.

    2002. 'The rational landscape in the Garden of Eden', unpublished Ph.D. thesis, Lincoln University, Canterbury, New Zealand.

Egoz, S. J. Bowring and H. C. Perkins. 2001. 'Tastes in Tension: Form, Function, And Meaning in New Zealand's Farmed Landscapes'. *Landscape and Urban Planning* 57, 177–196.

Egoz, S. J., J. Bowring and H. C. Perkins, 2006, 'Making a "Mess" in the Countryside: Organic Farming and the Threats to Sense of Place'. *Landscape Journal* 25, 54–66.

Ehrlich, P. R. 1968. *The Population Bomb*. New York, NY: Ballantine Books.

Ehrlich, P. R. and A. H. Ehrlich. 1970. *Population, Resources, Environment*. San Francisco, CA: W. H. Freeman.

Elster, J. 2010. 'One Social Science or Many?'. In *World Social Science Report: Knowledge Divides*. Paris: UNESCO Publishing, pp. 199–202.

Engels, F. 1971. *The Condition of the Working Class in England: Translated and Edited by W.O. Henderson and W.H. Chaloner*, 2nd edn. Oxford: Blackwell.

Eyles, J. 1985. *Senses of Place*. Warrington, Silverbrook Press.
    1989. 'The Geography of Everyday Life'. In D. Gregory and R. Walford (eds.), *Horizons of Human Geography*. Totowa, NJ: Barnes and Noble Books.

Featherston, M. 1991. *Consumer Culture and Postmodernism*. London: Sage.
    2007. *Consumer Culture and Postmodernism*, 2nd edn, Los Angeles, CA: Sage.

Feld, S. and K. H. Basso. (eds.). 1996. *Senses of Place*. New Mexico, NM: School of American Research.

Felstead, A., N. Jewson, A. Phizacklea and S. Walters. 2001. 'Working at Home: Statistical Evidence for Seven Key Hypotheses'. *Work, Employment and Society* 15, 215–231.

Felstead, A., N. Jewson and S. Walters. 2005. *Changing Places of Work*. New York, NY: Palgrave Macmillan.

Fogelsong, R. 1999. 'Walt Disney World and Orlando: Deregulation as a Strategy for Tourism'. In D. R. Judd and S. S. Fainstein (eds.), *The Tourist City*. New Haven, CT: Yale University Press.

Forrest, R. 2011. 'Households, Home Ownership and Neo-Liberalism'. In R. Forrest and N. Yip (eds.), *Housing Markets and Global Financial Crisis*. London: Edward Elgar.

Forrest, R. and A. Murie. 1988. *Selling the Welfare State: The Privatisation of Public Housing*. London: Routledge.
    (eds.). 1995. *Housing and Family Wealth in Comparative Perspective*. London: Routledge.
    (eds.). 2011. *Housing Markets and Global Financial Crisis*, London: Edward Elgar.

Foucault, M. 1976. *The Birth of the Clinic*. London: Tavistock.

Foresight Land Project. 2010. *Land Use Futures: Making the Most of Land in the 21st Century*. London: Government Office for Science.

Francis, M. and R. T. J. Hester. (eds.). 1990. *The Meaning of Gardens: Idea, Place, and Action*. Cambridge, MA: MIT Press.

Frank, G. D. 1971. *Capitalism and Underdevelopment in Latin America Historical Studies of Brazil and Chile*. Harmondsworth: Penguin.

Friedmann, J. 1995. 'Where Do We Stand: A Decade of World City Research'. In P. Knox and P. Taylor (eds.), *World Cities in a World System*. Cambridge University Press.
    2006. *The Wealth of Cities: Towards an Assets-based Development of Newly Urbanizing Regions* UN–Habitat Award Lecture UNCHS (www.unhabitat.org/forms/hsnet/docs/First_UN-HABITAT_Lecture.pdf; accessed 30/08/2011).

Froebel, F., J. Heinrichs and D. Kreye. 1980. *The New International Division of Labour*. Cambridge University Press.

Gans, H. J. 1962. *The Urban Villagers: Group and Class in the Life of Italian Americans.* New York, NY: Free Press of Glencoe.
1967. *The Levittowners.* New York, NY: Vintage.

Geertz, C. 1996. 'Afterword'. In S. Feld and K. H. Basso (eds.), *Senses of Place.* New Mexico, NM: School of American Research.

German Moltz, J. 2006. '"Watch Us Wander": Mobile Surveillance and the Surveillance of Mobility'. *Environment and Planning A* 38: 377–393.

Giddens, A., 1984, *The Constitution of Society,* Cambridge: Polity.
1990. *The Consequences of Modernity,* Stanford, CA: Stanford University Press.
2009. *The Politics of Climate Change.* Cambridge: Polity.

Gluckman, P. 2010. 'A perfect storm'. Opening Address by Prime Minister's Chief Scientific Adviser at the conference Degrees of Possibility: Igniting Knowledge, Wellington, New Zealand (www.nzclimatechangecentre.org/event/dop/programme; accessed 30/08/2011).

Glyptis, S. A. and D. A. Chambers. 1982. 'No Place Like Home'. *Leisure Studies* 1, 247–262.

Glyptis, S. A., H. McInnes and J. A. Patmore. 1987. *Leisure and the Home.* Sports Council and Economic and Social Research Council.

Goffman, I. 1969. *Presentation of Self in Everyday Life.* Harmondsworh: Penguin.

Gold, J. and S. Ward. (eds.). 1994. *Place Promotion: The Use of Publicity and Marketing to Sell Towns and Regions.* Chichester: Wiley.

Goldscheider, F. K. and L. J. Waite. 1991. *New Families, No Families? The Transformation of the American Home.* Berkeley, CA: University of California Press.

Gorman-Murray, A. and R. Dowling (eds.), 2007 'Home' *M/C Journal,* 10(4) (http://journal.media-culture.org.au/0708/01–editorial.php; accessed 2/06/2010).

Goss, J. 1995. 'Placing the Market and Marketing Place: Tourist Advertising of the Hawaiian Islands, 1972–92'. *Environment and Planning D: Society and Space* 11, 663–688.

Gottdiener, M. (ed.). 2000. *New Forms of Consumption: Consumers, Culture and Commodification.* Lanham, MD: Rowman & Littlefield.

Graham, S. 1999. 'Global Grids of Glass: On Global Cities, Telecommunications and Planetary Urban Networks'. *Urban Studies* 36, 929–949.

Graham, S. (ed.). 2004a. *The Cybercities Reader.* London: Routledge.
2004b. 'The Software Sorted City: Rethinking the Digital Divide' in S. Graham (ed.), *Cyber Cities.* London: Routledge.

Gregory, D. 1989. 'Areal Differentiation and Post-Modern Human Geography'. In D. Gregory, and R. Walford (eds.), *Horizons of Human Geography.* Totowa, NJ: Barnes and Noble Books.

Gregson, N. and M. Lowe. 1994. *Servicing the Middle Classes: Class, Gender and Waged Domestic Labour in Britain.* London: Routledge.

Greig, A. 2000. 'Project Homes or Homes-as-Projects: Fashion and Utility in Twentieth-Century Australia'. In P. Troy (ed.), *A History of European Housing in Australia.* Cambridge University Press.

Gumpert, G. and S. J. Drucker. 1998. 'The Mediated Home in the Global Village'. *Communication Research* 25, 422–438.

Gurney, C. M. 1997. 'Half of Me Was Satisfied: Making Sense of Home through Episodic Ethnographies'. *Women's Studies International Forum* 30, 373–386.

2000a. 'Transgressing Private-Public Boundaries in the Home: A Sociological Analysis of the Coital Noise Taboo'. *Venereology: The Interdisciplinary International Journal of Sexual Health* 13, 39–46.

2000b. 'Accommodating Bodies: The Organisation of Corporeal Dirt in the Embodied Home'. In L. McKie and N. Watson (eds.), *Organizing Bodies: Policy, Institutions and Work*. New York, NY: St Martin's.

Hall, C. M. 1992. 'Adventure, Sport and Health Tourism'. In B. Weiler and C. M. Hall (eds.), *Special Interest Tourism*. London: Belhaven Press.

Hall, C. M and D. K. Müller. (eds.). 2004. *Tourism, Mobility and Second Homes: Between Elite Landscapes and Common Ground*. Clevedon: Channel View.

Halle, D. 1993. *Inside Culture: Art and Class in the American Home*. Chicago, IL and London: University of Chicago Press.

Halkett, I. 1978. 'The Recreational Use of Private Gardens'. *Journal of Leisure Research* 10, 13–20.

Halpern, D. 2005. *Social Capital*. Oxford: Polity.

Halseth, G. 2004. 'The "Cottage" Privilege: Increasingly Elite Landscapes of Second Homes in Canada'. In C. M. Hall and D. K. Müller (eds.), *Tourism, Mobility and Second Homes: Between Elite Landscapes and Common Ground*. Clevedon: Channel View.

Hamilton, C. and R. Denniss. 2005. *Affluenza: When Too Much is Never Enough*. Crows Nest, NSW: Allen & Unwin.

Hamnett, C. 1999. *Winner and Losers: Home Ownership in Modern Britain*. London: UCL Press.

Hamnett, C., M. Harmer and P. Williams. 1991. *Safe as Houses. Housing Inheritance in Britain*. London: Paul Chapman.

Hampton, K. and B. Wellman. 2003. 'Neighbouring in Netville: How the Internet Supports Community and Social Capital in a Wired Suburb'. *City and Community* 2–4, 277–311.

Hardin. G. 1968. 'The Tragedy of the Commons'. *Science* 162: 1243–1248.

Harris, P. 2011 'As we plug in, do we drop out?' 3 February, *Good Living* 7, *The Press* Christchurch.

Harris, R. and P. J. Larkham (eds.). 1999. *Changing Suburbs: Foundation, Form and Function*. London: E & FN Spon.

Harvey, D. 1973. *Social Justice and the City*. London: Edward Arnold.

1989a. *The Condition of Post Modernity*. Oxford: Basil Blackwell.

1989b. 'From Managerialism to Entrepreneurialism; The Transformation in Urban Governance in Late Capitalism'. *Geografiska Annaler* 71B, 3–17.

Hayden, D. 1980. 'What Would a Non-sexist City Be Like'. *Signs: Journal of Women in Culture and Society* 5, 169–187.

1984. *Redesigning the American Dream: the Future of Housing, Work and Family Life*. New York, W. W. Norton and Company.

Healey, M. 2010. 'The good the bad and the digital'. *Good Living, The Press* Christchurch, 8.

Hegedus, J. 2011. 'Housing Policy and the Economic Crisis – Case of Hungary'. In R. Forrest N. Yip (eds.), *Housing Markets and Global Financial Crisis*. London: Edward Elgar.

Held. D. (ed.) 2000. *A Globalizing World? Culture, Economics, Politics.* London: Routledge.

Held, D., A. McGrew, D. Goldblatt and J. Perraton. 1999. *Global Transformations: Politics, Economics and Culture.* Cambridge: Polity.

Hirayama, Y. 2011. 'Towards a Post-Homeowner Society? Home Ownership and Economic Insecurity in Japan'. In R. Forrest and N. Yip (eds.), *Housing Markets and Global Financial Crisis*. London: Edward Elgar.

Hirayama Y. and R. Ronald. 2008. 'Baby-Boomers, Baby-Busters and the Lost Generation: Generational Fractures in Japan's Homeowner Society'. *Urban Policy and Research* 26, 325–42.

Hirst P, and G. Thompson. 1999 *Globalization in Question*, 2nd edn. Cambridge: Polity.

Hochschild, A. 1989. *Second Shift: Working Parents and the Revolution at Home.* New York, NY: Viking Penguin.

Holton, R. J. 1998. *Globalization and the Nation-State.* Houndmills: Macmillan.

Hunn, D., I. Bond and D. Kernohan. 2002. *Report of the Overview Group on the Weathertightness of Buildings to the Building Industry Authority.* Wellington (www.dbh.govt.nz/UserFiles/File/Weathertightness/Reports/pdf/bia-report-17–9–02.pdf: accessed 24/09/2010).

Hunt, P. 1989. 'Gender and the Construction of Home Life'. In G. Allan and G. Crow (eds.), *Home and Family: Creating the Domestic Sphere.* London: Macmillan.

Huntington, S. 1991. *The Third Wave Democratization in the Late Twentieth Century.* University of Oklahoma Press.

1996. *The Clash of Civilisations and the Remaking of the World Order.* New York, NY: Simon & Schuster.

Ingold, T. 2000. *The Perception of the Environment: Essays in Livelihood, Dwelling and Skill.* London and New York, NY: Routledge.

1994. *A Sense of Place, A Sense of Time.* New Haven, CT: Yale University Press.

Intergovernmental Panel on Climate Change (IPCC) 2007 *Fourth Assessment Report Climate Change 2007.* Cambridge University Press.

International Telecommunication Union. 2009. 'Facts and Figures' (www.itu.int/ITU-D/ict/material/FactsFigures2010.pdf; accessed 30/08/2011).

Internet World Statistics. 2011. www.internetworldstats.com (accessed 30/08/2011).

Jackson, J. B., 1994. *A Sense of Place, A Sense of Time.* New Haven, CT: Yale University Press.

Jacobs, M. 1999. *Environmental Modernisation: The New Labour Agenda.* London: Fabian Society.

Jansson, D. R., 2003. 'Internal Orientalism in America: W. J. Cash's *The Mind of The South* and the Spatial Construction Of American National Identity'. *Political Geography* 22, 293–316.

Jeanpierre, L. 2010. 'The International Migration of Scientists'. In *Knowledge Divides* World Social Science Report. Paris: UNESCO.

Jessop, R. 2002. *The Future of the Capitalist State*. Oxford: Blackwell.

Jessop, R. and Ngai-Ling Sum. 2006. *Beyond the Regulation Approach: Putting Capitalist Economies in their Place*. Cheltenham: Edward Elgar.

Johnston, L. and G. Valentine. 1995. 'Wherever I Lay My Girlfriend That's My Home'. In D. Bell and G. Valentine (eds.), *Mapping Desire: Geographies of Sexualities*. London: Routledge.

Kaltenborn, B. 1997. 'Recreation Homes in Natural Settings: Factors Affecting Place Attachment'. *Norsk Geografisk Tidsskr* 51, 187–198.

Kates, R. W. and I. Burton (eds.), 1986a. *Geography, Resources and Environment. Part I. Selected Writings of Gilbert F. White*. University of Chicago Press.

1986b. *Geography, Resources and Environment. Part II. Themes from the Writing of Gilbert F. White*. University of Chicago Press.

Katz, P., V. J. Scully and T. W. Bressi. 2004. *The New Urbanism: Toward an Architecture of Community*. New York, NY: McGraw-Hill.

Kearns, G. and C. Philo (eds.). 1993. *Selling Places: The City as Cultural Capital, Past and Present*. Oxford: Pergamon Press.

Keegan, V. 2007. 'Screen Grabbers on the Digital Frontier'. *Guardian Weekly* 30 November: 26–27.

Kelsey, J. 1997. *The New Zealand Experiment: A World Model for Structural Adjustment*. Auckland: Auckland University Press and Bridget Williams Books.

Kemp, P. (ed.). 2007. *Housing Allowances in Comparative Perspective*, Bristol: Policy Press.

Khondker, H. H. 2000. 'Globalization: Against Reductionism and Linearity'. *Development and Society* 20, 1, 17–23.

King, A. D. (ed.). *Re-presenting the City: Ethnicity, Capital and Culture in the 21st Century Metropolis*. Houndmills, Basingstoke: Palgrave Macmillan.

King, P. 2004. *Private Dwelling: Contemplating the Use of Housing*. London: Routledge.

Kneafsey, M. 2001. 'Rural Cultural Economy: Tourism and Social Relations'. *Annals of Tourism Research* 28, 762–783.

Kontos, P. C. 1998. 'Resisting Institutionalization: Constructing Old Age and Negotiating Home'. *Journal of Aging Studies* 12, 167–184.

Krottoski, A. 2011. 'Technology's saving grace'. February 3 *Good Living* 6, *The Press* Christchurch.

Laing R. D. 1969. *The Divided Self: An Extended Study of Sanity and Madness*. London: Pelican.

Langdon, P. (1994). *A Better Place to Live*. Amherst, MA: University of Massachusetts Press.

Larner, W and W. Walters. 2004. *Global Governmentality: Governing International Space*. New York, NY: Routledge.

Lash, S. 2002. *Critique of Information*, London: Sage.

1999. *Another Modernity A Different Rationality*. Oxford: Blackwell.

Lash, S. and J. Urry. 1987. *The End of Organised Capitalism*. Madison, WI: University of Wisconsin Press.

1994. *Economies of Signs and Space*. London: Sage.

Laxon, A. 2009. 'Leaky homes throw up $6bn repair bill'. *New Zealand Herald*, 19 September (www.nzherald.co.nz/nz/news/article.cfm?c_id=1&objectid= 10598216; accessed 5/05/2010).

Leonard, L. I., H. C. Perkins and D. C. Thorns. 2004. 'Presenting and Creating Home: The Influence of Popular and Building Trade Print Media in the Construction of Home'. *Housing, Theory and Society* 21, 1–15.

Levitas, R. 2005 *The Inclusive Society? Social Exclusion and New Labour* Houndmills: Palgrave Macmillan.

Lewis, M. 1999. *Suburban Back Lash: The Battle for the World's Most Liveable City*. Hawthorn, Victoria: Bloomings Books.

Lewis, P. 1979. 'Defining a Sense of Place'. In *Sense of Place: Mississippi* (eds.), T. W Prenshaw and J. D. McKee. Jackson, MS: University of Mississippi Press.

Ley, D. 1981. 'Behavioural Geography and the Philosophies of Meaning'. In K. R. Cox and R. G. Golledge (eds.). *Behavioural Problems in Geography Revisited*. London: Methuen.

Ley, D. and M. S. Samuels. (eds.). 1978. *Humanistic Geography: Prospects and Problems*. Chicago, IL: Maaroufa Press.

Lightman, E. 2010. 'Falafel in New York' (www.peopleil.org/detailsEN. aspx?itemID=30010&nosearch+t; accessed 01/02/2011).

Lipsey, R., K. Carlaw and C. Becker. 2005. *Economic Transformations: General Purpose Technologies and Long Term Economic Growth*. Oxford University Press.

Logan, J. R. and H. L. Molotch. 1987. *Urban Fortunes: The Political Economy of Place*. Berkeley, CA: University of California Press.

Loomis, T. 1990. *Pacific Migrant Labour: Class and Racism in New Zealand*. Aldershot: Avebury.

Loveridge, A., P. Graham, and P. Schoeffel. 1996. 'The Impact of Tele-Work on Working at Home in New Zealand'. *New Zealand Sociology* 11, 1– 37.

Lupton, D. 2006. 'Sociology and Risk'. In G. Mythen and S. Walklate (eds.), *Beyond the Risk Society: Critical Reflections on Risk and Human Society*. Maidenhead: Open University Press.

Lyon, D. 2003. *Surveillance After September 11*. Malden, MA: Polity in association with Blackwell Pub. Inc.

McCabe, S. 2002. 'The Tourist Experience and Everyday Life'. In G. M. S Dann (ed.), *The Tourist as a Metaphor of the Social World*. Wallingford: CABI Publishing.

McCracken, G. 1989. '"Homeyness": A Cultural Account of One Constellation of Consumer Goods and Meanings'. *Interpretive Consumer Research* 168–183.

McDowell, L. 1999. *Gender, Identity and Place: Understanding Feminist Geographies*. Oxford: Polity.

MacIntyre, N., D. R. Williams and K. McHugh. (eds.). 2006. *Multiple Dwelling and Tourism: Negotiating Place, Home and Identity*. Wallingford: CABI.

Mackay, M., H. C. Perkins and B. Gidlow. 2007. 'Constructing and Maintaining a Central Element of Housing Culture in New Zealand: DIY (Do-It-Yourself)

Home Building, Renovation and Maintenance'. APNHR Conference Proceedings: Transformations in Housing, Urban Life, and Public Policy 30 August–1 September, Seoul, South Korea.

Macnaghten, P. 2003. 'Embodying the Environment in Everyday Life Practices'. *Sociological Review* 51, 63–84.

2006. 'Environment and Risk'. In G. Mythen and S. Walklate *Beyond the Risk Society: Critical Reflections on Risk and Human Society.* Maidenhead: Open University Press.

Macnaghten, P and J. Urry. 1998. *Contested Natures.* London: Sage.

Madigan, R. and M. Munro. 1996. '"House Beautiful"': Style and Consumption in The Home'. *Sociology*' 30, 41–57.

Maginn, P. J., S. Thompson and M. Tonts. 2008. 'Qualitative Housing Analysis: A Meta-Framework for Systematising Qualitative Research. In P. Maginn, S. Thompson and M. Tonts (eds.), *Qualitative Urban Research: An International Perspective.* London: Elsevier.

Mallet. S. 2004. 'Understanding Home: A Critical Review of the Literature'. *Sociological Review* 52, 62–89.

Mansvelt, J. 1997a. 'Working At Leisure – Critical Geographies of Aging'. *Area* 29, 289–298.

1997b. 'Playing At Home? Emplacement, Embodiment and the Active Retiree in New Zealand/Aotearoa'. *New Zealand Geographer* 53, 57–61.

2005. *Geographies of Consumption.* London: Sage.

Marcoux, J.-S. 2001. 'The Refurbishment of Memory'. In D. Miller (ed.), *Home Possessions.* Oxford: Berg.

Marcus-Cooper, C. 1995. *House as a Mirror of Self.* Berkeley, CA: Conari Press.

Marcuse, P. 1995. 'Not Chaos, But Walls: Postmodernism and the Partitioned City'. In S. Watson and K. Gibson (eds.), *Postmodern Cities and Spaces.* Oxford: Blackwell.

2010. 'The Need for Critical Theory in Everyday Life: Why Tea Parties Have Popular Support'. *City* 14, 355–369.

Marcuse, P. and R. van Kempen. 2000. *Globalizing Cities: A New Spatial Order?* Malden, MA: Blackwell.

Maslow, A. 1943. 'A Theory of Human Motivation'. *Psychological Review* 5, 370–396.

Massey, D. 1984. *Spatial Divisions of Labour: Social Structures and the Geographies of Production.* London: Macmillan.

1994a. *Space, Place and Gender.* Cambridge: Polity.

1994b. 'A Global Sense of Place'. In *Space, Place and Gender.* Cambridge: Polity.

1994c. 'Double Articulation: A Place in The World'. In *Displacements* (ed.) A. Bammer. Bloomington, IL: Indiana University Press.

1995. 'Places and Their Pasts'. *History Workshop Journal* 39, 182–192.

1999. 'Spaces of Politics'. In *Human Geography Today.* (eds.), D. Massey, J. Allen and P. Sarre. Cambridge: Polity.

2004. Geographies of Responsibility, *Geografiska Annaler* 86, 5–18.

Meadows, D. H., D. L. Meadows, J. Randers, and W. W. Behrens. 1972. *The Limits to Growth*. New York, NY: Universe Books.

Meethan, K. 1996. 'Consuming (in) the Civilized City'. *Annals of Tourism Research* 23, 322–340.

Meiksins, P. and P. Whalley. 2002. *Putting Work in its Place: A Quiet Revolution*. Ithaca, NY: ILR Press.

Meinig, D. W. 1979. 'Symbolic Landscapes: Some Idealizations of American Communities'. In *The Interpretation of Ordinary Landscapes* (ed.) D. W. Meinig. New York, NY: Oxford University Press.

1995. 'Messy Ecosystems, Orderly Frames'. *Landscape Journal* 14, 161–170.

Memon, P. 2003. 'Urban Growth Management in Christchurch, *New Zealand Geographer* 59. 27–39.

Memon, P. A. and B. J. Gleeson. 1995. 'Towards a New Planning Paradigm? Reflections on New Zealand's Resource Management Act'. *Environment and Planning: Planning and Design* 22, 109–124.

Memon, P. A. and H. C. Perkins (eds.). 2000. *Environmental Planning and Management in New Zealand*. Palmerston North: Dunmore Press.

Miles, S. 1998. *Consumerism – As a Way of Life*. London: Sage.

Mitchell, C. J. A. 1998. 'Entrepreneurialism, Commodification and Creative Destruction: A Model of Post-Modern Community Development'. *Journal of Rural Studies* 14, 273–286.

Mobbs, M. 1998. *Sustainable House: Living for Our Future*. Dunedin: Otago University Press.

Mowl, G., R. Pain and C. Talbot. 2000. 'The Ageing Body and Homespace'. *Area* 32, 189–197.

Munro, M. and R. Madigan. 1993. 'Privacy In The Private Sphere'. *Housing Studies* 8, 29–45.

Newman, P., T. Beatley and H. Boyer. 2009. *Resilient Cities: Responding to Peak Oil and Climate Change*. Washington, DC: Island Press.

Nippert-Eng, C. E. 1996. *Home and Work: Negotiating Boundaries Through Everyday Life*. University of Chicago.

O'Connor, F. 1973. *The Fiscal Crisis of the State*. New York, NY: St Martin's Press.

Ohmae, K. 1996. *The End of the Nation State*. London: Harper Collins.

2000 'The End of the Nation State'. In J. Beyon, and D. Dunkerley (eds.), *Globalization: The Reader*. London: Athlone Press.

O'Loughlin, J. and J. Friedrichs. 1996. 'Polarization in Post-Industrial Societies: Social and Economic Roots and Consequences'. In J. O'Loughlin and J. Friedrichs (eds.), *Social Polarization in Post-Industrial Metropolises*. New York, NY: Walter de Gruyter.

Owen, O., 2007. 'Guinness is good in Nigeria'. *Guardian Weekly*. London: 14/09/07.

Oxley H. 1974. *Mateship in Local Organisations* Brisbane: University of Queensland Press.

Oxley, L., P. Walker, D. Thorns and H. Wang. 2008. 'The Knowledge Economy/Society: The Latest Example of Measurement without Theory'. *Journal of Philosophical Economics* November, 20–54.

Packard, V. 1957, *The Hidden Persuaders*. New York, NY: Pocket Books.

Paris, C. 2010. *Affluence, Mobility and Second Home Ownership*. London: Routledge.

Park, R. E. 1952. *Human Communities: The City and Human Ecology*. Glencoe, KY: Free Press.

Park, R. E., E. W. Burgess and R. D. McKenzie. 1967. 3rd edn, *The City*. University of Chicago Press.

Parliamentary Commissioner of the Environment. 2002. *Creating Our Future: Sustainable Development for New Zealand*. Wellington: PCE.

Pawson, E. and S. Swaffield. 1998. 'Landscapes of Leisure and Tourism'. In H. C. Perkins and J. Cushman (eds.), *Time Out?: Leisure, Recreation and Tourism in New Zealand and Australia*. Auckland: Addison Wesley Longman.

Peacey, B. 2004. 'E-Govtnz: a sociological exploration of e-government in New Zealand', MA thesis, University of Canterbury, Christchurch, New Zealand.

Pearson, D. 1990 *A Dream Deferred*. Wellington: Allen & Unwin.

Perkins, H. C. 1988a. 'Bulldozers in the Southern Part Of Heaven: Defending Place Against Rapid Growth. Part 1: Local Residents' Interpretations of Rapid Urban Growth in a Free-Standing Service-Class Town'. *Environment and Planning A* 20, 285–308.

1988b. 'Bulldozers in the Southern Part of Heaven: Defending Place against Rapid Growth. Part 2: The Alliance Strikes Back'. *Environment and Planning A* 20, 435–456.

1989. 'The Country in the Town: The Role of Real Estate Developers in the Construction of the Meaning of Place'. *Journal of Rural Studies* 5, 61–74.

2006. 'Commodification: Re-Resourcing Rural Areas'. In P. Cloke, T. Marsden and P. Mooney (eds.), *Handbook of Rural Studies*. London: Sage.

Perkins, H. C. and G. Cushman (eds.). 1998. *Time Out? Leisure, Recreation and Tourism in New Zealand and Australia*. Auckland: Addison Wesley Longman.

Perkins, H. C. and D. C. Thorns. 1999. 'House and Home and their Interaction with Changes in New Zealand's Urban System, Households and Family Structures'. *Housing, Theory and Society* 16, 124–135.

2000. 'Place Promotion and Urban and Regional Planning in New Zealand'. In A. Memon and H. C. Perkins (eds.), *Environmental Planning and Management in New Zealand*. Palmerston North: Dunmore Press.

2001. 'Gazing or Performing? Reflections on Urry's Tourist Gaze in the Context of Contemporary Experience in the Antipodes', *International Sociology* 16, 185–204.

2002. 'A Decade on: Reflections on the Resource Management Act 1991 and Urban Planning in New Zealand'. *Environment and Planning B* 28, 639–654.

2003. 'The Making of Home in a Global Context'. In R. Forrest and J. Lee (eds.), *Housing and Social Change*. London: Routledge.

2006. 'Home Away from Home: The Primary–Second-Home Relationship'. In N. MacIntyre, D. R. Williams and K. McHugh (eds.), *Multiple Dwelling and Tourism: Negotiating Place, Home and Identity*. Wallingford: CABI.

Perkins, H. C., D. C. Thorns and B. M. Newton 2008a. 'Real Estate Advertising and Intra-Urban Place Meaning: Real Estate Consultants at Work'. *Environment and Planning A* 40, 2061–2079.

Perkins, H. C., D. C. Thorns and A. Winstanley. 2008b. 'House and Home: Methodology and Methods for Exploring Meaning and Structure'. In P. Maginn, S. Thompson and M. Tonts (eds.), *Qualitative Urban Research: An International Perspective* London: Elsevier.

Perkins, H. C., D. C. Thorns, A. Winstanley and B. Newton. 2002. *The Study of 'Home' from a Social Scientific Perspective: An Annotated Bibliography*, 2nd edn. Lincoln and Christchurch: Lincoln University and University of Canterbury, New Zealand.

Piore, M. J and C. F. Sabel. 1984. *The Second Industrial Divide. Possibilities for Prosperity*. New York, NY: Basic Books.

Potts, L. 1990. *The World Labour Market: A History of Migration*. London: Zed Books.

Power, A. 1993. *Hovels to High Rise: State Housing in Europe since 1850*. London: Routledge.

Pred, A. 1983. 'Structuration and Place – On the Becoming of Sense of Place and Structure of Feeling'. *Journal for the Theory of Social Behaviour* 13, 45–68.

Privacy Commissioner. 2006. *New Zealand Website Privacy Notices: A First Look* (http://privacy.org.nz/new-zealand-website-privacy-notices-a-first-look).

Putnam, R. 2000. *Bowling Alone: The Collapse and Revival of American Communities*. New York, NY: Simon & Schuster.

Quinn, B. 2004. 'Dwelling through Multiple Places: A Case Study of Second Home Ownership in Ireland'. In C. M. Hall and D. K. Müller (eds.), *Tourism, Mobility and Second Homes: Between Elite Landscapes and Common Ground*. Clevedon: Channel View.

Rahmstorf, S. 2010. 'Climate change physics is irrefutable'. *The Press* Christchurch, 9 July, A15.

Redclift, M. 1987. *Sustainable Development: Exploring the Contradictions*. London: Methuen.

1999. 'Sustainability and Sociology: Northern Preoccupations'. In E. Becker and T. Jahn (eds.), *Sustainability and the Social Sciences: A Cross Disciplinary Approach to Integrating Environmental Considerations into Theoretical Reorientations*. London: Zed Books.

Reid, P. 1998. 'Nga Mahi Whakahaehae a te Tangata Tiriti (The Empire Strikes Back!)'. Haratua: Wellington School of Medicine.

Relph, E. 1976. *Place and Placelessness*. London: Pion.

Rehm, M. 2008. 'Judging a House by its Cover: Leaky Building Stigma and House Prices in New Zealand'. *International Journal of Housing Markets and Analysis* 2, 57–77.

Rex, J. and R. Moore. 1967 (reprint 1974). *Race, Community, and Conflict: A Study of Sparkbrook*. London: Oxford University Press for the Institute of Race Relations.

Ricci, I. 1980. *Mom's House, Dad's House, How to Make Them Homes*. New York, NY: Macmillan.

Ritzer, G. 1998. *The McDonaldization Thesis: Explorations and Extensions*. London: Sage.

Robbins, E. 1998. 'The New Urbanism and the Fallacy of Singularity'. *Urban Design* 3, 33–42.

Robertson, N., H. C. Perkins and N. Taylor. 2008. 'Multiple job holding: Interpreting economic, labour market and social change in rural communities'. *Sociologia Ruralis* 48, 331–350.

Robertson, R. 1992. *Globalization: Social Theory and Global Culture*. London: Sage.

Robertson, R. and W. Garret (eds.). 1991. *Religion and Global Order*. New York, NY: Paragon.

Robertson, R. and H. H. Khondker. 1998. 'Discourses of Globalization'. *International Sociology* 13, 1, 25–40.

Robertson, R. W. 1977. 'Second-Home Decisions: The Australian Context'. In J. T. Coppock (ed.), *Second Homes: Curse or Blessing?* Oxford: Pergamon.

Rodaway, P. 1994. *Sensuous Geographies: Body, Sense and Place*, London: Routledge.

Rojek, C. 1995. *Decentring Leisure: Rethinking Leisure Theory*. London: Sage.

Ronald R. and M. Elsinga (eds.). 2011. *Beyond Home Ownership*. London: Routledge.

Rudman, B. 2009. 'State needs to plug leaks scandal', *New Zealand Herald* 9 December, A13.

Sachdeva, S. 2010. 'Hassled in city, boy racers plague suburbs – residents'. *The Press* Christchurch, 27 May (www.stuff.co.nz/the-press/news/christchurch/3743915/Hassled-in-city-boy-racers-plague-suburbs-residents; accessed 23/10/2010).

Sané, P. 2009. 'Editorial No. 26: Climate Change: Rising to the Ethical Challenge'. UNESCO *Social and Human Sciences Sector Magazine*. October – December.

Sassen, S. 1991. *The Global City: New York, London, Tokyo*. Princeton University Press.

1994. *Cities in a World Economy*. Thousand Oaks, CA: Pine Forge Press.

1996. Rebuilding the Global City: Economy, Ethnicity and Space. In A. D. King (ed.), *Re-Presenting the City*. Houndmills, Basingstoke: Macmillan.

1999. 'Global Financial Centers'. *Foreign Affairs* 78, 75–87.

2007. *A Sociology of Globalization*. New York, NY: W. W. Norton.

Satterthwaite, D. 1999. *The Earthscan Reader in Sustainable Cities*. London: Earthscan.

2008. 'Cities' Contribution to Global Warming: Notes on the Allocation of Greenhouse Gas Emissions'. *Environment and Urbanization* 20, 539–549.

Savage M and R. Burrows. 2009. 'Some Further Reflections on the Coming Crisis of Empirical Sociology'. *Sociology*, 43, 762–772.

Saville-Smith, K. and D. C. Thorns. 2001 *Community-Based Solutions for Sustainable Housing.* Wellington: CRESA.

Schamalenbach, H. 1961. 'The Sociological Category of Communion'. In T. Parsons, E. Shils, K. Naegele and J. Pitts (eds.), *Theories of Society-Foundations of Modern Sociology.* New York, NY: Free Press.

Schänzel, H. A. 2009. 'Family time and own time on holiday: generation, gender and group dynamic perspectives', Ph.D. thesis, Victoria University of Wellington, New Zealand.

Schlosser, E. 2001. *Fast Food Nation: The Dark Side of the All-American Meal.* Boston, MA: Houghton Mifflin.

Schöllmann, A., H. C. Perkins and K. Moore. 2000. 'Intersecting Global and Local Influences in Urban Place Promotion: The Case of Christchurch, New Zealand'. *Environment and Planning A* 32, 55–76.

Scholte, J. 2000. *Globalization.* Houndmills: Macmillan.

Schuler, D. 1995. Public Space in CyberSpace. *Internet World* December. Social Perspectives.

Schulmman, S. 2006. *Undermining Science: Suppression and Distortion in the Bush Administration.* Berkeley, CA: University of California Press.

Sennett, R. 1999. 'The Spaces of Democracy'. *Harvard Design Magazine* summer, 68–72.

Shaw, L. and B. Brookes. 1999. 'Constructing Homes: Gender and Advertising in Home and Building 1936–1970'. *New Zealand Journal of History* 33, 200 220.

Sheller, M. and J. Urry. 2006. 'The New Mobilities Paradigm'. *Environment and Planning A* 38, 207–226.

Shields, R. 1991. *Places on the Margin: Alternative Geographies of Modernity.* London and New York, NY: Routledge.

Shields, R. 2003. *The Virtual.* London: Routledge.

Short, J., E. Williams and B. Christie. 1976. *The Social Psychology of Telecommunications.* New York, NY: John Wiley.

Shove, E. 2010. 'Beyond the ABC: Climate Change Policy and Theories of Social Change'. *Environment and Planning A* 42(6) 1273–1285.

Shove, E., M. Watson, M. Hand and J. Ingram. 2007. *The Design of Everyday Life.* London: Berg.

Silver, I., 1996. 'Role Transitions, Objects and Identity'. *Symbolic Interaction* 19, 1–20.

Simmel, G. 1969. 'The Metropolis and Mental Life'. In R. Sennet (ed.), *Classic Essays on the Culture of Cities.* New York, NY: Appleton Century Crofts.

Smith, M. P. and J. R. Feagin. 1987. *The Capitalist City: Global Restructuring and Community Politics.* Oxford: Basil Blackwell.

Smith, N. and P. Williams. 1986. *Gentrification of the City.* London: Allen & Unwin.

Smith, P. 2003. 'A Place in the Past'. *Air New Zealand* January, 82–89.

Smith, S. J. 2008. 'Owner-Occupation: At Home with a Hybrid of Money and Materials'. *Environment and Planning A* 40, 520–535.

Social and Human Sciences. 2009. 'The Ethical Challenges of Climate Change 5–7 Paris' *Social and Human Science Review*. Paris: UNESCO.

Soja, E. 2000. *Postmetropolis: Critical Studies of Cities and Regions*. Oxford: Blackwell.

Soler, J. 1989. 'The Incredible Document known as the Mazengarb Report'. *Sites* 19, 2–32.

Somerville, P. 1998. 'Explanations for Social Exclusion. Where Does Housing Fit In?' *Housing Studies* 13,6, 761–780.

Southworth, M. 1997. 'Walkable Suburbs? An Evaluation of Neotraditional Communities at the Urban Edge', *Journal of the American Planning Association* 63, 28–44.

Spellerberg, I. and J. McNeely. 2010. 'Biodiversity matters'. Christchurch: *The Press* 25 February, A15.

Spoonley, P. 1988. *Racism and Ethnicity*. Auckland, Oxford University Press

Stacey, J. 1990. *Brave New Families*. New York, NY: Basic Books.

Stanworth, C. 1998. 'Telework and the Information Age. *New Technology, Work and Employment* 13, 1, 51–52.

Statistics New Zealand. 2001. *Census of Population and Dwellings*. Wellington: New Zealand Government.

Stehr, N. H. 1994. *Knowledge Societies*. London: Sage.

Stehr, N. H. and H. von Storch. 2010. *Climate and Society*. New Jersey: World Scientific.

Stern, N. 2006 *The Economics of Climate Change*, London: UK Treasury.

Stern Report on the Economics of Climate Change. 2008. Accessed at http://webarchive.nationalarchives.gov.uk/+/http:/www.hm-treasury.gov.uk/sternreview_index.htm

Stiglitz, J. 2009. 'The Anatomy of Murder: Who Killed America's Economy'. *Critical Review* 21, 329–339.

Stoker, G. and S. Young. 1993. *Cities in the 1990s*. London: Longman.

Stone, M. E. 2009. 'Housing and the financial crisis', paper presented at the Australasian Housing Researchers Conference August, Sydney.

Stone, W. and K. Hulse, 2007. *Housing and Social Cohesion: An Empirical Investigation*. Final Report no. 100, Australian Housing and Urban Research Institute, Melbourne.

Stuart, J. 2008. *The John Wesley Code*. Wellington: Philip Garside.

Stymeist, D. H. 1996. 'Transformation of Vilavilairevo in Tourism'. *Annals of Tourism Research* 28, 1–18.

Sullivan, C. 2000a. 'Space and the Intersection of Work and Family in Homeworking Households'. *Community, Work and Family* 3, 185–204.

2000b. 'The Division of Domestic Labour: Twenty Years of Change'. *Sociology* 34, 437–456.

Svenson, S. 2002. 'Cottaging: A Tourist Takes a Vacation from Responsibility; The Cottager Makes a Commitment to Place'. *Alternatives Journal* 28, 30–32.

Sztompka, P. 2008. 'The Focus on Everyday Life: A New Turn in Sociology'. *European Review* 16, 1, 21–37.

Talen, E. 1999. 'Sense of Community and Neighbourhood Form: An Assessment of the Social Doctrine of New Urbanism'. *Urban Studies* 36, 1361–1379.

Thakali, S. Forthcoming, 'Interpreting and critiquing recent changes in environmental and development governance in high mountain regions; Mustang, Nepal, as a case study', Ph.D. thesis. Lincoln University, Canterbury, New Zealand.

The Press [Christchurch, New Zealand]. 2009. 'Detroit's descent into ruin'. Monday, November 23: B4.

Therborn, G. 2000. 'Globalizations: Dimensions, Historical Waves, Regional Effects, Normative Governance'. *International Sociology* 15, 151–179.

Thompson, C. J. and S. K. Tambyah. 1999. 'Trying to Be Cosmopolitan'. *Journal of Consumer Research* 26, December, 214–241.

Thompson, S. M. 1994. 'Suburbs of Opportunity: The Power of Home for Migrant Women'. In K. Gibson and S. Watson (eds.), *Metropolis Now: Planning and the Urban Community in Contemporary Australia*. Sydney: Pluto.

1996. 'Women's stories of home: meaning of home for ethnic women living in established migrant communities', unpublished Ph.D. thesis, University of Sydney, Sydney.

Thorns, D. 1992. *Fragmenting Societies? A Comparative Analysis of Regional and Urban Development*. London: Routledge.

2002. *The Transformation of Cities*. London: Palgrave Macmillan.

2009. 'Housing Booms and Changes to New Zealand Housing Affordability: The Policy Challenge'. *Journal of Asian Public Policy* 12, 171–189.

2010. 'Qualitative Interviewing', Chapter 662 *International Encyclopedia of Housing and Home* London: Elsevier.

2011a. 'Home Ownership in New Zealand; Continuing Dream or an Approaching Nightmare'. In R. Ronald and M. Elsinga (eds.), *Beyond Home Ownership*. London: Routledge.

2011b. 'Rebuilding Housing Polices in Response to the Current Crisis? Is Home Ownership the Solution?'. In R. Forrest and N. Yip (eds.), *Housing Markets and Global Financial Crisis*. London: Edward Elgar.

Thorns, D. C., P. Fairbairn-Dunlop and R. Du Plessis. 2010. 'Biculturalism, Cultural Diversity and Globalization: Issues for Aotearoa New Zealand'. *Korean Social Science Journal* 27, 93–122.

Thrift, N. J. 1983. 'On the Determination of Social Action in Space and Time'. *Environment and Planning D: Society and Space* 1, 23–57.

1999. 'Steps to an Ecology of Place'. In *Human Geography Today* (eds.),D. Massey, J. Allen and P. Sarre. Cambridge: Polity.

2003. 'Performance and Environment and Planning A' 35, 2019–2024.

2004. 'Intensities of Feeling: Towards a Spatial Politics of Affect'. *Geografiska Annaler* 86, 57–78.

Tönnies, F. 1956. *Community and Society* (Trans. C. P. Loomis). Michigan, MI: Michigan State University Press.

Troy, P. N. 1996. *The Perils of Urban Consolidation: A Discussion of Australian Housing and Urban Development Policies*. Sydney: Federation Press;

Tuan, Y. F. 1974. *Topophilia*. New Jersey, NJ: Prentice-Hall.

1975. 'Space and Place: Humanistic Perspectives'. *Progress in Geography* 6. London: Edward Arnold.

Tuan, Y. F. 1980. 'Rootedness versus Sense of Place'. *Landscape* 24, 3–8.

Tuan, Yi Fu. 1998. *Escapism*. Baltimore, MD: Johns Hopkins University Press.

United Nations. 1972. *Report of the United Nations Environment Conference* (www.unep.org/Documents.Multilingual/Default.asp?documentid=97; accessed 30/08/2011).

United Nations Centre for Human Settlements. 1996. *An Urbanizing World: Global Report on Human Settlements*. Oxford University Press.

2001a. *The State of the Worlds Cities*. Nairobi: UNCHS.

2001b. *Cities in a Globalizing World* London: Earthscan.

United Nations Second Conference on Human Settlements. 1996. Istanbul, Turkey (www.un.org/Conferences/habitat; accessed 30/08/2011).

Urry, J. 1990. *The Tourist Gaze*. London: Sage.

1992. 'The Tourist Gaze "Revisited"', *American Behavioural Scientist* 36, 172–86.

1995. *Consuming Places*. London: Routledge.

2000. *Sociology Beyond Societies: Mobilities for the 21st Century*. London: Routledge.

2002. *The Tourist Gaze*, 2nd edn, London: Sage.

2010. 'Sociology Facing Climate Change'. *Sociological Research Online* 15, 3, 1–3.

Valentine, G. 1999. 'Eating in: Home, Consumption and Identity'. *Sociological Review* 47, 491–524.

Vallance, S. and Perkins, H. C. 2010. 'Is Another City Possible? Towards an Urbanised Sustainability'. *City* 14, 448–456.

Vallance, S., H. C. Perkins and J. E. Dixon. 2009. *Compact Cities and Quality of Life: An Annotated Bibliography and Literature Review*. Auckland: School of Architecture and Planning, University of Auckland, Private Bag 92019, Auckland (http://researcharchive.lincoln.ac.nz/dspace/handle/10182/1428).

Vallance, S., Perkins, H. C. and Dixon, J. 2011. 'What is Social Sustainability? A Clarification of Concepts'. *Geoforum*. 42, 342–348.

Vallance, S., H, C. Perkins and K. Moore. 2005. 'The Results of Making a City More Compact: Neighbours' Interpretation of Urban Infill', *Environment and Planning B: Planning and Design* 32, 715–733.

Vertue, F. 2010. 'Virtually safe on line'. In *Good Living*. The Press Christchurch, 8.

Veblen, T. (1970) [1899]. *The Theory of the Leisure Class: An Economic Study of Institutions*. London: Allen & Unwin.

Wallerstein, I. 1980. *The Modern World System 11*. New York, NY: Academic Press.

2000. 'Globalization or the Age of Transition. A long Term View of the Trajectory of the World System'. *International Sociology* 15, 249–65.

Wan Jaffar W. M. 2010. 'On-line networks, social capital and social integration: a case study of on-line communities in Malaysia', unpublished Ph.D. Thesis, University of Canterbury, Christchurch, NZ.

Waters, M. 2001. *Globalization*, 2nd end. London: Routledge.

Ward, P. W. 1999. *A History of Domestic Space: Privacy and the Canadian Home.* Vancouver: University of British Columbia.

Wardhaugh, J. 1999. 'The Unaccommodated Woman: Home, Homelessness and Identity'. *Sociological Review* 47, 91–109.

Watkins, S. and C. Jones. 2005. *Unforgettable Things to Do before You Die.* London: BBC Books.

Watson, G. L. and J. P. Kopachevsky. 1994. Interpretations of Tourism as Commodity. *Annals of Tourism Research* 24, 643–660.

Watson, S. and K. Gibson. (eds.). 1995. *Postmodern Cities and Spaces.* Oxford: Blackwell.

Wearing, B. and S. Wearing. 1990. 'Leisure for All? Gender and Policy'. In D. Rowe and G. Lawrence (eds.), *Sport and Leisure.* Sydney: Harcourt Brace Jovanovich.

Werner, C. 1988. 'Home Interiors: a Time and Place for Interpersonal Relationships'. *Environment and Behaviour* 19, 169–179.

Wellman, B. and M. Giuha 1999. 'Netsurfers Don't Ride Alone: Virtual Communities as Communities'. In B. Wellman (ed.), *Networks in the Global Village.* Boulder, CO: Westview Press.

Wellman, B. 2001. 'Community Question'. *Canadian Journal of Sociology* 26, 1203–1228.

Wild, J. 1963. *Existence and the World of Freedom.* Englewood Cliffs, NJ: Prentice Hall.

Wild R. 1981 *Australian Community Studies and Beyond Sydney*, Allan & Unwin.

Williams, D. R. 2002. 'Leisure Identities, Globalization and Politics of Place'. *Journal of Leisure Research* 34, 351–359.

Williams, P. 2011. 'The Credit Crunch in the UK: Understanding the Impact Upon Housing Markets, Policies and Households'. In R. Forrest and N. Yip (eds.), *Housing Markets and Global Financial Crisis.* London: Edward Elgar.

Williams, R. 1977. *Marxism and Literature.* Oxford University Press.

Wilson, J. 2006. 'Unpacking the OE: an exploration of the New Zealand overseas experience', Ph.D. thesis. Lincoln University, Canterbury, New Zealand.

Winchester, S. 2003. *Krakatoa: The Day the World Exploded: August 27, 1883.* New York, NY: HarperCollins.

Winstanley, A. 2001. 'Housing, home and women's identity', Ph.D. thesis, University of Canterbury, Christchurch, New Zealand.

Winstanley, A., D. C. Thorns and H. C. Perkins. 2002. 'Moving House, Creating Home: Exploring Residential Mobility'. *Housing Studies* 17, 813–832.
2003. Nostalgia, Community and New Housing Developments: A Critique of New Urbanism Incorporating a New Zealand Perspective. *Urban Policy and Research* 21, 175–189.

Wirth, L. 1938. 'Urbanism as a Way of Life'. *American Journal of Sociology* 44, 1–24.

Wolfe, R. I. 1965. 'About Cottages and Cottagers'. *Landscape* 15, 6–8.

World Commission on Environment and Development (WCED). 1987. *Our Common Future*. Oxford University Press.

Whyte W. F. *Organisational Behaviour*. Homewood, 111 RD Irwin-Dorsey.

Yeats, N. 2001. *Globalization and Social Policy*. London: Sage.

Young, I. M. 1997. *Intersecting Voices: Dilemmas of Gender, Political Philosophy and Policy*. Princeton University Press.

Young, M. and P. W. Willmott. 1958. *Family and Kinship in East London*. Glencoe, IL: Free Press.

Zukin, S. 1991. *Landscapes of Power: From Detroit to Disneyland*. Berkeley, CA: University of California Press.

1995. *The Culture of Cities*. Cambridge, MA: Blackwell.

Index